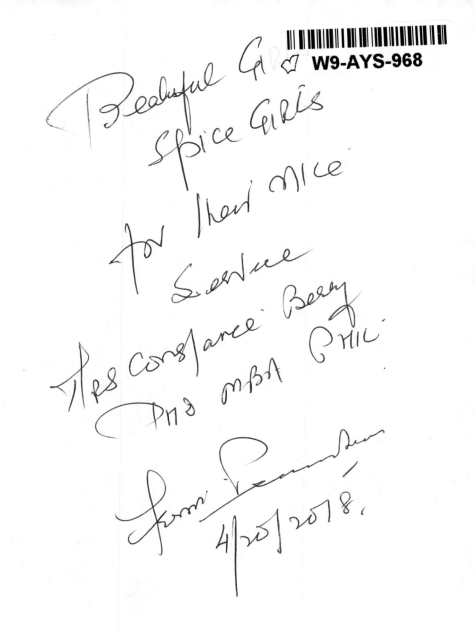

Beautiful Girl ♡ Spice Girls
for their nice
service

Mrs Constance Berry
PhD MBA PHIL

from [signature]
4/20/2078.

W9-AYS-968

My Connie

Pradeep K. Berry

authorHOUSE®

AuthorHouse™
1663 Liberty Drive
Bloomington, IN 47403
www.authorhouse.com
Phone: 1 (800) 839-8640

© *2017 Pradeep K. Berry. All rights reserved.*

No part of this book may be reproduced, stored in a retrieval system, or transmitted by any means without the written permission of the author.

Published by AuthorHouse 06/08/2017

ISBN: 978-1-5246-9510-1 (sc)
ISBN: 978-1-5246-9511-8 (hc)
ISBN: 978-1-5246-9509-5 (e)

Library of Congress Control Number: 2017908645

Print information available on the last page.

Any people depicted in stock imagery provided by Thinkstock are models, and such images are being used for illustrative purposes only. Certain stock imagery © Thinkstock.

This book is printed on acid-free paper.

Because of the dynamic nature of the Internet, any web addresses or links contained in this book may have changed since publication and may no longer be valid. The views expressed in this work are solely those of the author and do not necessarily reflect the views of the publisher, and the publisher hereby disclaims any responsibility for them.

Contents

In this great biography, I have tried to describe Connie in a short version. Her qualities were far from what I have written. It could take me another five years, if all the other qualities of Connie are to be written. It may be my next book. I know many other people have lots to write about their lives, and as such, I only want to detail a short version of Connie. "Forgiveness ends everything" was the approach Connie believed, and I respect that. My thanks to all my readers and well-wishers. Connie would bless me to follow that message, and that's what I want—to get her blessing all my life.

In memory of my beautiful, educated, and devoted wife, Connie Berry.
Never seek happiness outside yourself.

Life isn't about what happens to us; it's about
we perceive what happens to us.

Master your past in the present, or the past will master your future.

Life: A Book of Eastern Wisdom

1. Do not wake the following up: Snake, the king, the wasp, a child, other's dog and the fool. They better left sleeping. (They all becomes dangerous or disturbing when woken up from the deep Slumber.) (Chanakya Neeti, 301/120)
2. No disease is more deadly than (the sexual) desire, no enemy is more dangerous than infatuation, no fire is hotter than fire of wrath and no happiness is better than the self-knowledge. (Chanakya Neeti, 24/15)

3. One should always be satisfied (1) with his wife, (2) with his diet and (3) with his wealth; but never with (1) studies, (2) his austerity and penance (3) with his donations and gifts to the deserving persons. (Chanakya Neeti, 42/21)
4. Just one dry tree on catching fire can burn the whole orchard to ashes. Similarly, one incompetent, bad son ruins the whole family. (Chanakya Neeti, 52/24)
5. Never rely on someone who is a known betrayer. Poison is poison in all circumstances.
6. While protecting and collecting money leave the enemies out. Never insult a noble man.

A Very Special Memory of My Connie

(True) wife is she who is pious and deft (in her work), who is faithful to her husband, who loves her husband and who is truthful to her husband. (Chanakya list five qualities for an ideal wife: she ought to be pious, deft, faithful, loving and truthful to her husband.) (Neeti, 55/25)

A good husband always loves his wife, is faithful, respects her all the time, and creates a nice atmosphere for her. His wife is the most important part of his life. Both husband and wife are assets and keep their relations till death. The commitment for love and sorrow must be carried throughout life regardless of the circumstances. The wife is an incarnation of tolerance, and she should expect only one thing from her husband: love.

The Rich never (selflessly) contribute in the noble wok. (For They always seek their financial gain in whatever they do). (Chanakya 352/169)

Pradeep K. Berry, June 6, 2017

Author's Note

Writing has always been one of the prime skills that I have needed, from the sixth grade to the present day. From high school to undergraduate, postgraduate, and my professional career, writing skills were absolutely necessary. In addition, as I advanced my career, I developed a greater interest in writing and discovered that reading was the thing I enjoyed most. I must mention that my beautiful, educated, precious, priceless, and most loving wife of over forty-one years, Constance A. Berry, or Connie, always encouraged me to read and write in subjects other than my professional reports, newspapers, and research. I recall many incidents when Connie took me to different parts of the world, and interacting with people from different cultures was one of the most joyful things for us. Many people asked me to write books, and I considered doing so but did not act on those thoughts. Finally, Connie told me, "Pradeep, I wish you were a professor and a writer." Those words are still in my brain, in my heart.

I could never have imagined that my first book would be for my wife. After thinking of many titles, I invented a great one: *My Connie*. This is to honor her and to show our love. I decided on February 28, 2015, that I wanted to write my first book of our immortal love. This book is my life, my happiness, my sorrows, my power, my biggest strength, my companion, and my new life. There are many happy and sad chapters of our lives in this book. It is easy to understand that happiness and unhappiness are parts of life, but it's much more difficult to bear the reality. This is the difference between what we study in school and in the practical world: experience. Our love remains immortal.

I must thank many people, without whom it would have been difficult for me to handle the most tragic time of my life on February 28, 2015. They also helped edit and proofread *My Connie*.

My thanks to Mr. Sanjay and Mrs. Parina, who were with me when Connie was dying. Their help was timely when I was crushed with Connie's death, and later at the cremation, the interment of her ashes, and the chapel of peace services, which I wanted to have at the earliest possible time. Sanjay and Parina's help and support will always be remembered by me, my brother, and his family. I was successful because at my humble request, Elizabeth and Justine at the funeral home and Memorial Cemetery fulfilled my wishes, and everything was done on March 2–3, 2015.

Florida Harris, the caretaker of Connie, was a big support to me. I have written more about Florida under the "Death Episode" section. Connie was the president of the Condo Association for twenty-five years, and everyone in our building helped each other take care of mail and plants during vacations. After Connie's demise, our neighbors started picking up the mail and watering our plants in the house when I went to see my family thrice in India after Connie's death. At the same time, other residents were gracious to extend help to me, and I am thankful to them for attending Connie's last rites.

I would like to thank Judy Destefano, our neighbor, for introducing me to Jessica Harrison, who was a big help in the editing of my book until my first submission on August 19, 2016.

However, after two weeks, AuthorHouse asked me to revise many conflicting issues, which in my opinion were true for *My Connie*. They were absolutely true facts of our lives in the years 1989, 1999, 2000, 2002, 2004, 2005, 2006, 2011, and 2012. The worst were in 2013, and the most devastating and heartbreaking started in July 2014 and continued to February 28, 2015. However, since that date till today, October 30, 2016, the effects of all of 2014 and 2015 are hanging in my suffering and in my pain. They are getting deeper and deeper, transforming into different situations after the demise of Connie. I know how much revision I had to do to get this book published. I am now working by myself on all this. I am hoping I will be done with all these changes by November 4, 2016. They insisted I revise and take out some of the things relating to Connie's sickness and some family related issues. I did not, because the book had the true facts, and I was given full clearance by my legal attorney. However, later due to some publication issues, I had to rewrite a lot of different things while taking out some of the previous content suggested by the AuthorHouse. This is the third time I am making changes.

I also acknowledge Randi Merel, a good friend of Connie's and her finance advisor, for her support at the funeral services. My thanks to Akhil, a professional videographer, for covering the full services for two days. This video is my possession of my love and is important in my life if I want to see Connie's last rites.

I am very grateful to my biological brother, Mr. Arun Berry; his wife, Shobha; and their two sons, Ashiem and Ashish. Thanks also to Ashish's wife, Mona, and their two daughters (my grandnieces), Krishna (age ten) and Radhika (age five). My grandnieces cheered me during my depressing time. I have written a whole chapter of my life from February 28 to October 6, 2016, and going forward.

My uncle, Dr. P. N. Behl, a world-renowned dermatologist, was the first person in the family to have an English wife, Mrs. Marjorie Behl, and they were prominent in Delhi from the early sixties to today. Dr. Behl was more than a father to me in India until his death in October 16, 2002. His mother was my grandfather's sister.

I can't believe when I first visited India in July 1979, after close to four years of my arrival in the United States. While flying, my mind was wondering why I was so reluctant and depressed to come to the United States four years ago with seven dollars. Now I was flying back to India with my highly educated, beautiful, intelligent, and intellectual American wife, Connie.

I take pride that I am the second person to marry an American wife. Mrs. Constance A. Berry became the darling of the family. I never thought that

Pradeep would be the second person to marry an American girl. Dr. Behl was a shining star in India, and his influence on me as a child and teenager was great. Later, Connie's influence on my career, education, culture, world travel, arts, and adventures were her gifts to me. She succeeded in this mission with full capacity. I owe all this to Connie.

There were over one hundred immediate and extended family members waiting to receive us at the Delhi airport. I do not recall how we all went straight to my elder biological brother Arun Berry's house. For days, from morning till night, family members and friends came to us to visit. It was very common for family members to stop by with no phone calls or invitations. It was amazing.

My family and friends judged immediately that Connie, an American, was educated, self-made, polite, and intellectual. On top of that, she was my wife. She was the second daughter-in-law of the Berry family and the maternal family. I would not hesitate to say that after our marriage, Connie was the star of the family.

Now, Connie's loss has not only broken me but has been deeply felt everywhere. As a customer, I give thanks to Mr. Sanjeev Sachdeva of World Cyber in Delhi, India. I was spending up to twelve hours a day during 2015 and 2016 for my three trips to India, after Connie's demise.

Now, I cannot believe I came to the United States with seven dollars, and I was desperate to go back due to homesickness. I was well educated with no long-term plans. I was struck on foreign soil. How could I reverse all that? Why had I decided to leave India, leaving my family and my childhood partner, my biological brother Arun? My late cousin Anil had discouraged me to go to the United States and had told me that I would be absolutely depressed—no friends, no money, no wife, no certainty. I had very mixed emotions, and I truly never wanted to come. I was waiting for someone to say, "No way. You can't leave India." I mention in my childhood tragedy chapter that my biological mother, if she were alive, would have never let me come under such confusion. I never saw my biological mother, Shanti Mummy, because I was two months old (and my brother Arun was eleven months old) when Shanti Mummy died. Later, her younger sister, Kanta Mummy, was forced to marry my father for the sake of Arun and Pradeep avoiding having a stepmother. Kanta Mummy died when we were five and six years old, respectively, after the birth of my sister Pappi, who was two hours old. I remember her death, her dead body, and the cremation. However, I do not recall whether we had the emotions or the power of thinking about where Shanti and Kanta Mummy were. If they were alive, perhaps I would have never left.

It was a new life and a different culture. Looking at the snow and downtown was somewhat depressing, with large, high-rise buildings. The homesickness bothered me. I was desperate to go back, but I did not have the flexibility. I used to count on those who lived in India, came here for a week or two years, and then went back—but I was stuck until God knew when. These things were driving me crazy, and I was having withdrawal syndrome. When I started working in a suburb of Chicago for a short time, I met many of the actors of the great Second City, and they were extremely friendly and nice to me. I was staying on the second floor of a business house, in a five-bedroom apartment, with my own room and bathroom. There were three elderly Indian chaps on a temporary basis. I started writing their letters to their wives and children, as well as doing other errands, because they did not speak English. They were a big moral support to me, and I was great help to them. They too missed India. They had no plan to marry, but one thought to go back very soon. Connie and I discussed this point a few times, but there is no answer. I must write that my adult life was the best thing I could get, mitigating all the childhood tragedies and confusion. Neither do I want to know the answer to this word *if.*

Connie was the best wealth, wife, friend, sister, and mother. She was my life and will remain so till the next life. This is the most honest and truthful answer I have from my heart and soul. This is the most significant answer to my life, my heart, and my soul. I express all that in my own way by seeing Connie's pictures, writing her stories, reading her notes and research papers, and browsing her recipes. I look at them now and then close them as they become immortally attached to me, giving me pain because Connie has left this world forever, and I will never see her except in the next life. These things are more painful than a fish out of the water. I had never imagined that her memories would eat me day and night, that all her belongings remind me of her and are hard for me to give away. With everything she possessed, I am reminded she had an innovative mind. Truly she was disciplined and organized, and I never noticed that when Connie was alive. How could I have known all that? We were so happy among ourselves that my mind never thought to ask her to show me anything, because her love and her presence was more than enough for me. Now, her possessions and things haunt me. Why did I not ask her many things about her collection of those things? I would say that she was keeping them to enjoy for the next twenty to thirty years, but we both never expected her sickness in 2013. I am not going to mention anything about her sickness and or any good or bad medical treatments. I simply never expected that she would go so fast and suddenly. But it happened on that unlucky day for me, February 28, 2015, at 1:10 a.m.

Now, It is my solace that I want to be here in the house on Thanksgiving, Christmas, Valentine's Day, her birthday in February, and her death day All those days, I go to her cemetery as a way for me to give tribute. I was supposed to go to India for the Diwali festival of lights in India on October 30, 2016. I postponed it because I preferred to be with Connie in the house, writing and finishing this book so that I could start another one. I am never bored as long as I am in the house, because her blessings and her pictures all over the house are a big comfort for me. I listen to some of the sad, emotional songs of where two loves are separated. Those are great old love melodies from sixty years ago. Now the new generation has different a approach, which I do not know or want to know.

My mind is occupied mostly in my own sorrows of losing my wife. My friends, her siblings, my cousins, musical programs, theaters, movies, and anything else is far away from my life. I must admit that I am happy being alone and staying at home. I have no desire to meet anyone. Connie's death took away all my social and fun life. I have practically withdrawn myself from worldly things, including dining out and traveling anywhere (except to India to see my brother and his family, and my sister). Yes, I still have my aunts and uncles, but some of the other my mental happiness is a temporary happy over there. Inside this house, I am still with Connie. I therefore keep myself occupied in some sort so as to not make others less important. I wonder many times about meeting Connie and discussing the same topic if I had not come to the United States. However, then I would never had met Connie, who was to become my wife. That is one of the best things of my elderly life while forgetting my childhood tragedy. I am grateful to the Lord to make my youth life the most happiest life, mitigating the childhood tragedies. Connie gave me all the happiness one can expect from a wife and a friend, and that is why I call this book in my heart and soul *My Connie*. I had no idea of marrying anyone other than Connie, and the same would have been true for her because we had so much understanding. I wondered why all these things were happening.

It was very painful to start writing this book in March 2015, after her demise, along with cremation, ashes, a plot, the peace of chapel, and all the other mandatory legal paperwork. I was working about sixteen hours a day and night. I had to write the book to overcome my grief, which is still there. Sometimes it is difficult to write because Connie was and still in my mind. Connie was the darling of my immediate and extended family. I am the same Pradeep who came alone and was happy for forty-two years with Connie. Now I'm again alone in the United States. I wonder if it is a movie, if it's fiction or reality. It is a reality. I see Connie sleeping next to me every time. It looks like truth as I get some vibrations in the middle of night and in the morning when I get up. But when I see her side of the bed with her pillows and her favorite silk satin cover, it's upsetting. I pray there, as I would do in the temple or church. But why go anywhere? She is my temple, and her room and bedroom is now a new dimension of my love. I am very upset with unbearable pain. The truth is very painful.

Finally, my thanks to Dianne Hiatt and Joan Connors of AuthorHouse for publishing *My Connie*.

To end my notes, no matter what I write or say, there is no way I can ever forget my Connie. She was very special and priceless, and she was the one who made my life and my destiny. She will always remain in my heart and soul as long as I am alive. Connie, I am very grateful to you for all the help in my career and your devotion as a true wife and friend. I have lost the most important part of my life, a true partner, a diamond at this junction. You have left me too early. I can't say good-bye to you because you are always with me, in my heart and body.

Your loving husband forever,
Pradeep K. Berry
June 6, 2017

Preface

My Connie is the first book I have written, in memory of my loving and precious wife, my true friend, and my whole world, with whom I spent over forty-two years. My purpose was to write this book to give my tributes to my wife, and to let readers decide, think, and evaluate: Are we truly living in a good society? I want readers to make a special note: Never depend upon anyone. Test your relatives and friends when you are in trouble financially or sick. When you cry, you cry alone; when you laugh, they will laugh with you. Connie told me that in the United States, daughters take care of their parents in their old age, instead of the boys doing this in India. It was something new for me when we got married. During the course of our long marriage, her message was a reality. I can vouch for Connie: she was right. She emphasized that the biological brothers and sisters are raised with love and are very close to each other when young. Later, when people are grownup, married, and have children and grandchildren, the childhood love diminishes. Sometimes inheritance disputes and their own lives supersede the childhood love. I truly believe this. I saw it during my childhood, and I am still seeing it everywhere. An important saying in India is, "A blind person distributes sweets to his own." All parents give to their kids, and the same kids give to their own. This cycle keeps going forever. During the current period, there are so many disputes, greed, and bad relations among families all over; it is very common. Lucky are those who are past all this.

Connie and Pradeep were far away from all this. I can assert that I would never fight for my own inheritance back in India. I am contented and believe in earning with my two hands, as Connie did. That was her message to me, and I will follow that message till I die. Connie was instrumental in teaching me to save and work, and to never ask for a dime from anyone because no one will ever help. I do not want to be a burden on anyone. She never demanded anything from her parents after she finished her college, and the same was with me. That was one of the best things we discussed during our first meeting in the restaurant with her students, before getting married. She had valued education as the best thing, and so did I. She had a choice to ask for money from her parents, but she did not. I had no choice to ask from my father and my stepmother; as much as they were nice to us, I never wanted to ask, and a need never arose till October, 28, 2016. God has been great in that way. Connie and I have been givers and not takers, with the kind grace of God and our hard work.

Connie and I were not spared from certain inheritance issues, leaving bad marks in our lives, but we did not care because our love mitigated it, and we did not care for all that. My pain is not wealth, inheritance, or dispute, but the demise of Connie. Now it is haunting and has changed my thinking to not be involved in families and to carefully evaluate a new way to be happy in reading and writing, household work, organization of paperwork, teaching students, helping the needy, and visiting India to see my family for a short duration. Otherwise, as mentioned in other chapters, I do no more traveling anywhere. I am happy being in our home. As painful as it is, it's still better than wasting time outside the house. I would not try to find any companion; I would not marry again. Connie was more diversified in reading and writing, but my focus was on the different kinds of many readings and different issues. Now I will focus on that.

I have new experiences in my life after the greatest setback of losing Connie. The wife is the best friend of the husband, and vice versa. I have written a separate chapter of my childhood tragedy, her sickness, her blessings, her last four breaths, her demise, and the cremation and ashes in her plot. When she was dying in front of me, with her last four breaths before she was gone, I was shaking and lost the power to think. I was seeing her face and was at her side when she took four breaths. I was hoping what I saw was true, but it was possible that her good karma, and my love and devotion, would be heard by the Lord, and those last four breaths would keep her alive. I have seen many miracles and true happenings, where a dead person suddenly starts moving on the bed, or even in the casket. After her demise, I was with her body for over six hours, touching her feet, kissing her on her forehead, asking for forgiveness, taking blessings from her feet (a very powerful tribute in Indian and ancient culture). I failed and was reminded that I had to do her cremation, placing her ashes in her plot next to her parents.

I must write that there were no family members, not her one sibling or any of my first cousins. I wanted her last rites by myself because she was mine, and she did not want any funeral. In many ways, it was good that her siblings and my first cousins did not come. I never wanted to show to anybody how big the funeral was. I have seen many families showing how many guests were at a wedding, birthday, graduation, or even at a funeral. They have come to show off to society how popular and connected they are. This is shallow pride, showing oneself like a royal family, which they never were. Connie and I were academic and were not into this shallow show-off of false pride. Connie and I were modest and never asked them to come. I never informed them of the death of Connie. I never wanted them to come at the cremation, because they never bothered to call or visit when Connie was alive and sick. Now, why should I want them at her death? To show off how upset they were? It was an artificial formality to come with a crowd. They had no time to visit Connie when she was sick. They all the time for their daily and weakened parties. They never even called to inquire about Connie, knowing she was sick. Why inform these people? Her one brother knew, but he, his wife, and their two boys never gave us a phone call. Their younger daughter and her husband never came till January 2017. I do not ever wish to see them or keep any relations with them, as much as they would like to pretend. I promise my readers that I do not want any relations with them now.

Rather than coming, her brother was asking the morning Connie died, "Pradeep, do I need to know anything about her money?" I said no. He told me I'd better find out or hire an attorney, otherwise there would be a probate. I told him not to worry, and Connie had left money for his four grown-up children. His wife said to me, "Pradeep, that is good." They were more interested in Connie's than coming to her cremation. Now they are only asking about her money. They knew Connie died but never came to visit until after two years. Neither would they come to the cremation and give condolences to me. Now, I do not want any relations with them. Connie and I always hated all that kind of show-off stuff. We were very modest and private and not shallow. Many families live to satisfy their egos. We both believed in education, academics, and being constructive rather than wasting time on big events, marriages of five days, and asking people to come for funerals, imposing on working days. Very close family is okay, but not everybody. This relationship with all of them is over from my side, and I do not want to have any relations whatsoever.

I would have to find my own way of a new life, a new beginning. I'd have to find a way to keep myself occupied. It may be teaching MBA students, working as a senior management consultant, spending time alone watching the symphony and Broadway shows, traveling for a few days in different cities, or spending a few months a year staying with my brother and his family in India. It's the beginning of a new journey, like an eighteen-year-old. How difficult it is going to be for me? But what choice do I have? I would follow the guidelines of my Connie: what would make her happy? We never discussed this topic, except in December 2014. Connie told me that if something happened to her, I should go to India for a few months to be with my brother and his family, but I should not move back to India permanently. Upon my mentioning my old age, Connie told me that I should buy the Medical Alert device and put around my neck, for any emergency.

One painful conversation I remember was on June 16, 2006. We went to see her mother in the nursing home, 178 miles away from our house. We were going to stay in a hotel for two nights as always. Her mother had moved to nursing home due to some very controversial episodes from her one sibling, and it was a very difficult family drama. Connie and I were very hurt and would remain hurt all my life. That episode was one of the biggest events of her sibling relationship till January 1, 2017. Now the forty-three years of relations are all gone. We had planned to stay two nights in the hotel. This was the first time Connie and I had spent the whole day with her mother, and at 6:00 p.m., we cancelled the hotel room. Connie was very keen to get home. I will never forget in my lifetime everything relating to Connie. On that day, June 16, 2006, Connie told me, "Pradeep do you mind driving me back home after dinner?" I knew right away that she was going through so much pain due to her sickness. After one day, she was to meet another medical doctor for a second opinion. I was driving another three hours in the morning, and now also at night.

During that time, Connie told me, "Pradeep, thanks for taking me home. I do not know how to say it, but in case anything happens to me, please remarry."

It was a bombshell on my brain, and I was in pain. I told her, "Connie, I never want to see you going through this suffering and pain. You are going to live for many, many years. Please do not say anything else about marriage. Please take your words back. No way can I even think of any other woman in my life and in my heart." It was the most painful thing in my mind, and it still is at this moment on January 1, 2017. I cannot ever think of that at any cost. It is beyond my thoughts. I am now a widower and single, with no physical relations. It would be the biggest sin, showing the lack of my love, my character, my soul, my heart, my inner soul, to remarry and have physical relations. Connie was everything to me, and she would remain the same Connie for me. I wonder and ask many people who have remarried again how and why they opted for a second marriage. Everyone has different answers, but my answer is no way. I get upset and depressed, and I evaluate my thoughts over this. The answer is always no.

Connie and I had attended all the happy and sad occasions, including funerals, but it was in our blood to do our duty to attend funeral and say prayers. That was our ethical way, but Connie's death was absolutely different for me. My brother called one of my friends, Sanjay, to tell him that Connie had died and to please go to the hospital because I was alone. Sanjay came around eleven ten on February 27, 2015, and he was surprised that Connie was alive. He also went to his house to bring his wife, Prina. Connie was looking better, and I asked the nurse if I could use the restroom around 12:45 a.m. on February 28, 2015. I'd needed to empty my bladder since 3:00 p.m. I also called Arun, who was crying, and the cooking lady told me, "Uncle, your wife will be fine. We are praying hard to all the gods." I was positive that Connie would be fine, and that God had given her and me a new life.

But, when I entered the room at 12:56 a.m., Prina, who was reciting chapters from Gita, the holy book, desperately asked me to do my prayers because Connie was dying. Sanjay was on the computer watching her vitals and pulse. I was stuck in between the vitals and prayers. I could not believe it, but finally I saw her breathing going down. Now I too started praying and watching, praying faster next to Connie. I was absolutely shaken and dumbfounded. I lost my mind and kept watching Connie and the computer vitals. Finally, after the last four breaths, Connie was gone forever from my life. I could not do anything but look at her lovely face with no breath and her shining body. Breaths are life as the body remains the same. Nothing happens to the ears, eyes, legs, arms, head, shoulders, face, and the rest of the body. What is missing? Breaths. Death means sleeping with no breaths. God has given us these breaths free of cost, and while we're living, we do not realize how important breaths are. Are we grateful to God for those free breaths, which are life? Connie lost what? Her breaths. She was gone forever from me physically, but in my heart and soul and in every way, she was connected to me with my spiritual faith, devotion, and love. I have a great attachment forever that is absolutely pure.

When I came to the United States, I would say I had some hope. Now, I am a stranger in the United States. I am here, but Connie is no longer with me. All I have is empty paper to start writing about Connie and my past.

The last day of my years with Connie and holding her hands and forehead ended on February 28, 2015, at 1:10 a.m., and finally again at the her cremation on March 3, 2015, at 11:45 a.m. I was seeing the most terrible thing of my life, this human body in the cremation machine burning— the lovely body of my Connie. I was crushed beyond imagination, and my friends held my hands. I was able to see and bear all that was the end of our life. Death is a difficult thing to watch. A burning body is a much harder thing to do and watch. Ashes to see and hold is another painful thing. Ashes were buried in her plot on March 3, 2015. This was the most devastating thing I did by myself, with few friends and no siblings or extended family. I was very happy that they were not there in any case; I wanted that way. I must mention that I hold no ill will to anyone for this. It was my and Connie's decision that we never wanted her siblings to come. I am glad that they did not come I wanted to be alone at a private funeral without those who never came or called when Connie was alive. I never want to have any more relations with them, and I hold myself very lucky that I had to see this by myself. It's a part of my life, and I will never forget this while I am alive. All the past things are now memorial possessions, happy and sad thoughts in my mind and soul. Only I can feel those, and now I have to start a blank page, writing different parts of our lives.

I had never thought in my life that I would have to face the death of my beloved Connie. This is one of the most tragically upsetting, heartbreaking, unforgettable scenes, crushing mind and soul. How I could handle all that, seen all that, brings back the most upsetting memories of my life, the worst memory. Too much love is good, but it can be painful. I was helpless on both sides.

We both were very close from the moment we met. During our working years, I had to travel for my professional career in leverage and mergers, commercial lending, and crisis management as a senior to evaluate large loans to our borrowers all over the United States and Canada, as well as a few trips in Europe. I used to take Connie with me whenever she could come. She was everything to me, and I was everything to her. During my travels, when Connie was home, we were connected over the phone four times a day. When time permitted, she would travel with me and explore the city or town where I was working. She was the most innovative adventurer I will ever know in my life. I left my high-paid professional career on September 1, 2005, but I did a few projects in the West Indies in December, 2005, and in Chicago in July 2006, as well as some marketing strategies projects at home. I decided not to travel for work, but I would for our vacations in the United States and cruises in Europe. We'd go to Hawaii, Sanibel, Captiva, and Marco Island to escape winters. Most of our travels before and after 2005 were excellent cruises in the United States,

Europe, and India. We wanted to spend every minute of our lives together because we both were lovebirds.

The idea of writing tributes to my love has long been in my mind. I would say since 2005, the thoughts there, but no writing was in place. My laptop and my troubled mind started to write this love story in March 16, 2015. There was no going back, but idea was to move forward to write a book, and in a few weeks, I started writing daily. That result is *My Connie*, a true story of my life and the death of my mind.

I must mention that Connie's brother and his family, as well as my first cousins, were all a one-hour drive from my residence. They never came, and I don't want them to come. I hereby declare I mean no harm or bad feelings, and I would come over these family matters and try to forgive them. That said, I do not want to have any relations and would rather be by myself. Let God take its own course. I will eventually forgive all of them, and they all will be happy to have me included in their family, including her brother and their four children and grandchildren.

Pradeep Berry
June 6, 2017

A Very Special Note for This Book

Please note that I was very angry with my father, and with my third stepmother, Uma Mummy, and their children but I have forgiven them now. This is because Connie's lost was much more painful than that. Now when I am writing this book, I realize what my father must have gone through after losing our two mothers and his two wives. I have all the good feelings for my father but not a good feeling for his third wife and his children.

Regarding Connie's family, I don't have anymore relation with them. Only God will take care of them for their acts and their bad karmas.

I was angry when I started writing this book, immediately after the demise of Connie on February 28, 2015. Now it's June 6, 2017, and I concentrate on doing humanity work for my Connie. Please let me make it clear that by any means or anger, Connie is not going to come back except in our next lives. I am sure we will be a great couple again in our next lives. Keeping it in view, I would rather concentrate on doing good things so that I can get Connie back in the next life. By this thought, I don't want any more bad feelings for Connie's family or my family. My darling Connie would not be happy to see Pradeep Berry is annoyed with her family or my family, so I have no bad feelings for anyone. I am angry and upset as to why Connie died, and I wish she had lived till I was gone.

I think of good for all the humans and animals of the Lord. I am extremely interested in Connie's happiness, and this is the best way to come over my sorrows and my suffering from Connie's demise. At this junction of my life, I want to keep the best memories of my life with Connie darling, my beautiful wife and my world. Connie is still with me in my life and heart, all hours of each day. It will remain that way throughout my life. This hope will provide me with some soothing in my mind. I don't want to live in anger for Connie. Let the world keep going in peace and love. God bless Connie and Pradeep Berry, because we both had beautiful and best lives. How lucky I am to have my Connie in my life as the greatest partner for years and years. Very few people get this love, in my opinion. I would pay my highest priority to Connie and the good deeds she did for me, as well as the charitable institution in her life and after death. I truly appreciate Connie's loss and presence, but her good deeds keep me going forward. I don't have time to think bad feelings for my family and Connie's family. There are plenty of better things to do rather than be angry with anyone. People do what they know for Connie's loss, and her peace of mind and body and soul. Constance Berry will be alive in my life every moment of the day and night.

A wonderful and beautiful thing happened to me. Connie was the first and last choice of mine, and I was hers. The best things happen to lucky people, and we both were lucky. I will never get tired of naming Connie in my book and my soul. This is a very strong message for the love of a wife and a husband, and the wife played an extremely important role in the marriage, at least in my marriage and family. Connie was the first time I achieved happiness, and Connie achieved the same happiness. That is why Connie and Pradeep Berry were a very special couple in eyes of the world.

Pradeep Berry
June 6, 2017

Introduction

Connie the Light

My Connie was an extremely rare, priceless, precious destiny, and she was a special gift from God to me. We were two bodies with one soul. Before starting this biography of my true love, I have to give my highest tribute to my Connie and how she became an immortal love for me—a love that will perhaps be immortal for us both. I write this book to share my love and to give maximum credit to Connie for destiny and for lifelong love. This book, with valuable messages about the nature of love, is a creation of the love, hope, and faith we shared. Imagining this destiny and love is the only comfort I have left. I had never realized how life can be changed by love. Because of my devotion in fulfilling Connie's desires, I am sure God will fulfill my wish and hers. Perhaps her illness was a difficult test of life, an exam we had to face in order to pass again with a gold medal in our next love. In this book, I examine how destiny and love have shaped the course of my life.

It is extremely important to mention that Connie's demise created the most painful and shaking trauma in my mind every moment of my day and night. Even before sleeping, I have dreams. When I get up, pain and thoughts wander in my brain. I feel as if I am dreaming, but while getting up, I have to face the facts of my life. Connie's love is in my mind every minute of the day, maybe except when I am sleeping. However, the moment I am up, my pain is extreme. In addition to thinking about her, I am still avoiding the reality and don't want to believe at all that Connie has left me. I go through the pain that upsets in my mind, body, and soul.

I don't know what to do and how to cope. I start looking at her pictures, videos, computer, chair, walker, and whatnot. I can't decide whether I am getting peace of mind or more pain. Then I try to compromise by praying by her pictures and touching her chair, computer, and walker. That gives me some peace mixed with pain, and the lights in her study room are a small solace. It still looks as if I am on a business trip and will be with her on Friday. Once I dreamed that she was no more, which made my pain extreme. That time I was in a world of thoughts—specifically, how intelligent, intercultural, and intellectual she was. I have never met any person like that. I have compared her to too many of my family and friends, but I can't find anyone like her.

I then suffer from extreme, unbearable pain. I go deep into my thoughts and stop whatever I am doing, sometimes for a short time and sometimes for a long time. I then have to force myself to concentrate on the things I was doing or was planning to do. This much distraction is due to the love we had for each other. After that, I want to be alone and be isolated. I read one anecdote. "Life asked Death, 'Why do people love me but hate you?' Death responded, 'Because you are a beautiful lie, and I'm a painful truth.'" Yes, it is painful and unbelievable that God didn't fulfill my prayers. Is God is so cruel to his followers? These things are still rattling in my mind. It's painful when you love someone so much.

True Love and Great Destiny

True and pure love of anyone, whether that person is your significant other, parent, or sibling—is a double-edged sword that brings pain and joy. If on the one hand, you were never gifted with that love, you would not feel as much pain when the loved one passed. However, if you have been blessed with a deep love, the downside is that the pain is that much deeper after the loved one is gone. According to Lebanese author Kahlil Gibran, life and death are one, "even as the river and the sea are one." Gibran also wrote that "Like seeds dreaming beneath the snow, your heart dreams of spring." He says to trust in your dreams, for in them is hidden the gate to eternity.

I also turn to the holy words of Lord Krishna, as recorded in the Gita, a Hindu religious text that is used in courts of law. In this book, when Arjun was grieving over the death of his son Abhimanyu, Lord Krishna told him, "Why grieve? What son? Whose son? It was a mortal relationship and with death, mortal relationships break for good. Soul has already taken a new birth. Do your duty by killing your enemy brothers who betrayed you and killed your son, otherwise they will kill you and your four brothers." This true episode is one of the most popular and powerful in Indian history, as recounted in the Sanskrit epic history the *Mahabharata*. The story of the *Mahabharata* can be found in texts, films, and Internet searches. Many American and Indian stage actors have acted in this episode on the stage all over the world.

Speaking of the fleeting nature of life, Lord Buddha wrote, "Our body is given by our parents and nourished by food; therefore, it will be destroyed one day." This quote comes from one of the books on Lord Buddha that I read in school. A saying in India is "Sadanaam parmatama ka hai," which means "God always exists, but there is no relation with anyone before birth and after death." It speaks to the fact that our existence is temporary. However, in spite of this knowledge, it is not always possible to relieve this pain we experience when a loved one leaves us. The knowledge provides no solace, and it is extremely painful to lose a loved one. The degree of pain we each feel depends upon the love or the closeness of our relations, and we may feel more pain for the loss of some loved ones than we do for other friends and acquaintances. It depends upon the depth of love that we feel. With that love, we may hope that it will become easier to cope with our loss, although that may not be true. Rather, as time passes, sometimes the pain gets worse and dampens our former desires to travel, dine out, and do other great things that we did with our lost ones. The pain leaves us wanting to live an extremely simple life.

Mathematician, statistician, physicist, and astronomer Pierre Simon Laplace said, "Thinking of you much at this difficult time. What we know is not much. What we do not know is immense."

Consider also this poem by Edgar Guest,

One or the Other
One or the other must leave.
One or the other must stay.
One or the other must grieve
This is forever the way.
Braving what has to be borne
Hiding the ache in the heart
One whomsoever adored, first will be summoned away
This is the will of the Lord.

Yes, these are great words and philosophies about the loss of loved ones, but they may not hold universal truths or be true for everyone. They definitely don't provide me with any comfort, solace, or peace of mind. The loss I feel has extinguished all of the comfort I once took in spiritual and religious learning, and it's left me with unbearable pain that will last my lifetime as I withdraw from the world we explored together. Our relationship was and still is extremely strong, built on true love, attachment, and devotion to one another. The death of one half becomes a living death for the other half.

Our True and Pure Love

Now, I will write about my most precious love and the friendship that I had with my darling wife of over forty-one years, Mrs. Constance Ann Berry, or Connie, was born Constance A. Fuller. We not only loved but worshipped one another with our pure and true love. I can say with great pride that we were truly two bodies with one soul. Our love was a special gift granted by the supreme Lord. That kind of love is, in my opinion, extremely rare and results from a unique destiny. I am reminded of a line in a book I read, though I don't remember the name. "It is a wonderful song cum poem of love." The pain of losing that love rattles me to the bone. At the same time, I cannot believe the whole happiness of the world is over for my other half.

The Painful and Sad of My Life

The sad chapter of my life and the trauma I went through began when my darling Connie fell down from her bed at home on February 20, 2015. She was taken for a checkup at the hospital. Although her results were normal, the hospital kept her for two days for observation. Connie was to be discharged on February 22, 2015, however this never came to pass. She suffered cardiac arrest and, after six days, died on February 28, 2015. That was the day we were to travel home from the trip we had planned to Sanibel Island, where we had been going for the last ten years to be away from the cold and snow. We had canceled the trip in November 2014 after a negative report from another hospital.

Connie had been so considerate, and she had said, "I hope you're not disappointed that we can't go. If you want to go, you can go."

I had replied, "1No way. I would never go without you anywhere. I cannot even think about that. I will be with you no matter how much cold or snow I have to suffer." I was taking full care of her with great happiness. The saying "Do your duty. Life is a duty, and you must perform your duty with happiness" came to my mind. "If you cannot perform your duty, sit outside the church, temple, or road and ask for alma (money)." I believed this message about duty all my life, but it pained me to think of staying in town. For my love, it was not my duty but necessary for my wife. It was my love and care from my heart and soul, and for the first time I rejected this message of my childhood. I may or may not pass this message of duty onto others, particularly the young generation. However, for Connie it became a hurtful message. I asked myself, *What duty, which duty, whose duty, why duty? Why is this word in the dictionary?* Duty may be bothersome, but not when love is involved; then it becomes a true purpose.

My purpose was to save my beloved Connie from demise, but I lost that battle, and it bothers me all the time. I ask God: "Why did I lose that battle?" I was serving her like we served God. Why didn't God see the true devotion and pure love, with no more demands for anything other than her life? We were one loving couple and were extremely happy with each other. The Lord had been watching this for years and could give me one thing only: Connie. There was a time when Connie acted as mother, my sister, and of course best friend and wife. Now, when Connie was sick, especially starting in June 2013, our devotion, love, pain, and worries for her life were in the hands of the Lord even though we both were doing our duties, humanity work, and taking care of needy people. I even begged God to take some of the years from my life and grant those to Connie, because she was more important to me than material things. I also prayed, "My supreme Lord, please grant Connie a long life by taking some of my good karma, if I have some. Let both of us share by extending and curing Connie." I begged like a mother who always asks for her child. In the Bible, the Lord would say, "I will help you, my child." What happened to that?

I have great knowledge of spirituality, death, and birth. These are things over which we have no control, especially death. In spite of this, I was not ready for Connie's demise. She had told me her family had a history of long life and good genes, living to the ages over ninety. She was very positive and had tremendous good health throughout our marriage. She was intelligent and active. She said she would live a long time because she had been swimming regularly, golfing, walking, doing all the housework, cooking, shopping, teaching, and driving for years. In addition, she spent hours reading, was well versed in computer technology, served as the president of our building association for twenty-five years, had knowledge of building laws, watched all the best movies, traveled extensively, pursued higher education, and lived a healthy life. She was extremely careful about our diets. I believed she would be given that inheritance of long life. However, I was not sure about my own longevity, because my birth mother died at age twenty-six. My younger aunty, my mother's sister, was forced to marry my father to avoid bringing a stepmother in our family. She was married to my father for five years and died at the age of twenty-five, two hours after giving birth to my sister. My sister is still alive at age eighty-nine, but my father died before her at age eighty, on November 14, 2003. My paternal grandparents died at eighty-one. My maternal grandmother died at age fifty-six, and my maternal grandfather died at ninety-three. I was quite convinced with Connie's positive approach, we would live to ninety.

I mentioned my childhood pain. Connie is not with me, and that brought back the pain of my childhood to some degree. But Connie's loss is more painful than the childhood pain. Perhaps as part of my tributes to Connie, I am writing about this chapter of my life. Otherwise, I would not have written too much pain of my life and my brother's life when we were young in India. Now, the loss of Connie is the only thing on which I concentrate. Her demise, her separation, and her absence are the most terrible and devastating things. I mean this very seriously: her loss has absolutely broken me to no end. It is hard to believe that Connie is no longer in this world, I can't see her, I cannot talk to her, and there is no place on this earth where I can find her. She truly was the greatest wife for forty-two years. Two bodies got married, and till her disappearance at 1:10 a.m., I saw the same body, the same Connie I was serving food and watching movies and seeing her in the house, car, dinner, bedroom; giving clothes; sending messages on my cell phone; and cutting jokes. I loved seeing her smile and her beautiful, shining face till February 22 at 6:28 p.m., when she had cardiac arrest.

After that when she was on the artificial breathing, being intubated, I was watching, and she was talking in body language. Though painful, she wanted to say something. She was forcing herself to say something to me, and I was very close to her mouth, holding her hands. She had wanted to say something for six days. That scene, that moment of the day, will stay in my brain and heart all my life. What was in her mind, what she was thinking, and what she wanted to say—not know is very upsetting. What exactly did she want to tell me? What particular topic was it that she was trying to get to me? There was something in her mind for sure, which she was forcing to tell me, but she could not. I wish I could have known what her desire was. I wish I could hear her what was in her mind. I am dumbfounded when those scenes are crystal clear, and I go into hours and hours of thought as to what she wanted to convey to me. It's extremely painful, and only Pradeep Berry can feel that. No other person can even think of the depth of my experience of those six days. Only I can feel that, and not a single person on this earth, including my family, friends, neighbors, or any human being can answer. I pray to God. At least some miracles happen, and I hear the voice of the supreme Lord in my ears. God has given me the answer that Connie was saying this. Maybe if my devotion is true, one day through her soul, God's messenger, some dream, or some power, I will hear the message coming from somewhere. Then I would know that Connie wanted this particular thing. I would not take second to fulfill that desire. I would follow that desire like an order from the army general or vibration coming from the Lord.

I have read many books about this in Indian civilization. It happened to great saints and great swamis, holy people who had totally surrendered to God, dismissing their families and worldly things and waiting for enlightenment. Buddha is one example. Bandit Ratnakar, who was into the act of killing and looting people, was taught by saints. They crossed the jungles and enlightened Ratnakar, and from a great bandit, he become enlightened after twelve years of 100 percent devotion to Valmiki, who wrote the great holy book Ramayan, on Lord Rama. Kabir Das was enlightened by Lord Rama. Tulsidass was obsessed with his wife and in one incident (mentioned in this book) became a disciple of Lord Rama. Surdass was fascinated with all the woman, and he was enlightened to change himself. He poked his eyes and became blind so that he could not see any women anymore. These people came so close to God that they could sense and declare in advance as to when and where they would leave their bodies and take their last breath. These people are called Tappasvai—absolutely devoted to the Lord. To do that, it needs lots of sacrifice. However, in my case, I was still lacking this much devotion. I didn't where, when, and how I should start to become one of them, so that I could find out what was the last wish of Connie. My love and devotion is very close to these people, but I need some teacher to encourage me and show me the path to become one of those people. I have tried, and especially when I stand a few hours at Connie's granite stone, I ask the same question and same power. At that time, I am absolutely lost in my thoughts and far away from the worldly things. My thoughts, mind, and soul are pointed only on her granite stone with the engraved words I chose.

Constance Ann Berry
Best Friend & Most Precious
Darling wife of 42 years
Death—Feb 28, 2015.

This place under which her beautiful copper and gold urn with her ashes is sitting, is a great holy place for Pradeep Berry, with flowers spreading all over. The trees add to this holy place under its protection. I go to this holy place any day and any time to pray, at least three to four a weak. I must be honest, whenever I went to India in the last two years (three times), I made it a point one day before going and the day I landed back in the United States to go to this place to get power, peace of mind, and some soothing but painful vibration. Cold, snow, hot, rain, darkness—I go there regardless. If it is pitch dark, I turn on my car lights to see and stand there. Death is a truly a very dreadful thing to watch, and it takes away all the education, wealth, and human investment. How much education and knowledge has the world lost from these people who were teachers, doctors, presidents, CEOs, and thousands of other professions? How much schooling, PhDs and other professional knowledge is sitting under the grass or in the caskets? Buddha was right when he stated that the body is given by parents and nourished by food, and it would be destroyed. Another Saint in India stated with death, the world looses the deepest ocean of water in the shape of knowledge and education. Even the ocean does not have a space to accommodate all that knowledge after death.

It is a terrible thing to see, and death is what I saw, with Connie having cardiac arrest. It was my first experience to see both. No one can understand, and neither they can feel that pain expect Pradeep, who was there with Connie every moment. I could not do anything but watch her vitals on the monitor go down and down, going from forty seconds to zero. The last four breaths was killer for Connie and me, watching with my eyes and body. I saw and heard the four breaths, and my world was over right away. I had hope the medical doctor who was to come later to examine Connie's dead body would say that Connie could be revived. That hope went thousands of miles away when he uttered to me, "Mr. Berry, I am sorry, but your wife, Constance Berry, has died." I was stunned and kept sitting and kissing her face, forehead, feet, ears, eyes, and hands. All were absolutely gone. I kept sitting there, along with Prina, Sanjay, Florida Harris, and a nurse, till her body was taken. Everybody had to leave the room for half an hour when it was time to wash her body. I saw that but closed my eyes because I never wanted to see that scene of Connie's body being washed. I opened my eyes when the two nurses covered her body with a sheet and some clothes. Later she was taken in a blue bag. Sanjay, Prina, and Florida came inside, and we stayed till they were coming to take her body. I left at that time because it would have been very painful to watch them take her body to the funeral room, to the place where dead bodies were kept. Nurses asked me, "Mr. Berry, do you want to see when her body is taken?" I said no. They also told me that was better that I not see her body being taken, because it was not an easy thing to watch. Very upsetting, very scary.

When her body came in the casket after two days and was to be cremated in the cremation machine, I was not ready to give her body to that machine and kept delaying. I told the people who were wanting to place her in the burning machine to stop many times. Finally, after my last sixteen kisses on her mouth, forehead, feet, eyes, and hands, that was the last time I saw Connie and her shining body. After few minutes, I helped to pull her casket closed and pulled it inside the cremation machine. I waited ten minutes. Finally, when the cremation people were waiting in their cold ways inside, the cremation room was making everyone suffer. I did the most horrific thing. I pressed the red button, and Connie's body went inside the machine. Connie's body in the casket started burning, and I was shaken and wept. The cremation staff and my friends gave me comfort by holding my hand, head, shoulder, and shaking body. They kept me from falling or having a nervous breakdown or anything else.

The next day, her ashes were in her beautiful urn, and I held them at the peace of chapel. Thanks to all those friends and neighbors who were listening to the priest and my half-hour tribute to Connie and her qualities, without preparing a prewritten speech. My tributes poured from my heart, and I did not even write even the bullet points. It was pure, genuine speech and tribute.

Later, the ashes were in my hand, and people were waiting to put those ashes and the urn in her plot. There were six blue chairs for the visitors to sit in, and snow was giving its blessings. After half an hour and my last kiss to the urn, it went down in the ground. I watched, the last two hand to cover the grass over her hole were the hands of her beloved husband, Pradeep Berry. Was this life, or was this death? Regarding where Connie went and where she is, if the Lord lets me, I will go to that place no matter how far or how difficult it is. Only a miracle of God can do that. Man has no power to do that. Here comes the end of our beautiful, pure love and marriage with the great world-traveling memories.

Now, I have my prayers, Connie's pictures, and her home and her car. I am binding in that house and the other things that I find are just a survival to live on, to keep doing my duty toward humanity. Her memories, good and bad, are in my heart and soul. That is what my life is now. Please note that this writing is from my heart without forethought. I am pouring my heart on this book, typing whatever my heart is telling me to write. It is for my love to Connie. I thank my readers as they read and understand what our love is, even to this day. Who would do all that? Only her beloved lost husband Pradeep Berry. No one else has gone there, except a few neighbors of mine and my brother's daughter in-law, Mona, and her two daughters, Krishna (aged nine) and Radhika (aged four) during their first trip in March–April 2015 from India to the United States. It was the day the stone was to be placed, on April 10, 2015. My neighbors D, M, and M, as well as Florida Harris, were with me. In May 2016, Mona, Krishna, and Radhika again came to the United States, and they went there. My brother lives in India, and that is why no one else from my family can visit.

I must make it clear, other than these mentioned people who went there once, no other family even knows where Connie was cremated. This my choice. I do not want anyone else to know, and neither do I want them to go there. This is because Connie was very special to me, and that is why I titled the book My Connie. She was very precious, and she was mine. I am not worried about worldly affairs, the formalities of life with no true feelings and artificial tears. some use to show how much they are upset. If I find anyone who is sincere, he or she is welcome. Otherwise, I am not going to leak this immortal secret of Connie. Connie and Pradeep are the ones who matter to me. The rest of my friends and relations are only relatives and friends, nothing beyond that. Only I can feel that love. I do not intend to offend anyone, including my readers, but I am sure that readers are very bright and can understand my feelings. I would be very grateful to them for understanding what I have written for my most precious and darling wife of forty-two years.

My brother and my sister were raised by our grandparents. After the demise of my parental grandparents, my father and stepmother, and two of my uncles' wives, started treating us mostly good. But a mother is a mother. I had to do so many different errands, counting thousands of huge delivery boxes from eighty trucks into our warehouses for inventory count at 4:00 a.m. After that, I had small breakfast, studied, went to school, did homework, was a Boy Scout and Eagle Scout, and took lunch for my uncle when he was in the hospital. Later, I went to the best college in the country. I had job offers but decided to go for higher education, and I finished my chartered accountancy, a high-powered postgraduate degree. During that time, I would take dinner to my elder uncle in the hospital, studying and sleeping there like a nurse. These paternal aunties would give us food, but after a while, we felt that they were obliging us rather than caring for us, although all our living expenses were met by the family business.

This situation greatly bothered my father's elder brother, but he was at a loss regarding how to help us. To fight against four others was a losing battle. After his marriage, my elder brother was asked by my aunts to take his own separate kitchen, apart from the rest of the family, even though he and his wife lived in our family mansion. Later, these aunties tried to insist that we pay for the electricity and water bill, but my father's elder brother intervened and insisted that there was no way he would allow us to pay anything. That was a great gesture, and we never had any bad feelings with anyone.

I want to tell a true story about witnessing my grandfather's grief for the death of his son, my uncle, who was only thirty-two years old. When Grandfather Berry came to the cremation and saw Grandfather Mehra, he realized that he had not understood the pain of Grandfather Mehra regarding the loss of my mothers, his two daughters. Grandfather Berry broke down and apologized sincerely and from his heart, saying that now he knew what it was to lose a child. He felt deeply for Grandfather Mehra's losses as well. This touched me deeply as a child, and I look back at that moment sometimes when I think of my Connie. Her loss brings my childhood suffering back to me. All of these forgotten things come back to haunt me. I am still willing to forgive and forget, but the pain of Connie's loss is killing me. As powerful as that moment was, it is lost in my pain for Connie.

Four months later, Prime Minister Pandit Nehru died in 1963. When he died, I was in my uncle's room, and my grandmother was lying on the floor, weeping. In reality, she wept from the shock of Nehru's death, but it brought back feelings from the loss of her son. I was also weeping for Nehru, whom I had met many times and regarded very highly. I truly grieved for him. My grandmother told me, "Pradeep, why don't you attend Nehru's last rites?" I told her that it would be too difficult for me, because the security would make getting across the city almost impossible. She told me that I should go see if it would heal me. I realized that I wanted to go, and immediately I thought that maybe I should wear my Eagle Scout uniform. I also had my Boy Scout bicycle, and I went to get it. Right away, I started pedaling. I crossed all of the roads and crossed police lines. No one stopped me. In fact, they started saluting me, because the Boy Scouts were very renowned at the time. I was able to get close to Nehru's body, and I saw his funeral. I was happy and sad, and when I returned home, my grandmother was pleased that I had gone to see Nehru's cremation. It was healing for her to know that even Nehru, a powerful man, could die unexpectedly, as her son had.

I wanted to give this speech at an Eagle Scout ceremony for my cousin's son in April 2012, in the United States, but I could not due to time constraints.

After this Boy Scout function, Connie told me she would not attend his next function on July 14, 2012. It was my birthday, and she wanted to take me out for dinner. I regret and ask for forgiveness from Connie. Why did I give her so much pain to deprive her from treating me for my birthday? I chose to go to this cousin's daughter's graduation and make them happy while sacrificing the desires of my wife. There was loud music and noisy atmosphere. We could not socialize over the loud music. We sat with a nice American couple and tried to talk, but we all began to feel the noise. Connie was offended and left the party early, leaving me. I immediately followed her because she was furious. After that, no one from that family including my other first cousins and spouses and grandchildren, called us. Neither do I call any of them. I know I could have called them myself, but I did not because it was painful for me, especially because no one ever called us about why Connie wanted to leave. My love for Connie was so huge that I decided I would never go to any of their functions no matter what. My cousins called me twice to invite me for the marriage of their nephew, who is also my cousin's son and whose business is close to our home. He never called or came, and there was no way I was going to go to his wedding or even call him. That relationship has vanished forever. He always wanted my help on many things. Now I am very strongly writing that there is no way I would ever do any favor to all those people who were not in touch with Connie. I loved Connie, and anyone who did not call her and talk to her no longer exists in my life. For me they exist on the other planet.

My cousins called me to inform that this nephew's younger brother, in his late thirties, died in India. They wanted me to come for the prayers. It was a one-hour drive, and I could not go because I was out of the country. I did not go, and neither did I give my condolences. I want forgiveness from my readers for writing these angry acts of mine, but Connie's demise made me very upset, and I truly did not want to bother with them. Had they come to see my Connie from time to time, or even called to ask about her, my reaction would have been different. But from the very beginning, Connie and I knew that they all wanted to have Indian friends, and it's a shameful act that they have not developed any American culture or American friends in the last sixty years. They have made friends who all are Indians and India – little-little India, per Connie. We must respect the country and men of a country that has been kind to provide jobs and other amenities. If I had to live that way, I would have moved back to India to remain Indian. But Connie was my life, my American wife. America gave me my butter and egg and my success, and my forty-two years of marriage to Connie is strong evidence that I have lived my career and life as American without forgetting my roots in India. This is India for me. I was more hurt than anybody else from the demise of Connie. Now, I must openly write that Connie's death has made a wall in my heart so that I do not talk to any of my many friends, relatives, or cousins living one hour away from me. This has been expected in my mind, my soul, and in my brain.

You can see from my wording and writing my open views, and I'm breaking all ties with those friends and relatives. I am happy being alone and enjoy being alone. I truly do not want anyone to come to see me, and neither do I want to see them. Pradeep Berry can handle living alone without meeting any of my relations and friends, except the few outside friends in the health club or when I happen to buy groceries. These activities of going out for shopping and talking to the cashier are enough. I recall, during college in 1966, a friend of mine told me, "Pradeep, hello, hello." That would always last a lifetime, and too much meeting and depending upon the long-term friendship cannot replace hello and hello. I find they're worth a thousand words and have depth. I am seeing that had Connie not died, my reaction would not have been so strong, bitter, and angry while writing all in this in my love book.

When Connie had some illness in March 2005, I left my senior position and, per Connie's desire, traveled more and did so much all over the United States and in Europe, including many cruises and different trips, till March 2014. During this time, I rejected all the senior positions and my consulting, and I totally surrendered to be with Connie. I am lucky and happy that I did. I have no regrets except wishing Connie had not gone so early. I would have never thought of going back to work. It was all right to do some projects from home once a while, but working outside or traveling was history in my life. That strong love was the main cause. Connie meant a lot to me. During her sickness, I had many job offers for senior positions, but I refused them because I wanted to be with Connie.

For the last forty-two years, I have wondered why, and I think the reason is that I wanted to leave the painful atmosphere of my family home. Now I am convinced that it was my destiny to have Connie as my wife. I am happy that I forgot my Indian career and would take Connie as my destiny over wealth and a great career in all my future lives.

Only I can feel my loss, no matter what family, friends, and outsiders tell me. The comfort they try to give me has no effect on my loss. I only want Connie. I am not ready to follow anyone's advice or to try to forget the past. I want to bear this loss alone, grieve alone, cope alone, and find some temporary ray of light, although darkness will always be in my heart and soul. I am trying to stay healthy, keeping myself busy by working on legal cases and housework. I feel that the cleanliness of our home is important, because Connie was a perfectionist and always kept a spotless home. I have written a separate section about the importance of her housekeeping.

I have lost my one love. I am well aware that people die suddenly, but I am angry that God did not listen to my prayers and devotion. It has taken my happiness and left me with pain and withdrawal from the world. I no longer do the things I did with Connie. Now, my life is limited to traveling to India to visit my brother. I don't want much of a social life. I make business calls, run errands, speak with people from vendors and marketing people, and teach new MBA students.

Knowledge Theory vs. Practicality for Myself"

At some point, we must come to the following realization of death: everyone has to die. Man is born alone and will die alone. Does death become destiny, or does destiny become death? Everyone has his own faith in this dynamic puzzle, and some try to cope with the imminence of death early in life, whereas some choose not to think of it depending upon their love. When we lose a loved one, we all think that if the perceived cause of death would not have happened, perhaps death could have been avoided. For example, if he or she would not have traveled, had not driven, had not gone out in the night to attend a wild party, had not ridden in a car without a seat belt, or hadn't gone boating in the night, then perhaps death could have been avoided. Yes, we all realize that death will come, but when it does, we are filled with regret. That is the first reaction of someone to death. However, the old sculptor Vedanta says, "Death or its destiny." This comes from our ancient beliefs that I learned when I was sixteen years old.

Was it destiny that Connie's death was coming, or was it due to other reasons? Some people commit suicide; some shoot others and then kill themselves. Alcohol and accidents take lives. Connie and I always remembered one incident that happened thirty-five years ago. I was driving on the Edens Expressway with Connie around midnight, coming back from Oak Park after a party. We both saw a big man in his forties speeding on his motorcycle. Connie and I were surprised by his speed. Connie told me, "I do not understand how some people are so daring and take their lives in their own hands. Look at him. He might be going over a hundred miles an hour." Connie and I discussed how bold this person was to drive at such a high speed. Connie said, "I am surprised that he is taking such a risk—and without a helmet." She mentioned that she worried about him slipping on the wet road because it was raining, and we should pray that nothing would happen. A few minutes later, we saw him coming toward us, going south in the northbound lane. He crashed into the wall and died on impact. Cell phones were not available in 1983, so we went to look for a phone booth, but before we had gone far, three police cars arrived on the scene. Would you call this his destiny, or the result of his lack of common sense? Connie always told me to drive defensively and with full concentration, and to avoid driving at night, especially when we went to parties and functions. She was always careful to make sure that we had just one small drink. I had the habit of drinking three or four scotch and sodas, whereas Connie never liked me drinking that much; she would only have one drink and had good control over her habits. I don't know how she put up with me at that time, and I ask her forgiveness for my childish habits. Although I didn't see it at the time, now I know I was wrong. I regret it, and I think about her love, her care and concern for me, which she had from the first time we met. I even think of that time, that place, and our expressions and happiness.

I see that moment in my thoughts and have gone to see that place many times and stay there for hours, thinking. The place is there today: the windows and stairs and neighborhood and street are still as they were, except for minor changes on the side roads. The street names and roads are still the same, and the place where I lived when we met is there. We walked together on those streets for safety. She had to put up with my childish habits, although it made her angry. I realized her advice was right, and she wanted me to cut back on drinking. God helped me one day in 1989, and I decided I would try not to drink the next day; it was a Saturday, when I would not have to go to the office. I had a wonderful meal and a lovely sleep. Since then, I have never touched wine or beer. My relatives and friends were shocked and begged me not to be a saint and to have just one drink, but I'd made my decision. A few times when we were flying first class, I was tempted to have a few drinks, but I decided not to start alcohol again. When we used to drink, I had the habit of continuing to buy wherever there were great sales. Connie asked me why I would stock up on liquor, which took up space in our home. Once I quit, Connie was amazed by my determination. My brother and friends were also amazed. Why drive in the dark when you can drive in the sunshine? During snowstorms, drive in the morning when you can see more clearly. It has been over fifteen years since we found out that the motorcyclist in the horrible crash was not drunk, but driving and speeding for fun. Connie and I discussed that accident with many of our friends, and they agreed that he must have been stupid and brainless. Vedanta would say it was his fault, and that if he did not speed, he would not have died. After Connie's demise, even if someone offers me millions of dollars, I will not drive on the highway for more than a few miles.

Our life was most wonderful throughout the forty-one years we had together. Every moment of those years are on my fingertips and are running in my head all day like a movie, and it is painful. I must write that our love was so special that her death crushed me forever. This is because of our love. I cannot help repeating many parts of our love. Now her death moves around in my mind all the time, and I openly write and admit that I do not like to deal with anyone. Every moment, Connie comes into my brain, my mind, and my soul. I always keep with me her pictures—in my pocket, my jacket, and on my phone. I wear some of her unisex chains and watches. I do not want to give away many of her things, and neither do I want to sell them no matter what someone offers me in cash. Our love and sadness during her last few months from 2013–2014 was worse and worse, and February 2015 was like a death for me when my Connie died. I cannot ever forget our forty-one years of marriage, and I can say that each and every moment is like a photographic memory for me. Six years ago, Connie and I attended lots of parties, and I loved driving at night, drinking, dancing, and going all over the city.

In India, and perhaps in other old civilizations, people are of the view that when death has to occur, it takes the person to that place where death is to occur. To some degree, I believe this because I have seeing many instances of it in my life. I will give a few examples to demonstrate. At the same time that some people's deaths seem predestined, other people fall asleep and simply never wake up in the morning. People get heart attacks while driving, while in the house, and while in the ambulance. Some get saved, and some die. Who or what should we believe, and why? Do we justify the reason of a loved one's death for our solace as God's decision? Or do we place blame on a series of events and decisions to explain why the person went to that place of death? Would they be alive if they had not gone there? I think no one knows this answer, and if someone says he knows, perhaps he is justifying death to himself and to others. However, even those who believe that life and death are in the hands of God and fate will still question whether a loved one might have lived if particular events had never come to pass.

Going back to death or destiny, I want to mention a true story involving a relative of my close uncle, Dr. P. N. Behl (PNB), and his English wife, Marjorie Behl (MJ). Their marriage is proof that love is blind. Dr. P. N. B. was a world-renowned dermatologist who studied and practiced in the UK and the United States before eventually returning to India permanently with his wife. He traveled the world for conferences and served as a visiting professor and numerous institutions. MJ's parents would frequently visit her and my uncle in India.

In the early 1920s, a young Indian Muslim boy, Dr. Rashid, left India for the UK at age six. Eventually, he was befriended by my aunt's parents, who raised Rashid like a son. Rashid remained a bachelor his whole life and lived with MJ's family, Mr. and Mrs. Hopkins. In time, Rashid became the surgeon general of the UK, where he met a young PNB at a hospital and decided to give the young student an internship chance. In this way, they had a father and son kind of relations.

In 1971, there was the death of Mr. Hopkins, whom I met in India in 1968 and spent lots of time with. He was very decent person in spite of being rich. MJ went to the UK to visit her mother, Violet Hopkins, and her godfather, Dr. Rashid. She came back after few months. I was looking after PNB; his son, Anil; and Vanita, an elder brother in the absence of busy schedule of PNB, while finishing my education and teaching Hindi to Anil. In this way, we were closer to Anil and Vanita, and later my elder brother, Arun, was part of all that. After a few years, Mrs. Hopkins was coming to visit MJ. In 1972, Mrs. Hopkins became very sick, and MJ went to England along with Anil and Vanita. We missed all of them. PNB was alone with his mother, and I used to visit PNB all the time. It is important to mention that while Anil was in India, he went to medical school and also met his girlfriend, NH.

MJ met with a serious car accident in Brighton, England, where they had their houses and resorts. MJ was sick and as a result was stuck there two years. NJ was left without Anil, and she used to meet me near PNB's house to inquire about Anil. She was very upset. I too was upset with all these things. PNB was and his mother, who was a true jam, was a big support to all, including the servants in PNB's house. In my own Berry mansion with joint family, I was responsible for maintaining the balance and being with them, being with my brother, and later thinking of starting my CA practice. PNB said that he was going to England to bring home his wife, but due to some conditions, he was gone for a week and had to come back. Finally, he asked his son Anil to come back, and then we were happy. NH was very happy with legal work. Her mother and Rashid came to India for a six-month visit. This was Rashid's return to India after eighty years living abroad in the UK. At the end of their stay in Delhi, my aunt's mother and Rashid planned to leave for their return to the UK on a Sunday night. However, Rashid chose to stay two extra days for work. My aunt's mother, V, flew back alone, but upon her arrival at home, she got a call that Rashid had passed early Monday morning. His body was immediately buried according to tradition. V returned to Delhi and tried to take Rashid's body back to the UK for interment, to no avail. For the next several years, my aunt's mother continued to travel between the UK and India to visit her daughter and family.

Many years after Rashid's death in 1976, my aunt called me to say that her mother was coming to visit me and Constance in the United States. A day later, my aunt and uncle called again to say that V had passed away in Delhi. She was cremated and buried next to Rashid in Delhi. Was it her destiny to die in India much as her adopted son had, or did this come to pass by chance?

Another story that happened was the tragic death of my cousin, Dr PNB's son, Al. We were very close growing up, and he was a gem of a person. I taught him Hindi when he was young, and we became great friends, as close as brothers. I was like an elder brother to him and his sister, V. Al was studying his medicines and was dating a girl, N, who was like a sister to me too because of Al. Al was crazy for N, and they were very close to each other. Al went to England for four months with his mother, and while there, Mrs. PNB had a car accident and was seriously injured. Dr. R and V called Dr. B and told him many times to come see his wife, but he did not go because he was devoted to his work, and some unavoidable circumstances came too. At that time, Al was away from N for two years, and I used to talk to her every week to tell her about Al. I used to stay some time with my uncle and his mother too. Finally, Dr. B called Mrs. PNB and said that he was coming to take her, but PNB was again stuck due to his new clinic and some legal things regarding his building and hospitals, where they wanted him all the time for serious burn patients. His visit was not more than a week. After his return, he was stuck in between the UK and India. It was a difficult thing, and that made me somewhat aware of life. However, it was just a theory and experience.

PNB called his wife to send Al to Delhi. Al started studying his medicine in another state—two hours by plane, or eight hours by train. Being away from N who had sacrificed for all these years was difficult for Al, and he saw his own suffering for N. I used to go with him to be with him during his exams and on some other occasions. I must ask for forgiveness that Uncle PNB was not aware Al was so lonely without N, and that I was going back and forth for moral support. I must say, I did lots for PNB, Al, and my aunt. Perhaps that was the time I should h had focused on my career. PNB was telling me that I should forget all that and focus on my career. I was wondering whether I should go for my profession, the family business, or get away to the UK or the United States. All these things were on my mind, and suddenly a miracle happened. I decided to come to the United States. I was to come here, and I am sure my destiny was to meet Connie. I would say this was the best thing I got in my life, my Connie.

That is why I am writing this book in her memory. My love, my homage, my tributes, and my life—I give everything in this book. It's not simply "In memory of my wife." I want to write my heart out for this book because

Connie was my world. I am crushed without her, and the pain I am going through is unbearable. I have talked to many people, and they have been advising me that I should not feel that way. But how do I stop thinking about her? That is a big issue in my life, puzzling me all the time. Yes, we had a wonderful marriage and had the best time of our lives. Not too many people get to travel around the world as we did. All the dinning, all the Broadway shows, and all the other plays around the world. The symphony in Chicago, Vienna, London, Italy, and Ireland. Many concerts watched on the TV during Christmas. We were even lucky to see Mozart's house while going with a group from Budapest to Vienna, Germany, and Amsterdam for seventeen days, on a river cruise. There are other places in the world, as mentioned in the section about travel.

"Finally, they got married." I was already in the States at this point and had not been there long. I got a call from my family telling me that Al was killed in a car crash. I sent a telegram to Dr. and Mrs. PNB, as well as N, who had a one-year-old daughter, N. When I went to India after four years of our marriage, Al was gone, but I saw Dr. and Mrs. PNB. It was a new experience, and they both brought new life to all of us. PNB, who had not been happy that I had gone to the United States, was now happy to meet Connie, and so was his English wife. It was a happy and sad occasion for them and for me. Connie was new and met them for the first time, and they reacted very well due to her education, character, and intelligence. Both my uncle and aunty got new strength now that we were part of the family again after four years. They found no changes in me and forgave me for leaving them four years ago. Our success and our true love was a great happiness for them, and that was a true blessing to Connie and me.

In the same vein, I can vouch for my father, my brother and his family, my sister, and all my other extended family. There was a new bond, a new wave of life after meeting Connie. Connie was the name everyone was saying to me, and I was overjoyed that they truly loved her. My mother and father were already in Delhi, and they also came to the airport to receive us. They were delighted in every way. After ten days, we took a flight to Kashmir Valley. I had few friends there, but Connie wanted to stay in the best hotels in Kashmir, while considering staying on the large riverboats, which includes a whole day of riding in the boat, with rooms inside and home-cooked meals three to five times per day. Connie and I loved it, and there were several American tourists in that boat, called the *Shikara*. Later, because of Connie's intelligence, she discovered that the purity of the water of the river was an issue, to avoid getting sick. The boating and *Shikara* people assured us that they got special, clean water for all, and no one wanted to get sick. We decided to come daily for rides but stayed in a nearby five-star hotel. My friend was not happy that we were staying in the hotel. Later, to please him, he agreed to provide his taxi business to us all the time for no payment.

The coincidence was that the friend was married to a girl right across our Katra Neel house. The two girls were right across our home, and they were keen to be friends with us like sisters. My brother and I were shy and never talked to them. They didn't initiate because that was modesty, although inside we all wanted to be friends. This sheltered life was the main reason that boys and girls never used to talk; it was only if the families approached each other for marriage. There was no shortage of brides, but I was not keen. I am sure Connie was my destiny, and she was a beautiful, highly educated girl. I could not ask for anything better than Connie. Connie was the brightest wife compared to others who were keen to marry me. Connie was much more educated, intelligent, and self-dependent. Our marriage, our tune-up, our rhythm of understanding academics, and her intelligence was much more solid and was the foundation for my success.

During that period, I told Connie about this girl from Katra, adding that I could have married her. Connie stated that who knew what kind wife she would have been. I noticed that she was very happy to see us because we were from the same place. I noticed she was slightly sad that we couldn't stay longer, but we had limited time because our flight was booked for coming back. They came to the airport to say good-bye and, that was the last time I saw both of them and their two daughters. I wonder where they are now?

It was my happy destiny that I came to the United States and immediately met Connie. I cannot believe that forty-two years went by like forty-two seconds, and that thought shakes me. I wonder, is it the end or beginning of my life with Connie? What and how many changes does one have to go through in this life, what am I experiencing at this junction? Did our ancestors also go through the same kinds of life? I want to say yes, but when Connie comes in my mind, I convince myself no. My Connie was extremely special, and perhaps no one else had that kind of love. I am not trying to be arrogant in writing this, but my loss of Connie is making me think of all that. How many readers will like my book? I do not know, but I hope they will respect me for my love to a different culture in the United States. I feel I am the wealthiest person with Connie as my wife. Money is immaterial. The saying "Money is everything" comes from those who have not seen money. Money is good, but too much of that can also be a disease, bringing disputes and other friction. I believe a comfortable and great life with happiness is more powerful than stacking up money in the bank. We believed in a good life, traveling, dining, and having all sorts of fun with no compromise, while also doing humanity work. My maternal grandfather and my Berry family were an amazing thing for all of us. Later, Dr. B adopted a son, S, and they loved him very much. He had no profession as an adult, so Dr. B made him a businessman. Later, S got married, and V was very nice to him. They had to work through difficulties but resolved those with my help, and now everything is okay. At N's daughter's wedding in August 2003, which Connie and I were able to attend, N's daughter was able to able to include the memory of her father and grandfather, and she gave tributes to them, as well as to me and Connie.

Life and Death Episode Message

On September 1, 2005, I was confused about whether or not to go to India for two weeks. I was not sure whether I wanted to go or stay. I came home at 3:00 p.m. Connie asked me why I didn't go see my family, because I had already planned to go and had purchased the tickets. I said, "I cannot leave you, because you will be alone for two weeks."

She said, "Pradeep, I can come with you, but last-minute tickets are very expensive, and we will have separate seats. I don't think it is fair to spend double or triple the money for a two-week trip. After your return, we are going on a Norwegian cruise, and then Hawaii. I think that would be too much travel for me, and I would not be able to do your packing for the cruise because we are going with the top alumni and professors of the University of Michigan. I think if you want, you should go and come back in one week, and we will talk on the phone every day."

I agreed and found I had no good undergarments. Connie surprised me and told me that she had already gone shopping that morning while I was at work; she'd bought me new undergarments, socks, and shirts. I was in tears and told her, "No, I want to wear them when I am with you. I can buy new ones in India." She had purchased two dozen pairs of special underwear in my size, which were difficult to get due to some ban on imported clothing. I used only a few and saved them for years. I wore them all, except for a new packet that was still unopened in my drawer. It is worth a million dollars to me today, because it reflects her love for me in doing my shopping. The shirts and ties she bought me are sitting in my drawers, and I was saving them to use with her on trips to different climates. Lastly, she bought me four silk shirts to wear to special functions. She wanted me to wear those shirts, which were very expensive, designer made, 100 percent silk, and cost over $150 dollars apiece. Connie started getting sick and hoped that I would wear the shirt to please her. I regret that I was saving it because it was an expensive present. That polo shirt is still sitting in my drawer. I see those often and regret that Connie never saw me wearing those things. They are sitting in the closet along with cardigans she bought me from Carson's, and two expensive jackets that cost $350 each are sitting with their labels on, along with many other lovely clothes.

Connie died suddenly due to those shameless doctors. She desired to wear them in March, when going anywhere—stopping for cake at Benson's Bakery after a doctor's appointment, or to get something from Harry and David's, or to get her cheese and chocolates and her favorite frozen yogurt with chocolate from Whole Foods. She would have one every night. One bar is still in my freezer waiting for Connie, but Connie is gone. I thought I could eat that bar of ice cream, but my hands started shaking, and I did not want to eat it. My love for Connie has made me think of that bar of frozen yogurt that she was to eat on the night of February 20, 2015, but she was tired and told me that she would eat it the next day. I have written that she fell down on the night of February 20, and she never made it back home. That frozen yogurt is still in the freezer.

One friend of mine showed up because my brother from India had called him to say that Connie had died and I was alone. He came at 11:00 p.m., and I surprised. He was surprised to find Connie alive. He stayed and said it truly looked like false news. We were at peace because Connie seemed fine then. He told me to let him bring his wife to the hospital, but I said no because it was getting late. He insisted. I asked the nurses if I could go to the bathroom, because I had holding my bladder since 3:00 p.m. At 1.10 a.m. Connie died on February 28, 2015. I was a king when I talked to one lady while coming back to Connie's room. She told me nothing would happen to my wife because our devotion to each other was marvelous and rare. I was extremely happy, but I was not truly a king. The moment I entered the room, I saw my friend by the computer with the vitals, and his wife was next to Connie's bed, saying, "Pradeep, Pradeep, come. Connie is going, she is going."

I was shaken and was absolutely broken. I looked at Connie, telling her, "Connie, Connie, please do not leave me. Please, Connie, do not give up." I asked the nurses to do something. I saw her last four breaths. Darling Connie died next to me. I was absolutely gone and wept and fell apart. My friends, along with Connie's caregiver, gave me great support.

In spite of this setback, I was still positive that my Connie would live. A great thought came to me: never deprive someone of hope when hope may be all he has left. I thought that miracles happen every day. These messages brought us great comfort. I began to ask God to make Connie normal again by a miracle, like when Jesus brought Lazarus back to life. That prayer was heard, so why couldn't my prayer save my lovely wife? At the same time, I thought of Savitri and Satyavan, a miracle that took place in India one hundred years ago. Through Savitri's devotion to God, her husband's life was returned to him. Thinking of these two miracles made me stronger, and I felt ready to fight anything. During her treatment, it was a struggle for Connie to go to doctor's appointments, and even walking too much in the house was difficult because she had to rely on a walker and oxygen. This was not pleasant for us, but being together and seeing each other's faces gave us great happiness.

Ultimately, I saw my darling's last four breaths and was present for her death. A couple of close friends were with me. I could never have imagined her death. It was one of the most painful, shocking, and uncalled for things I have ever witnessed. My mind went totally blank. Connie's body, and her face—I have no words for the pain that I felt in my entire being. Could it be true that I would never see her, talk to her, live with her again? I was left alone. I thought of the miracles. Was it possible that God might reward me by granting her life again? All those thoughts ran through my mind. Even now, as I write on August 20, 2015, every day since her death, these questions and thoughts run through my mind day and night. I relive that painful episode, and it gives me panic attacks.

I stayed with Connie's body for five hours, until it was taken to the funeral home for cremation. I will never forget that trauma as long as I live. After two days, I had her cremated and put her ashes in her plot next to her parents. Doing this was heartbreaking. I suffer from that pain and have withdrawn from life. The pain and suffering I am left with are incorporated into my mind and heart. I must mention that after Connie's demise, I asked Florida Harris if she would be willing to stay with me during the night in my study room, sleeping and studying; she could leave in the morning. I asked for this till I could overcome my fear of staying alone in my bedroom. I was crushed. It would have been a very big issue had Florida had not agreed. She does not like to stay in anyone's home and liked her apartment with her dogs. She agreed to come at night and leave in the morning. I would eat, and she would sit and talk for an hour and then go to my study room and sleep or study while watching TV the whole night. I was not used to the TV on the whole night, but she was sensible, and the study room was lit the whole night. I would go to my bedroom, lock it from inside, do paperwork, and sleep until around 5:00 a.m. I had so much legal work and many other things. Florida was surprised, and most of the mornings, she was gone and closed the door from the outside. Sometimes, I would hear her voice, and I would get up to say hello or see if she wanted to have breakfast. She ate many times. I hope Connie admired that.

We had an excellent car. Connie was driving, and her main car was meant for Florida after Connie. Since March 15, the same car is with Florida. That joy she had was unbelievable as she expressed her gratitude. Whenever she meets or calls me, I think there is some power that all this happened. It is very bothersome sometimes that a personal thing of Connie's and mine is with Florida now. But Connie's soul must be happy. I want to apologize to Connie. I do think now that Connie is gone, hopefully I will have more courage to give away some other things. This was another shock, a crushing thing. Some would not even imagine all that.

It has been very common in the families in India that some relatives stay with someone who lost someone for up to fifteen days. That is a culture difference between the United States and India. It may be happening more in America; I do not know. However, I am sure some families have this tradition. I have written separately how I passed through March 20–21 at Prina's home, till Mona and her two daughters came to spend one month with me on March 22.

I was absolutely nervous to sleep alone on the March 20 and 21. Mona Berry and her two daughters, Krishna (aged nine) and Radhika (aged four), were lucky to get US visas and flew flying from Delhi to Chicago, arriving on March 22, 2015, at 7:30 a.m. I was worried that I was alone for these two days. I called Parina, and she was very gracious to bring dinner and eat with me in my house at 7:00 p.m. She stayed till 3:00 a.m. and her husband, Sanjay, came at three fifteen after doing research at the university near our home. I was happy and thanked them, and they were gracious. Before leaving, Parina put some of the lovely necklaces of Connie on my neck and rings on my fingers, telling me that these would give me the power to overcome this fear. I must mention that those necklaces and rings were lifesavers for me. I still feel some power in them. I am sure it is my love that is blended in them. Whatever it is, I wear them all the time and do not take them off when I go to the health club. I must preserve them, and they are the most important part of my life. I find peace and power of Connie and in her rings, especially her marriage band. At one point, I never used to wear because it was loose. But now I cover them with other lucky rings. I am wearing them now and will continue wearing them till I die.

Parina took me for shopping for Mona and the family on the morning of March 21. Then she brought dinner in the night and took me to sleep in her home. She had offered to pick up Mona and family in her SUV. I delayed Prina on March 21 because I was cleaning the house. Prina and I left around 1:00 a.m. I was on the phone, and Parina was driving. Once we reached her home (not too far from my home), she offered me some food. We chatted because her husband was to come soon. However, we had to get up early, by six thirty, to go to the airport. I called my brother and nephew in India, asking them to call me in the morning as an alarm clock. Parina went to her room and slept, and I had a fantastic three hours of sleep in their guest room.

After getting the wakeup call from Arun and Ashiem Berry from India on my cell, I quickly got up, had tea, and woke Parina. She drove to pick up Mona and the family. It was a new experience in my life after Connie's death. Her demise affected me badly. Florida kept in touch with me when Mona was here, and she offered other help. We went to dinner and other places together.

Mona Berry and her two daughters, Krishna and Radhika, came from India on March 22, 2015. I took Mona, Krishna, and Radhika to Disneyworld, Animal Kingdom, SeaWorld, and other places in Orlando for ten days, They loved it because it was their first trip to the United States. Later, back in Evanston, Chuck E. Cheese was one of the favorites for the grandnieces, as well as different Indian restaurants and shopping. That month was great because they were with me, and I was not alone. Florida Harris also met Mona and the girls.

Connie's granite stone was placed on April 10. I had invited all the building residents. Some came, and I took the people to Hackney's Restaurant. Mona, Krishna, Radhika, Mary, and Florida enjoyed it. I was extremely happy when they got their passports and visas so quickly. Mona and her family left on April 20, 2015, for India. I was supposed to go with them to India because it had been close to four years since I'd seen my brother and others. No way could I have left Connie to go to India when she was sick. I never thought of leaving her alone. After Connie's demise, I got the power to stay myself, working sixteen hours a day to handle all the legal formalities and write this book. It was too much work for me by myself, but I made the decision that I would never ask anyone to help me because I was angry.

I went to India on May 17, 2015, to spend time with my brother and his family, as well as other relatives. I did not even disclose Connie's death until Arun, with anger, informed my sister and other family in mid-June 2015 about Connie's death. I cannot say that I truly enjoyed India as much as before. It was a change, but my anger and thoughts were the same. I was doing very little and was sleeping late, writing the book on Connie. I mixed some fun with my sorrows. Krishna and Radhika were the main entertainment, and my brother's family was excellent, but they could not help me overcome my loss.

I came back on July 23, 2015, and was busy again doing many things. After that, I went to India on October 17 and returned on December 21. My India trip was the same as it was in May, and I had the same life back in the United States. However, I am always happy to be at my home with Connie's memories. I still prefer to be with my memories. I do miss my family and Connie. I am living in a mixture of two worlds. For Thanksgiving, Christmas, Valentine's day, and Connie's birthday in 2015, I celebrated by myself with her memories and pictures. I plan to do the same in 2016. In my three trips to India after Connie's demise, God wanted me to do some humanity work in India and in the United States. I was able to donate blankets to the poor in India, sent money to blind schools, and provided money the education of poor slum children. In the United States, I was able to donate money to hospitals, charities, individuals, and needy people for clothing. My aim in life is doing humanity work. I think of Connie and surrender to God. I also want Connie to give me the power to get over my anger and forgive all the people who betrayed Connie and me. I do not know when that will happen.

On May 24, 2016, Mona, Krishna, and Radhika, came to the United States a second time. I took them to California to see Disneyland and other parks, and we stayed at Hilton properties, having nice dinners and nice rides. I met a childhood friend, Sanjay Seth, and his family. He and his wife were very happy and joyful. Sanjay; his wife, Pratibha; and their daughter, Karuna, were nice and took us to a few places, including dinner and their home. They later dropped off food for two days in the hotel due to the incident described below.

There was one incident where Mona and Krishna got sick in Disneyland. It was a very upsetting thing that scared me. They got sick while having rides in the theme park. On top of that, when I was walking fast with two wheelchairs, Mona and Krishna, I lost control with my dark sunglasses and my mind on taking the pictures of this sickness. It made me fall so badly, but I did not break anything. That day was a nightmare, and I was nervous. On February 28, 2015, I'd lost Connie, and now there was this incident. Disneyland was very kind to give us extended help immediately, and they provided all the medical and emergency services. They also returned our three-day pass money, which was a struggle due to their policy—one problem after another. But at the end of the day, the tunnel was open.

For the last three days, we flew from California to Las Vegas and stayed three nights in a Hilton. I must admit that Mona, Krishna, and Radhika had the maximum fun in Circus Circus Hotel. I cannot imagine that Krishna (age 10) and Radhika (age 5) were in the United states twice and saw both Disney World and Disney Land, SeaWorld, and other theme parks, shows, and restaurants. They'd experienced four fourteen-hour, nonstop international flights from Delhi to Chicago and back. I'd only had seven dollars when I'd come to United States forty-one years ago. That was change for me.

I flew back with them on June 26, 2016, and came back on August 5. My trip was 80 percent writing this book, though I did a few things with the family. I was only waiting to come back home to do humanity work and lectures. I went to Connie's gravesite the day I came back from India and have gone four times since. I plan to go there twice a week to get blessings from Connie, clean her stone, and check the gardening and flower services I have engaged. This brings the most happiness now in my life. I want God to bless Connie. Connie, you were instrumental in helping people in many ways. Not too many people would do that. When you were sick and used to call them for any help, they were takers and never came to see you while you were sick. Neither have they called me till October 5, 2016. I therefore never want to have them in my life. Such an inhuman thing I have never seen. This includes so many close relatives, though I do not want to reveal them. In the ancient days and even now, neighbors, unknown poor, rich, and whoever else will give tribute to the departed. I have seen dogs cry and come for the deceased till last rites are done.

Connie's cemetery is my place to ask for blessings from Connie. Since my arrival, I have gone three to four times every week. Connie's grave is well looked after, and that is my priority and happiness. I can say that I would sacrifice any of my dining or anything so I wouldn't have to compromise with money for Connie. I wish I had done lots of things for Connie when she was alive. I think about her every moment of my life. I would give anything to get Connie back in my life, and there would be no compromise there. I do not plan to go anywhere but sit in the house, write, read, or go walking. I have no idea what the future holds for me. I can assure one thing to myself and the world: no other woman will ever come in my life. Connie was my wife and was everything for me. I have only one true love, and that was Connie. That's why I am writing this book from my heavy heart and soul.

I never imagined that so many things come in life. Connie's sickness worsened in November 2014, and she died on February 28, 2015. After legal work, cremation, peace of chapel, and eighteen hours of work during many stages. I could not find time to go to the health club. My friends in the health club were worried about where I was. Connie's demise had absolutely broken me. It was one of the biggest tragedies I had seen in my life after my childhood suffering. I disconnected from TV, newspapers, magazines, credit cards, bank accounts, real estate taxes, other payments, income taxes, and loads of paperwork.

Connie and her sickness, her fall, the emergency call, the emergency room, eight days of her stay, my staying with her all the time, her cardiac arrest, –her demise, her cremation, the ashes ceremony, the memorial services—I do not have to elaborate on everything other than this. I must mention it was the most difficult time in my life. I had forgotten all the childhood tragedy and hardship. That looked very easy compared to the loss of my love. In India and childhood, I had hoped, and I had time and education. Now, I have education and a comfortable life, but no Connie. I realize that one of the biggest reasons for depression and loneliness is due to the loss of Connie.

Connie had met Mona for half an hour in February 2004 when she went to India to attend my elder nephew's wedding. When we came back to the United States, none of my family in India saw Connie, and Connie didn't go to India. She was not up to long flights and preferred to go to many European cruises, traveling in America. We took six cruises to Europe and went to Hawaii twice. There was Sanibel and Marco Island every year, Las Vegas, Houston, Wisconsin, and other places from 2004 till 2015. We attended a few alumni events, went for dinner every day, swam, and saw movies and shows. From 2014 till her death, Connie was home and went out to see the doctor's appointment. Our last long trip was in November

2014, to one state that was six to seven hours' drive each way. We spent five nights in a hotel but did not go out for dinner and had food delivered to our room. That was also upsetting all the time, as much as I try to forget, but I am helpless in my love. Connie was absolutely great and would do anything for anyone.

My immediate family has asked me to move back to India, however I can't because my mind and soul are in my home, where we spent forty-two wonderful years.

Today is July 11, 2016, and our marriage anniversary was on July 10. I prayed and prayed and then donated money to a school for the blind in Delhi. I spent two hours with the administrator, some of the staff, and a student. My brother Arun and nephew Ashiem were with me because they often drive in Delhi and know the roads. This is the first time in my life that I have seen a school for blind students, and they are very bright, studying for their MBAs, JDs, and government jobs, and going to top colleges and high schools. It was the happiest and most painful experience in my life, and I donated cash in memory of my beloved wife, Constance Berry. This is going to bring some peace to my mind, and I am sure my darling wife was watching me do that noble cause. This is the way I will spend my life until death, and we will meet in our next life. Connie and Pradeep will be together in the next life.

This book has two parts, happiness and sadness. Sadness has taken over happiness. Sadness is hard to define, and no one can understand that pain but me. I don't know what I can do while waiting to face the rest of my life, however I will have to be strong to survive Connie's death. For me, the world is lost. I no longer travel, dine out, go to Broadway shows, read, or watch TV or movies, I do not meet any friends, and I don't attend any parties or functions. I want to be absolutely alone in a sort of Robinson Crusoe situation, where a man lives alone and does everything himself.

In ancient times, many scholars and learned people took sanyas, during which they would totally surrender the world to get enlightenment and peace, and to leave a legacy of learning to the world. Around the world, many generations of people learned from these hermits, who withdrew from the world to gain knowledge. In my opinion, today we live in a world in which different generations do not share and pass on knowledge in the same way, and the young ignore the knowledge of their elders. The youth of the twenty-first century has also contributed to great technological innovations, and the world has gained. I believe in applying both ancient and modern knowledge to keep the balance in my life. Connie was also of this view and never criticized anyone. We both respected the beliefs of others.

Mahatma Gandhi

I thought of Gandhi, who fought for equal rights during the British Empire. In spite of the fact that he was a barrister of law, he was not allowed to practice in England. In South Africa, he was thrown from a train by whites because he was considered dark skinned under apartheid. That incident shaped him to fight to free India from the British. He was involved in all the Satyagraha, or strikes, and was imprisoned many times. One time, Gandhi was in his jail cell, and his fellow inmate told him that he should write a book, which he refused to do. The constant, persistent pressure from that inmate led Gandhi to start writing his book, which captured the world market. That book was an autobiography: *My Experiments Living with Truth*. This book has so much wisdom and many good messages for humanity and for nonviolence. Ben Kingsley acted as Gandhi in the Oscar-winning *Gandhi* in 1984. One can see his devotion and the sacrifices he made to free India. Pandit Jawaharlal Lal Nehru, the first prime minister of India; Maulana Abdul Kalama Azad; and many great leaders were the freedom fighters who supported Gandhi's movement.

Gandhi, who is called the father of the nation in India, is well respected. I feel upset that his approach of nonviolence was not followed for a long time. For the past sixty years, the world has changed, and nonviolence looks like it is gone from the dictionary. John F. Kennedy was a great president, along with Abraham Lincoln, Franklin Roosevelt, and others who did so much for the United States. Dr. Martin Luther King Jr., Nelson Mandela, and other great leaders also did so many great things. George King, the father of her Highness Queen Elizabeth of England, who had a speech problem, finally gave a wonderful speech during wartime. The film based upon this true story, *The King's Speech*, won an Oscar.

Connie's death crushed me, and I was absolutely broken and lost my mind and brain. I can never forget her condition and her last breaths. One cannot imagine what I had to go through because of Connie's death. That death was the first I saw in my life. How could someone even wonder why I was struggling to save her? She was dying, and that ruined my life, my happiness, and my world. I had forgotten all about my hardship during childhood struggle and all the sacrifices and hard work. I was weak in thinking, but I kept getting my strength from the knowledge that I had to keep my mind and my brain focused; otherwise, anything could happen to Connie and of course to me. I had to worry about her cremation and her wishes for ashes in her plot, and the chapel of peace.

I started praying, and I started thinking of many leaders and how they could do such great things. Gandhi was able to say to the British Empire, "It is time you left India." This was a powerful tool, and I was ready when Connie was taken to the cardiac unit. She was mentally alert and wanted to speak to me. I was there twenty-four hours, watching her like she was my small daughter, and I thought, *She is my wife. God, can I ask if you can grant me one thing? Give my Connie back either as a wife, sister, mother, daughter, or a small born child, but do not take away this second body of mine. Take whatever you want from my karma; I am willing to do anything to get her. I want only one thing, and that is Connie. I am willing to sweep the tables, clean the bathrooms, and do any small or big work for humanity, just like we have been doing since we met.* Unfortunately, my rhythm was very low. With a diminishing theory of lower returns, I decided I needed food, clothes, and our beautiful home, which Connie had beautifully decorated better than an outside professional. Connie's death took away all my happiness and desire to go to any restaurants or travel anywhere, except to see my brother and his family. Even today, I would do whatever God wants me do to do to get Connie back. I was sure God was listening to my thoughts, and perhaps watching me at the bedside of Connie; he would definitely grant me my Connie.

Another true example of love happened during the Mughal Era of India. One of the kings, Babar, came during Babar and Human. When Human made eleven round circles around the bed of his dying son as he lay dying,

God granted his wish, and his son's life was granted. I tried that, but due to the position of the bed, I was able to do more than eleven, but not in circles. God knows that I am trying round circles, but in the hospital bed with all the tubes and equipment, I could cause more damage if I started moving. It was not my home where I could do what I wanted. However, my intentions and the theory were the same. I was still very hopeful, and that is how I thought of Savitri and Satyavan and other miracles in the world. I was confident that miracles happen every day, and that God would definitely perform miracles as Connie did for her parents, for her students, for humanity, for the universities, for the library, and for the Mexican people by her giving free education, teaching, and writing songs and many research papers for them. She was a Spanish teacher and had seen many good and bad things happening there, and in every part of the world.

She was fully devoted to humanity and the idea that what God wanted was to get me to my door alive and take care of my people. That was what she did for everyone. I was the same way to some extent, but she was the engine in my life for everything: this marriage, our house, the household work, laundry, shopping, accounting, the budget, taking sick and elderly people to the grocery story, and helping many neighbors. One neighbor was ninety years old, and Connie took her every week, sometimes twice a week, for her shopping. We were even taking her out 70 percent of the time for dining out, movies, bringing her what she wanted, driving her to her appointments, cleaning her house, and more. Connie did that for over twelve years. Even when Connie was sick, Connie took care of her. It stopped when that lady moved to an assisted living home in her late nineties.

However, all these thoughts and faith was not granted to me by the Supreme Power. Perhaps there is some sin I must atone for, some slackness somewhere from my current life or past life that was still due, even after my childhood tragedies of losing my biological mother and her younger sister, whose devotion and sacrifice were unbelievable and painful. My aunt sacrificed her great career and had to take care of my father, my elder brother, and me. How hard it would have been to be my second mother, Kanta Mummy, who was a few years younger than my biological mother,

Shanti Mummy. Both our mothers had died. Kanta Mummy died when I was five and my brother was six. Kanta Mummy died two hours after my sister was born. We brothers remember that death very well, including Kanta Mummy's body and my sister of two hours having her thumb in her mouth. I was playing with her. I knew and saw everything, but I don't recall any emotions or being devastated.

The true death and tragedy came before and after Connie's death: all her cremation, the interment of her ashes, her ceremony for two days, placing the headstone, and then visiting her cemetery more up to four times each month. This death and shock is mental agony, and it is the most extremely painful thing in my life. It will remain that way as long as I live. I know that for sure.

After losing our two mothers, another tragedy was waiting for us. My father married Uma Mummy, from another family, and our maternal grandparents were not happy about it, knowing that she may not be nice to the children. That fear was in the whole family. My sister was already brought up by my parental grandparents, but we two brothers had my grandparents' mansion, where there was a big joint family. We were very good students, and we used to get ready for school with studies, outside laundry, and good food. If we were eating with our parental grandfather, then we would get to taste all the thirty different varieties of food. If we ever ate alone, then maybe there were fewer delicacies. We therefore preferred to eat with our grandfather in his big mansion, where he had this private, huge space, with many rooms and special privileges. It fit all the eighty family members, including his brother's son, and grandchildren. Because of his wealth, he was looking after us by bringing up his brother's children and grandchildren. He was like the head of the state, and no one could disobey him. He was a well-wisher and charitable, and he would spend his wealth equally for all.

Pradeep and Arun were sixteen age when Uma Mummy wanted to move out from our huge mansion to a newly built large bungalow. My father and Uma Mummy's two sons moved out to a newly built home a one-hour drive (forty-five miles) away. My father asked if we two wanted to move with them. We told him no, and that was the end of our wealth inheritance chosen by my brother, me, and my sister. Because of the three of us, my mothers' parents wanted Uma Mummy to be part of our family and more or less adopted her like their daughter. I remember Uma Mummy was nice and loving, and she had some passion for us. She was part of our studies up to fourth or fifth grade. The change came because of all the expenses of the joint family of over one hundred members, including Grandfather Berry's four children, grandchildren, and three brothers and their children. Grandmother Berry's family, their children and grandchildren, outsiders, and so many extended family members were all paid by for by Grandfather Berry. Grandfather Berry was very wealthy. We would have loved to get our two expired mothers gold and diamonds. Shanti Mummy and Kanta Mummy each were given four kilos of gold and diamonds, a very exclusive dowry that we feel should have come to the two brothers from Shanti Mummy and Sister Pappi from Kanta Mummy.

But Uma Mummy kept everything. We did not mind including after all she was our third mother. I must admit that we have no grudges because we have no desire to get anything from her. We have cordial relations, and we are happy that God helped us to make our own destinies with our education. Uma Mummy now realizes some of her errors, and Pradeep, Arun, and Pappi have good relations with her. Once again, we have no grievances, and I write very clearly that Pradeep Berry declares all the wealth was distributed after the Berry grandparents were gone, when I was twenty-two and had finished my postgraduation degree and my chartered accountancy. I should have started working and would have achieved the highest position while making a big salary, and perhaps we two brothers would have bought a house. Real estate is extremely expensive in India, especially in Delhi. We still have some of our ancestral houses, although some of them have been sold. I could not even think of buying that; it costs millions of Indian currency.

I think that if we had not lived in our big house with Grandfather Berry, we would have been with my mothers' parents' family. My mother had seven sisters and two brothers. During those days, having lots of kids was culturally valued by the rich and wealthy families. Things are different in the last fifty years. We refused to take anything from Berry but education, Boy Scouts, sports, clothes, public transportation, and pocket money (which was very small). We only received our basic necessities. We two boys were the first who'd finished high school, college, and postgraduation. I did another four years of chartered accountancy to make my own destiny. We were residing there and were given the food and basics, as well as some small pocket money, until my brother finished his postgraduation degree and got a job. I had one year to finish and two years to complete my chartered accountancy, and then my brother started taking care of me because he was told to separate his kitchen from our main kitchen, meant for thirty-eight people, though the house could accommodate over three hundred people. But slowly, every other uncle and the Berry family members of my grandfather were being supported.

I used to depend upon my brother because doing chartered accountancy is one of the toughest degrees, with 3 percent passing. Then I worked an apprenticeship from nine to six each day with no salary or stipend, because no scholarship was allowed for this course. After I finished that, I was confused about which way to go: start my own practice, join the family business, or join the army. I was C certificate and would have been a major after three months' training. I kept refusing great job offers from banks, foreign institutions, the US embassy in Delhi, Australia, the United Kingdom, and anywhere in India. It was a confusing battle, and I had no money to travel. I made a great mistake by not looking into my career at that time, but I am extremely happy that all of this happened. Connie was my destiny and was waiting for me. I was waiting, and God had other plans for me after suffering with my rich family and never receiving my share of the inheritance. I've never even seen a nickel of the inheritance my grandfather left to distribute among my family.

I do not have any bad feelings for my father and Uma Mummy, and I truly have great respect for her. She too is extremely fond of Arun and Pradeep. In fact, had Uma Mummy not been old and slightly sick, I would have brought her to my home in the United States, and she would have been very comforting to me. It would have been a great moral support in my life after the demise of Connie. Uma Mummy has knowledge of karma and spirituality, and I could serve her food, juice, and fruits as her best meals. She likes fruits, milk, tea, and almonds. I would have fulfilled her desire to travel in business class, and I'd take her around. But this is not possible. Connie would tell me many times, "Pradeep, what are you taking for Mummy?" Connie had no bad feelings for my father and Uma Mummy; she truly loved them, and they loved her. My father died in November 2003. Had he been alive, I would have called him too, and he would have been devastated to know that Connie had died. I am sure Uma Mummy is very upset about Connie, and the next time I go to India, I am going to spend time with Uma Mummy. She will be happy to be with me and talk about Connie while healing my wounds, pain, and suffering. It's a common tendency that wherever there is big family and money, there are always disputes and hindrances. However, when the time comes, we do not fight or become enemies. Blood is blood. Nails always remain part of the ten fingers. We all fight and later are friends. Time heels everything. In the end, to live with anger is a dirty plan. Anger is death. God is the supreme power.

Connie was the biggest inheritance and I would take her anytime over any money, inheritance, or whatnot. I simply want Connie. When I met my Connie, all of that money became worthless to me. I couldn't buy my Connie for all the money on the planet. She was my wife and my Kohinoor diamond. I wanted her for myself. Now, I am heartbroken and living an isolated life after the loss of my precious Connie. That loss is much more painful than any of my childhood suffering. I do not want that inheritance. Connie's loss is the thing that has broken me, and I will always suffer.

I will continue to live a simple life of high thinking, with my outings limited to the health club, her grave, and once in a while going somewhere by myself. My company is in night and nature: the moon, stars, and sun. I find happiness in Connie's study room, and in sleeping with her beautiful pictures in our king-sized bed on my side. Each night, I prepare her bedside table for her with a glass of water and her sandals by the bed. In the morning, I put out her water glasses in her study and in the kitchen, and I look at her beautiful pictures hanging in the living room. Our house is a great museum of science and art. This is my happiness. I can go to India to see my brother and his family for a few months, but now I am living in the happiest of places, my Connie's house. It is ours, but I call it my Connie's house, her temple or church. This is the way God wanted me to find happiness. I am not happy without her, and I think of her each second, but I have to follow the law of nature and God's order, because we are all puppets in his hands and have to do whatever he asks of us. So her house is very soothing for my troubled mind. I have no other choice. I have resources to travel anywhere, but I will not, because Connie's memory would follow me wherever I go; we both traveled extensively in the United States and Europe.

India holds no fear for me because I am with my brother and his family. Connie's room and all the big rooms are decorated with her pictures, so that is very comforting. I have my grandnieces, two nephews, and my niece by marriage who are very kind to me. My brother, his wife, his two sons, and his two granddaughters are fun and take away some of the pain I feel for Connie, but Connie is in every part of my body. I will never touch another woman in my life. Never. I will wait because I am sure I will meet Connie in my next life. I am certain this will happen.

Today, April, 25, 2016. I went to the Connie's cemetery and cleaned the granite, the grass, and a few other things. I generally spend one hour when I visit her grave. I could easily spend four hours, and I would even not mind going daily. That is my love for Connie. I was thinking what a shame it is to Connie's memory that her only sibling, his four children and their spouses, and his grandchildren did not ever visit her. I was standing close to Connie's beautiful granite stone, where I had them inscribe "Constance Ann Berry. Best friend and most precious darling wife of 38 years." Suddenly, I wondered why I did not have them write forty years, because there were some errors in my troubled mind. I chose the inscription, the granite, the color, and the design of her headstone. I was the only person making those decisions because Connie's one sibling and his family have had no relations with me after Connie's passing; it would be very painful for me to see them without Connie. Neither do I want them to visit me, because I am happy by myself. Connie's death made me totally different.

Connie had one college student, Roberto Ciera. At the same time, I have a great friend in Mexico, Alfonzo Penna Ciera, whom I was thinking of calling. He worked under me along with thirty-six other people when I was the senior management consultant in 1998–1999 in a suburb of Chicago. Alfonzo came from a rich family, and I used to bring him home to meet Connie. Connie immediately told me that he was from a rich family. Later, he tried to come to the United States and wanted me to join him in San Francisco with his business. I didn't join him, and so he went back. If I ever go to Mexico, or if he comes to United States, I would be very happy to meet him.

Dogs are serious and faithful to their masters without thinking if people are rich. They give unconditional love and eat anything given to them. They are faithful to their masters even if they have to kill themselves to save their beloved masters. They can judge the character of humans in no time, even from miles away, and they stop bad people from coming near. I wish Connie and I had had a dog before she put the evil eye on my Connie. A dog would have torn her apart from this evil from the earth, just as great Lord Rama was in creation of God to kill the great scholar Ravana, king of Sri Lanka. I might write a note about this in the book. I got on the Internet and read about the Diwali festival in India, or Lord Rama and Great Ravana. This true story happened five thousand years ago in India, and it revealed the sacrifice of Rama's half-brothers and how they ran the kingdom of Ayodyapuri until Lord Rama returned from his fourteen years of exile along with his wife, Sita, and younger brother Laxman. It talks about how the younger half-brother looked after the kingdom without sitting on the throne but by touching Rama's wooden sandals, until he came back and took his throne. That is what I am doing: touching Connie's sandals in the morning and night; and placing her water glasses in the kitchen near her computer, and on her side table. That is the most healing thing for me, as well as praying to that noble soul's pictures and sleeping with her framed picture. The picture shows how she was sitting on her chair with a walker in front and another walker with her clothing. That place is a church, a cathedral for me. On this visit, I was upset that I should ask Connie to be with me.

Constance Ann Berry: Best Friend and Most Precious Darling Wife of Forty-two Years

Throughout the two years of Connie's illness, she seemed normal in the course of her daily life: reading, writing, working on the computer, keeping our accounts, watching films, and discussing things. We were both still happy because being together was nothing but happiness, and we were filled with the hope that Connie would live at least another ten to fifteen years. She was an avid reader and learned that new medicines and treatments were being released. I read the same and was also positive about our prospects.

In ancient Egypt, people mummified the bodies of their dead as a way of coping with the loss of their loved ones. I think it was right for those people to be able to see the bodies and feel that their loved ones were still with them. I could never have done that with Connie, who asked to be cremated. I never thought I, her loving husband, would have to oversee her last rites. Why was this my fate? Connie's pictures and our pictures together fill my house. In this way, my life is a combination of happiness for the memory of our life together, and sadness for her loss.

While she was ill, my life was dedicated to serving Connie. I brought her tea and juice in the morning after she got up to go to her study with her walker and oxygen. Later, she would make the painful trek to the kitchen for breakfast. Making and serving her the best breakfast food was my greatest happiness. I felt the same about cooking her dinner, helping her shower, and bringing her a glass of water first thing in the morning and last thing at night. Taking care of her and bringing her to the hospital for appointments and treatments was a mixture of pain and joy. Helping her prepare for these appointments brought both pain and happiness to my heart and soul.

Throughout her illness, Connie was extremely positive. but inside she was most unhappy, not knowing if she would ever get better. I used to give her positive feedback based on my own faith in God and the miracle of Savitri and Satyavan. I was absolutely devoted to Connie and was hoping God would listen to me. However, I lost that battle and was absolutely broken and devastated. After her death, I was only sleeping three to four hours a night, and there was lots of work to do. Most important of all was to have her cremated and put her ashes in her plot next to her parents, and then putting the stone on her ashes (as per her wishes and the wishes of others). God helped me to do all that, and by my aggressive approach I was able to get the cremation done in two days. I didn't want my darling's body sitting in the funeral home for a long time. She was not a charity case, and I told both the cremation and cemetery people that money was not a problem. I also told them that I wanted the best casket, urns, and priest at all the services, including the cremation, the memorial in the chapel of peace, and later at the burial of her ashes in her plot. The same was for the headstone. I was firm and would not compromise anything for money. I provided lunch for the people who came to pay their respects to Connie. I also hired a professional video maker for two days to cover the ceremonies of Connie. It is not a pleasant video, but all those sad memories can stay with me to provide me some happiness. They may give me pain, but they also take away some pain. I watch those videos quite often. What I think and how it affects me, I do not know, but I feel that it provides me something.

How much pain and suffering was going on in my heart and soul to see my wife's funeral, which I never thought I would have to do? She was the one I'd married, and now I had to arrange her funeral services. I am extremely upset about it. I was not ready to lose her and to never again see that great person who played the role of best wife and best friend. It reminds me what Sahajahhan must have gone through at the loss of his wife, Mumtaaz Mahel. After her death, he built the Taj Mahal in Agra, India. It is an example of love and is one of the seven wonders of the world. No outsiders can understand my pain, which is in my heart and soul, always haunting me. I know if I start talking about this with relatives and friends all the time, they will not understand my pain; if they said something, I would not listen or follow their advice.

Now I understand what Great Buddha, who was silent for two years after his enlightenment, said upon breaking his silence. Many Gods were worried about his silence and requested that he speak, but he refused. After many requests from all the gods, he broke his silence by saying, "People who understand me know my silence, and if I say something, they would not understand me and think negatively about me. I therefore decided to be silent. My message is even if I can change the life of one person out of millions, my purpose is accomplished." How wonderful were those thirty-nine and a half years we had? I pray to God to take away some of my possessions and give my darling Connie back, but I am sure we will be husband and wife in our next lives. This hope gives me strength, and I am willing to struggle in whatever way I have to, but I want Connie back in my next life.

"The Story of Sati Savitri" is taken from the Internet. In my opinion, it's for the world to see that these kinds of things happened in India. I encourage my readers to read the whole episode on the Internet via Wikipedia or by googling Savitri and Satyavan.

I would also like to share a true story about faith in religion and greed that I read long time back. This is a true story. There was once a rich and very generous merchant who never refused alms to anyone. His neighbor was an evil old lady who would curse everybody going for alms. A few years ago, some true saints went out asking for alms. The merchant gave them a generous amount of wheat flour, and the saints left happily with their blessings to the merchant. The evil old lady started shouting abuse and curses to the saints and the merchant. The saints continued on, and while they were traveling, a flying eagle dropped a dead rat into their wheat flour. The saints ate the flour and died. People asked their religious leaders, "Who is to be blamed for their deaths: the merchant, the woman, or fate?"

The learned religious men replied, "The merchant gave in good faith, so he is above blame. The evil woman is to blame because of her bad tongue and bad intentions. Finally, fate is responsible for their death." I have met some people who were not able to fulfill their daily needs, and others who are amassing wealth out of greed. I think this story is right: it is the greed for more that is killing the sages.

Lord, you are everywhere, omnipresent, omnipotent, and omniscient. You are perfect. Your pattern and design of the world are perfect. We accept your orders without question.

The rule of Nish Karma, daily duty: do your duties, deeds, and karmas without identification of self with it or its reactions. This is self-realization. We are puppets in the hands of God, and we have to perform whatever role he wants us to play.

In the kingdom of God, every event and situation is preordained to happen in its proper time. There is a chain of cause and reaction. But God has allotted a function and duty to everyone. No man, however great he may be, should interfere with it the conscience and lifestyle of another man. Therefore there is so much discontentment, frustration, and crime in the world.

To practice religion, there are certain rules laid down by ancient worship.

My Loss and Pain for Connie

My loss compelled me to repeat the same things I wrote before. I can say for sure there was no lack in my devotion for Connie throughout our lives. However, when Connie was first diagnosed with cancer in 2002. Throughout her illness and until her death, the devotion and love for both of us was at its peak. Many of our friends, the hospital staff, our neighbors, and even strangers wished that they were blessed with that kind of love and devotion. Further, when the Mayo Clinic declared palliative care on November, 8, 2014, my devotion and prayers to the Lord to make Connie well again was at its peak. Her body was like a god, and I prayed over that weak body, her walker, her oxygen, her clothes, and any object that was a favorite of hers. I was convinced that God would see my devotion and would give more strength to both of us, and that a new enlightenment was coming to save her at any cost. I knew miracles happened every day, and our good karma (or rather, Connie's best karma) would convince God to change the process of palliative care to normal life, and he'd choose to give her fifteen more years to live. That what the only thing I was asking God, and that what she asked as well.

We both shared good karma, which was far greater than any small bad karma. We began to feel confident that she would have a full, long life. We believed in miracles and knew of many miracles that had happened. We were sure that she would live another fifteen good years, and she had already gone through cancer treatments. Connie would tell me, "God helps those who help themselves." God has the power to do anything, to take and to give life. We were not asking God for immortality. We knew that someday I might be alone with only God for comfort. I wanted my service to God to save Connie. I decided that I would fight her sickness all by myself, without asking for the help of my friends and relatives. I had read true stories of life in the jungle, of the suffering of animals and people, and how they were granted new life. When these things came into my mind, I grew stronger and was better prepared to handle the stress of Connie's struggle. My love and devotion to my precious wife increased immeasurably, and I cherished everything about her, down to her daily routine. I gained confidence that God knew how much love I had for Connie. The saying "If one truly asks God for something with devotion, hard work, and does anything to reach out to him, God is kind to grant that wish" came to my mind. It happened centuries ago during the Mogul era. Hamayun, Babar, and Akbar, the great Mogul kings, asked God for help. They were granted what they wanted. My devotion perhaps exceeded theirs. I know medical science and serious illnesses result in the end, but the saying "Nobody goes as long as God is protecting them" also has truth.

There is a true story that was told by three ladies we met in 2006, narrated in front of three top medical doctors. The doctors had told these women that they had only a few months to survive. They told them to say their last prayers because the end was coming. The women prayed and waited. They waited and waited, but still they lived. It so happened that many years later (sixteen years for one, nineteen years for another, and twelve years for the third), these ladies returned to their doctors for a minor illness and asked if they recognized them. These doctors were astonished that their diagnoses had been incorrect. These ladies were childhood friends and neighbors, and my family was in touch with them. I had a few friends who also experienced a similar situation. This gave me confidence in the ways of life and death and God. Connie and I were so confident that she would survive. I had one uncle in India who'd lived with cancer for thirty-three years, and a woman I knew survived cancer for twenty-three years.

These were positive examples that made us stronger. However, Connie used to read the obituary column in the *Chicago Tribune*, and I noticed some died within only a few years of being diagnosed with cancer. There were encouraging and fearful thoughts, but we chose to be positive. I truly did not want anyone to know how ill she was. First, I was very angry with my friends and relatives who had not reached out to us in several years. I took an oath in 2012 that I would not call them or tell them that Connie was not doing well. I would not be open with those friends who were only interested in paying lip service to our friendship. They never once told us that they were with us and that we could count on them. I could read the difference between lip service and sincere friendship. I know everyone has problems, but we had always gone out of the way no matter what. We still called them to inquire after their well-being, their families, and more. Connie was in touch with their sorrows, so why did we not get that dedication from them? At that time, I turned to the Lord and said, "It is our battle; please help us, who have such good karma." I was totally in the hands of God, and so was Connie. Yet we lost that battle. Later, at the time of her cardiac arrest, I had another chance to fight the doctors and medical staff like a tiger to protect Connie. It was ten against one. God helped me to fight and be strong like a boxer, a tiger, or the ambassador of God. But I did not win; instead, I lost the most important battle of my life. I will never forget this lost battle of love and my future.

Another Painful for Connie and Pradeep

I am the biggest loser because my darling Connie is no longer with me. It's a terrible loss in my life. Perhaps I am writing this sad family episode to share my loss. I pray to God that one day, I can forget the past and forgive people for their behavior. It takes years and years to make friends and develop love with family and friends, but in one second or at one incident, the love can be gone forever. However, I find peace by writing Connie's biography, which gives me happiness and sadness.

Further, I want to share my own childhood tragedy. My mother, the respected Shanti Mehra, was born in 1921 in Lahore and Lyallpur, now in Pakistan after India's independence from British rule, which was achieved on August 15, 1947. She was highly educated and wanted to go into the civil service during the British Empire. But can we play with destiny? My maternal grandfather was not wealthy, but he was well off. He was convinced by his close friend, Puran Chand (whom I never saw but am still angry at), that ladies do not go to the UK for jobs and should be married. He suggested the boy of an extremely wealthy merchant in Delhi, India, as a possible husband for my mother. My mother was absolutely devastated and did not want to marry; instead, she wanted to work toward a great career. I am still very angry and ask why she was forced to marry my father, Mr. Ram Prashad Berry, born in 1921. My paternal grandfather was extremely wealthy.

Shanti Mummy bore my elder brother Arun and me before dying tragically young. Arun was twelve months old, and I was only two months of age when Shanti Mummy died. I did not see my mother. My family suffered a big loss and thought that because my father was twenty-seven years old and would remarry, we two boys would get a stepmother who would neglect and ruin us. My maternal grandparents forced my mother's younger sister, Miss Kanta Mehra, to marry my father in order to avoid having a stranger stepmother. Respected Kanta Mehra, who completed her double master's in English and was going for a great career, was devastated and did not want to marry. She had no choice but to marry my father. I am extremely upset with my grandparents and my father for forcing her to marry. We two brothers remember her being a great mother, and she was extremely beautiful and educated. She loved us like her own children. But God had other plans. She bore one daughter, my sister, and died after her birth at the young age of twenty-five. Arun was six and half, and I was five and half when we lost our second mother. We both remember her death and funeral.

I was upset when my father died in November,14, 2003 I, Connie was upset that my father died and asked me that I go to India and attend the last rites. However, I was busy, and flight schedules made it difficult to arrive in time. I stayed with my brother, and two half-brothers connected on the phone from the United States to India all the time. We all pooled money for my father's death. Connie also gave her share for his last rites and tributes, and we had no grudges against my half-brothers and Uma Mummy. I must mention again if she was not old and sick, I would have brought her to America and asked her to stay with me for as long as she wanted. She would have been a great support to me because she has some way of healing the pain. She is and was extremely fond of Connie. Connie was her favorite daughter-in-law. She truly loved her. It did not matter whether she gave money. Her love late for Connie was always there, from time they met in 1979 till today. After my father's death, she loved my brother, me, and my sister more than her two boys.

I want to be fair about her. We do realize our mistakes and our deeds sometimes in this life, rather than in heaven or hell, as people talk. I wish I could bring her and serve her. Connie would have done the same thing if she was not sick. After my father's death on October 14, 2003, I don't know whether or not I felt sorrow for his loss.

Greed is ruining humanity everywhere. However, the world continues to exist because there are good people, and some of them are very compassionate. Connie was the most ethical, honest person, and I am the same way, as is Arun. My great uncle, Dr. P. N. Behl, advised me about the family war over money. He told me, "Son, either fight or forget." He told me to give him my power of attorney, and he would get my share, because he was very well connected and had a way to get us our share of the inheritance. Arun and I did not listen to him. According to Indian law, grandchildren have the first right to their grandparent's property and assets. Connie told me to fight so that we brothers would not lose our inheritance, especially my brother Arun in India. We both refused. Connie also told me that there was no reason to fight or ask for anything; we'd better let them have it because we were comfortable, and living costs were very expensive in India. Uma Mummy and all my family members used to tell me, "Pradeep, you are very lucky having Connie as your wife. She allows you to visit India every year." Wives in India make a huge deal if their husbands go somewhere even for two days. It was Uma Mummy who was crazy for Connie, and she was very happy to see us. We always maintained very good relations.

Few of my relatives have ever visited us in America, and Connie went to India seven times. Our family members and friends were highly impressed with her manners and simple life. She never demanded any special food or any privileges, and she accepted whatever was offered to her. It truly impressed people. Now, when I think of all these qualities and her special intelligence, I go into the deepest pain of losing my Connie. For each and every day of our forty-two years together, there are love and care movies in my brain, mind, and heart, as if I am watching a movie. I am storing all these memories in my mind and heart. No matter how I try to explain it, no one will ever understand how I live with my memories. Even a doctor or a psychologist will never figure this out. This is due to the special bond between me and Connie: we had no boundaries, and it was an unbiased love like the smile of a small baby, the soothing effects of the ocean, the early morning voices of the birds, or the beauty of stars, moon, and sun.

Many people told me they knew how lovely and great she was. I would like to tell them that they are not able to convince me of her greatness because I'm the one who truly knows her. Some feel they have already defined it to me, but they could not have known her. Connie was one in ten million.

Many times while traveling on cruises or staying in hotels, I asked Connie if I should give a tip or buy a present for the general manager, thinking he or she may not be offended. Connie replied, "No one would say no to a present or money." I found this to be true all my life, except for a very few situations. Connie also told me many times that we should leave a little early to go anywhere, because unexpected traffic or other problems could arise. It is better to be at the airport early rather than to risk missing a flight. Whether traveling or meeting friends at restaurants, punctuality was her theme.

I have forgiven my stepmother since I met Connie. Connie's her love, devotion, charm, and beauty, as well as my true love and devotion to her, made us extremely happy. My darling Connie was my wife and friend, sister, and mother. This may seem very strange to people—that a woman can be my wife, best friend, sister, and mother. She took all my pain on her shoulders and heart, and she loved me so much. My love to her was tremendous. We were made for each other, and our love was true and pure. In the ancient Indian Vedanta, it is believed that a great wife can play all these womanly roles.

To Prove This and as Part of My Tributes to Connie, I Would Like to Share Some Remarkable Quotes I Studied and Knew, but Now I Am Taking Them from the Internet, to Put the Exact Words

This quote is by Chanakya, in 520 BC. "A good wife is one who serves her husband in the morning like a mother does, loves him in the day like a sister does and pleases him like a prostitute in the night." I personally would not use the word prostitute, but Chanakya went in-depth by using this word, and maybe he was right. My world-renowned dermatologist uncle told me, "Son, marriage is an art, and you have to understand your wife because she is very sensitive. A husband's love is very important for her, more than anything besides necessity of life and comfortable living. A wife surrenders herself to her husband." I have written more on this under my uncle's advice. In our Vedanta, it is written in Sanskrit as:

A. Kaysha: Devotion, career, keeping the house in order. Though, I also believe husband must contribute more for the house and cooking and be the greatest help for his wife. I was very happy to do everything, including cooking and cleaning, to make Connie's life easy. But she did a whole lot too, and we valued each other. She balanced her career and our travels housework, and learning.

B. Kasrrmeshue: Giving good advice to her husband and to others. I was the same way, and we had the best understanding. We valued everything equally.

C. Bhojeshue: Good food for husband. and I did the same for her. We both valued everything equally and had no egoistical sense that she was a woman and I was a man. She was everything for me.

D. Shaileshue: The love of wife and husband and in whatever forms it takes. In the old centuries, women and men married for physical relations: to have a good marriage and to have kids. Love was there.

More Quotes by Chanakya

I read Chanakya's books *Arthashastra* and *Chankayaniti* during high school. Chanakya was an Indian politician and strategist who gained a great knowledge. He was considered a great politician and was one of the best strategic planners in 520 BC. This picture is from the Internet, from Chanakya Quotes, a public site. The following are some of his many quotes and aphorisms.

1. **"A man is born alone and dies alone, he experiences the good and bad consequences of his karma/deeds alone, and he goes to hell or the supreme abode."**

Connie and I practiced this message throughout our lives. I am therefore positive that Connie is with the supreme, and that gives me some consolation. However, I still live with pain in my heart and soul. I would do my best to reconcile and to survive by doing more good karma and helping humanity but, I will never be able to forget Connie as long as I am alive. She was everything for me. I truly do not want to go to those places we used to go to. Everywhere I go, I miss her. It is extremely hard for me to believe that I will never see her again, except maybe in my next life. But I want the exact Connie, with the same face and same external and internal beauty. My faith tells me God will fulfill my request, and this hope makes me strong as I try to do better and better things.

2. **"As a single withered tree, if set aflame, causes a whole forest to burn, so does a rascal son destroy a whole family."**

Connie only had one brother. I believe that it was Connie's brother and his wife who destroyed her family with their greed. Her brother and sister-in-law definitely destroyed the whole happiness of their own mother and father, and most important Connie's happiness. Now, when I think of Connie's brother, who is her only sibling, he and his four children and grandchildren were truly proven with this quote. They were nice to us the first five to six years of our marriage, but later we had a relationship of love and hate. Now, after the demise of Connie, none of them came for her last rites, and no one sent me condolences. My forty years of relations with them vanished. I have no desire to talk or see any of them. Anyone who was not nice to Connie will not ever be my friend; neither would I like to talk to them or meet them. This is all due to my love for Connie. Were she alive, my bitterness would have been forgiveness, but not anymore. Connie is gone, and so are they gone from my life. Perhaps, they don't care. They only care for money.

3. **"Treat your kid like a darling for the first five years. For the next five years, scold them. By the time they turn sixteen, treat them like a friend. Your grownup children are your best friends."**

I am convinced that this quote is true. When I was in college and studying my chartered accountancy, I was convinced that when your children are about sixteen, and especially when they reach 18, they are your best friend. I have seen this even at the age of six or seven. I was raised in a very strict atmosphere, and my brother and I were not allowed to disobey our grandfather or any member of our joint family. However, after finishing my undergraduate, chartered accountancy, NCC, Eagle Scouts, and other things, I was treated as a friend by my family in India.

In spite of this, I still object to that friendship because my own Berry family, including my own father and uncles and aunties, saw to it that my brother Arun, my sister Rita Revri, and I never got a penny from our inheritance. It is bothersome, but after the loss of Connie, I don't want to think of or need any inheritance. My loss of Connie is the deepest and most hurtful thing now. As far as I am concerned, other than my brother Arun and his family, no other family member of the Berry and Mehra families have a close relationship with me. If I call or meet them, they will go out of the way to meet me with love, hospitality, and respect. I have no enemy. I am simply angry and devastated that Connie is gone. That loss takes over all of my happiness and joy, and I experience withdrawal. It would be nice if they came to see me, however the old love will never come back.

I was told an important saying by Mrs. Violet Hopkins, Dr. Behl's mother-in-law. She told me, "Pradeep, you can break a glass bowl either by accident or by falling. You can fix it with glue, and it will look the same; however, some marks of the broken bowl will also show. If differences come between friends and relatives, it can come back or not, but even if it comes back for the sake of formality, the true feelings are gone." Now I see the parents of young children treat them with love, and especially after eighteen or even after they get married, they are best friends. I especially hurt, even more than Connie did, when she and I noticed the behavior of her brother. His four kids were young, and we treated them like our own children. We were all very close, and Connie's sister-in-law was a good host. But when the children grew up and had their own children, lots of distance came between us. It is natural all over the world. All of this started some twenty years ago, and it got worse with time because of distance, responsibilities, and many other reasons. We had our own lives, and this is the way this world operates. We were invited for Thanksgiving and Christmas, and during the summer for two days. That was enough for them and for us due to distance and other things in our lives. Twenty-five years ago, I suggested that we should all go on vacation to India or Europe, or for a cruise, or even for dinner. But they were busy with their friends, and we enjoyed traveling by ourselves. Our style of late nights and their style of early nights conflicted.

Connie went to the UK with her fellow teachers and friends, and I was happy that she should go. None of the other spouses wanted to go, so I told Connie, "Please do not deprive yourself. Go enjoy yourself." I was very happy, but she was guilty that she went with her friends. I told her, "Don't I go to India for two weeks alone, to see my brother and family?" At that time, my father, paternal grandfather, and Dr. and Mrs. Behl were alive, so I was happy to go. This argument convinced Connie to go to the UK for two weeks, and we five husbands went to the airport to drop them off and pick them up. I called Connie twice a day in the UK, or a few times a day when she went with her teacher friends to Cancun, Mexico. Taking Connie to the airport, picking her up, and talking to her on the phone no matter how much it cost was my true happiness.

While writing this, my memory is photographic, and I am in pain. My mind is 100 percent on the movie playing in my head. But that is not happening. Connie is gone. That is very upsetting and painful, but I have to finish her book.

4. **"The life of an uneducated man is as useless as the tail of a dog which neither covers its rear end nor protects it from the bites of insects."**

5. **"A person should not be too honest. Straight trees are cut first, and honest people are screwed first."**

Connie and I have both gone through this message. However, we always followed the same message, regardless of the consequences. Although there have been so many painful things we suffered, Connie suffered more. This reminds me of an episode in 1984. I visited a huge client of my employer (the largest finance company in the world) in California and took Connie with me. Connie would drop me off in the morning and pick me up in the evening. She would go to library and shopping while waiting for me. This client was one of the largest in his own industry in the United States and had taken a big loan from my company. I was introduced to the chairman of the board and all the senior management, with whom I spent whole day talking about the business, plans, expansion, and related matters. Later, they introduced me to their lady accountant. I was highly impressed with her knowledge and grace, and I thought that she knew the business very well. She was super.

During lunch, she asked me if I wanted to go for lunch, and I said yes. She told me that she couldn't go, so I decided to order food for her, and I paid for that as part of my business expenses. We were extremely busy because a lot of work was to be done, and she closed her office. We both had lunch. She told me her story, which I will never forget.

She told me that she and her husband owned this huge company. She trusted their employees and her attorney very much. In fact, she adopted that attorney as her son when he was a kid and put him through school, college, and law school. She had a large customer in Mexico and owed the company many millions of dollars in accounts receivables. The customer was in tight cash flow, and she gave that account to her adopted son attorney and asked all the employees to cooperate as a team. Suddenly, the company was forced into liquidation, and she and her husband lost everything. She later found out that her own son attorney took all the money from that customer. He later bought back the company and made the plant supervisor the president. Now she was reporting to him as an accountant. He made her husband go to work as an ordinary worker at their company.

She further told me that since they'd lost the company, she and her husband had never received a call from the Rotary Club, the Lions Club, and other charitable clubs where they used to give charity and host dinners. All their wealthy friends disappeared. She stated that the only people who came forward were the food vendors, who brought their trucks to the company to sell breakfast, late snacks, lunch, and dinner to her one thousand employees. Those food vendors bought them a small place to live, gave them food daily, and met all their expenses. All of their rich friends and cultured socialites were gone, but these vendors helped them to survive. They went from riches to rags and lost their entire world.

It was such a heartbreaking thing for me. While agreeing to approve the new loan for the company, I put in a clause stating that we would only lend the company this huge amount again if she was made the chief financial officer, replacing the current one—who knew nothing and was making fifteen times more money than her. I openly stated that unless she was in that position, because she knew the customers and the business better than anybody, we would not grant them a loan. I also stated that the attorney would have to face the penalty for his crime because he'd cheated our previous loan. The deal was approved, and the attorney was given some sentence. We recovered our loan and lent more while making that lady the new CFO. She was extremely happy with her new life.

I finished my work early on Friday afternoon to be with Connie, who came after checking the hotel. We enjoyed a long drive on Friday and stayed in California's Orange County for five days. Connie was in tears when she heard this story. I am writing this as great tribute to my darling Connie, who is no longer with me physically. However, the whole scene of her picking me up and driving through Palm Springs is with me as a photographic memory. In fact, the whole of our lives and love, our travels and everything for forty years, is a movie in my mind and heart twenty-four hours a day. Throughout my career, I dealt with many such episodes. Connie was very supportive and helpful in giving me moral support, and sometimes she accompanied me on some very hostile borrowers, who played with fraud and other unethical things for our worldwide finance company. I was given the most troubled, difficult, large, borrowers with over millions and millions of dollars in loans. Three of them were in Chicago; two were in Michigan; two were in Columbus, Ohio; three were in California; and two were in Houston. They were small and large cities all over America. Also, a few jobs were in France and Germany.

One of my jobs took place in Ohio in 1987. The owner defrauded my employer one of the largest finance companies in the world. I was working for this organization as a senior management person. Many junior and middle-management field examiners went to his office. The owner had run away and was hiding for months, and he had given instructions to his two senior management staff not to allow anyone from the lender; they were all denied access to his premises. Let me explain that because we were secured lenders, we had the right to enter, and even to do a surprise walk-in. However, we had a practice that we should notify our borrowers that it was time for due diligence and asking if it was convenient for them to provide the documents we needed. We used to send borrowers a list of our due diligence requirements. Again, it was our courtesy to do so; previously, we had relied on surprise.

I was an expert in crisis management and was asked to go. I showed up at the borrower's office and presented my business card. They were truly nice and asked me to sit and have coffee. I told them, "You three people did not allow in my four juniors, and now you are reluctant to let me enter and see your books." They said no way could I review the books, and I told them, "I have a right to do anything, and if you do not let me, I will report to my senior management. We will take strong action against you that you will regret for the rest of your lives. Please know that I am not letting you play this game. Let me see whatever I want to see, period."

They told me, "Mr. Berry, you are very strong and determined, but we are helpless because our boss had told us not to allow anyone."

I told them, "Let me talk to your owner and boss, because I am not leaving like the others. You'd better be careful and let me talk to him. If he has refused to give his number where he is hiding, tell him the senior management person is here and is determined to be here until the whole thing is discovered."

They were panicky and went behind closed doors to talk to the owner. Slowly they told me, "You can only see a few records, and we cannot provide anything else."

I was determined and told them, "I am even going to go through the locked room of your boss, and you'd better be ready to cooperate with me. Otherwise, you will be part of the fraud, and if we have to go to court and take orders, you will all be involved for protecting your boss. Perhaps you should think of yourself, your wife, and your children. You do not want to be involved in case the issue is turned over to the senior government agencies. Now, listen either to your boss or to me."

They both went to a room and came out after twenty minutes. "Mr. Berry, we are going to do anything for you because we do not have the money and salary, and we would lose all. Go ahead. Also, do us a favor. We have not been paid for three months and have been working for free for him in anticipation that we would be paid all our dues soon."

I assured them that we would make sure they got paid, but they should let me do my work. We could go for lunch or dinner to talk and be friends. "I am here to save you and your boss, if he cooperates with me." They were happy. I took them for a nice lunch and an exclusive dinner.

At dinnertime, they told me, "Mr. Berry, it has been over six months since we had dinner, drinks, and desserts. You truly are a gem, and we feel that you are going to do good things to us. We are with you because we do not want to go to prison or pay heavy fines. We can't find other senior positions and would be doomed forever."

The next day, I worked and worked. I went to the owner's room and was thrilled to find a stack of locked files. It was clearly mentioned and signed by the owner regarding his scheme to defraud my employer, and there was a conspiracy between the owner and his largest customer, the largest US company. I took all those documents and told them that I was going to the Federal Express office because some information in the office was important to overnight.

Now, Connie came in the picture. I told her about it, and she was worried about my life. I was as well. I kept flying from Chicago to Ohio for two months, from Monday to Friday. Connie was instrumental and withstood all that heavy travel of mine; internally, we were both concerned. However, she was strong and encouraged me. This is America, Pradeep. Don't think anything. You have been doing these kinds of hostile situations, and you have earned your name in your senior job. That is why they had promoted you to this senior position. I take pride in you. I am with you. I can accompany you for few weeks, and I even get my vacation and teach during school and college break." She did take a week off and went with me, staying in the hotel for dinner and all.

I told my employer, and they were thrilled and told me, "Pradeep, please take Connie. We will pay for everything." It was advantageous to both of us, and they knew I would detect the large fraud. That perhaps was my last Friday, and I was to meet the owner in the office at 9:00 a.m. I did not tell Connie that I was slightly worried about what the owner would do, and neither did I disclose this to my employer. God is great. Somehow or the other, he had found out that I knew everything. I went to him. Connie was sitting in the restaurant downstairs in case of some violent, to help me. That was the greatest support I had.

I went to the owner, and surprisingly he stood up, shook my hand, and asked me to sit down. He ordered coffee and some bagels and closed the doors. Only the two of us behind those big, closed doors. I bluntly told him that I knew everything, and perhaps he knew too. He agreed to cooperate with me and said, "Mr. Berry, I do not want to go to prison. Please tell me how you can help me."

I politely told him, "Mr. Z, please cooperate with us. Admit it to us. How are we going to get those funds? You have defrauded us, and you know well that you can go to prison. Please ask your customer to help you because they have deep pockets and would not want it in the paper or on TV that they were part of the crime." He was asking me for mercy, and I was regretting it. He was crying that he did it all and was willing to do anything and cooperate. We also needed him because he was an expert in turning millions of dollars' worth of raw material inventory and work in process inventory into the finished goods to sell and get paid on a COD basis. He could start paying our full loan and we did not have to take any write-off in our P&L and financial statements.

The owner cooperated with us for six months, and he and his company worked hard while we funded the payroll and stated paying the IRS part of his liability of loans. In one year, we were paid back the large loan. The owner had to sell his home, car and everything for any shortage in our loan. He was practically on the road. We helped him to refinance his home and find a decent job. He was an engineer and expert in his field. I took the initiative to help get his three senior managers get other jobs. It was one of the wonderful things in my career, and I kept doing the same kind of difficult situation in my career.

The same types of episodes happened in Michigan, Austin, Columbus, California, Seattle, Indiana, Baltimore, New York, New Jersey, Chicago,

Denver, Philadelphia, Phoenix, and many more cities. I will always wonder how I was able to do all that. I would like to describe all of these as a case study for the upcoming young blood to gain knowledge in the field of crisis management. These were extremely great challenges, and I am lucky that my employers gave me the jobs. It was a win-win situation for them and for me. I know for sure that there are many other brilliant people with lots of things to teach, but I would also like to add some of my knowledge as a legacy, in Connie's memory.

Michigan was special. For three months in 1981, I would travel to Michigan every Monday through Friday to liquidate our borrower or sell the company, to avoid any write-off on our large loans. Connie was on a two-month vacation from teaching and was busy doing her research in the hotel where we were staying, while I was working at the office. We had breakfast, lunch, and dinner together and went sightseeing on the weekends. These things are important to me because my traveling job had become a joy.

The best work travels I had was when I had to go to Germany and France, and I asked Connie to join me so that I wouldn't be lonely. It was in September 1996 for over two weeks. I never felt lonely and was amazingly happy. When I think of all these times, I practically start shaking and become absolutely devastated. Everything is fresh, as is every single day's activities: dining, driving in Germany and France, sightseeing on weekends, going to the winery. I can write an entire book about our traveling, and it would have over six hundred pages. I will see if God's and Connie's blessings are showered on me. Now, I do not think I can travel even for a night, except to visit my brother and his family in India. How much has changed in my life due to one person, Connie. Many people will never understand this, but I am happy writing for Connie and myself. If someone appreciates my book, I am extremely grateful to them and feel obliged that they are giving tribute to Connie.

I worked until September 2005. After that, I spent every day with Connie except twelve days each year, going to India. In between all those days, I was with Connie every moment. From India, four to six times a day, I used to call her and talk to her for hours.

In eighth grade, we learned about the true story of Oh Master Ji (Oh My Teacher). This took place during the early 1940s, and it concerns a Hindu teacher who worked at a small school in a village. This teacher took great pain to teach his Hindu, Muslim, Sikh, and all other students with love and compassion. Suddenly, riots broke out between Hindus and Muslims. Villages started burning, and there were sectarian killings. At that time, there were many Hindu and Muslim bullies fighting against each other. So it came to pass in this village that conflict began between Hindu and Muslim. One Muslim boy went to the teacher's home and brought his daughter to his own home. Later that day, when the teacher came home and found his small daughter missing, he was devastated. His neighbors, who had seen the boy take the girl, told him where to look for his missing daughter. The teacher, thinking the worst, was extremely upset and took a big knife to kill the Muslim student who'd taken his daughter. On his way to his house, he was sad and asked God, "Why would my student take my daughter? I gave my love to all my students and took lots of pain in teaching them like they were my own children. Why would he do that to me? What evil did I do to him, that he should do such a thing?" All these thoughts were wandering through his mind, and the teacher was determined to kill his student.

From half a mile away, the teacher saw the boy and started running to kill him. He came across to him with every intention of killing the boy. Suddenly the Muslim student said, "Oh, Master Ji, I have been looking for you. Thanks to God, you are safe. Your daughter is with me, safe and sound. I brought her to my house like she was my own sister, before anybody could harm her. Please come and rest. I will send you and your daughter with ten of my friends for protection." Master Ji was overjoyed that his devotion to teaching all students paid off, and he apologized from the bottom of his heart for the negative things that had been in his mind.

Connie and I have tried to apply this true story throughout our lives. But now it is bothersome that our selfless, unbiased love and respect for all our relatives and friends did not make them realize our pain in difficult times, especially when Connie was alive. God gave me the power to reciprocate my love for Connie when she became more ill. That power, which came from love, was more than the strength of 150 people. This is all due to our true love toward each other. I also chose not to inform anyone of her illness and decided to cope with my loss via Connie's power. However, everything from our forty-one years is like an ongoing movie that plays in my mind and soul all the time, and it is very painful. Some of our dear people, whether family or friends, never called to find out about Connie. Some of my friends did not show me compassion after her death. Many sincere people came at last rites, sent cards, and called. Outsiders were more generous and upset at Connie's loss. Some of the men and young girls from insurance companies, Medicare, the airlines, and telephone and credit card companies have talked to me for two hours, and they even sent me cards. Some outsiders in food stores gave me flowers for her cremation, free on behalf of the organization, which I had to accept as a small token for Connie. That's what I call people who care for you. That's what I think humanity is. They are the ones who have humanity and care. I am angry and bitter over Connie's loss. If Connie could only return to me, I would forgive everyone and treat them nicely in my lifetime.

6. **"Whores don't live in the company of poor men, citizens never support a weak company, and birds don't build nests on a tree that doesn't bear fruit."**

Connie and I have been very sensitive about this message throughout our lives. We cared for the weak and never cared about the rewards.

7. **"He who is overly attached to his family members experiences fear and sorrow, for the root of all grief is attachment. Thus one should discard attachment to be happy."**

Yes, it is a good quote like many others, and I've quoted it many times. However, it is not practical for me at all, and I will never leave that attachment to my Connie.

8. **"O wise man! Give your wealth only to the worthy and never to others. The water of the sea received by the clouds is always sweet."**

Connie and I applied this message all our lives. Connie left a generous donation for charity to her alma maters, Carleton College in Minnesota and the University of Michigan, to provide scholarships for needy students. She also gave to the Red Cross, the American Cancer Society, Mayo Clinic, Northshore Medical Care, and many other foundations, I have started giving on an annual basis to all of the organizations she favored. This gives me happiness. Connie always followed this message until her end, and I will keep doing the same thing.

I have seen people give great support to many noble causes after the deaths of loved ones. Hospitals, educational foundations, schools, colleges, churches, temples, and mosques are patronized in honor of the deceased. I am sure that these noble gifts heal the loss of those people. I think there is great healing power in giving to charity in the memory of a loved one. Connie and I have never gone against the wisdom of this quote.

9. **"Do not put your trust in a bad companion nor even trust an ordinary friend, for if he should get angry with you, he may bring all your secrets to light."**

How true it is, and we both went through this in our lives. I have become more careful after Connie's demise. Among my friends and relatives whom I considered our well-wishers, I see a big gap in their trustworthiness after Connie's loss.

10. **"The fragrance of flowers spreads only in the direction of the wind. But the goodness of a person spreads in all directions."**

Connie had that quality of goodness, and she did not have to practice—it was in her blood, in her brain, and she left marks on many people all over the world. I get so many letters and appreciation from people all the time, and they bring joy but pain as well. Connie went so suddenly that I can't believe she is gone. I have to then see the reality every day, every moment, wherever I am.

11. **"Education is the best friend. An educated person is respected everywhere. Education beats beauty and youth."**

Connie and I tried to live by this message all our lives, and I am extremely grateful for that. We both had great educations and kept actively learning throughout life. Education stops after completing schooling and attaining degrees, but knowledge has no end. That is why Connie was reading so many newspapers and magazines, and watching intellectual TV programs such as *60 Minutes*, the news, *20-20*, *Night Line*, *Mystery*, and other public programs covering different world events and music. She took intellectual tours with scholars all over the world, listening to lectures, reading books, visiting the library, and watching intellectual movies, rather than wasting time gossiping and holding stupid conversations on shallow topics. She would research such diverse things as new recipes or new medical treatments from books and the Internet for our greater knowledge. Although from childhood I have had a foundation of seeking knowledge, Connie installed this further in my life, and that is helping today. I will never be able to repay her.

12. **"It is better to live under a tree in a jungle inhabited by tigers and elephants, to maintain oneself in such a place with ripe fruits and spring water, to lie down on grass, and to wear the ragged barks of trees than to live among one's relations when reduced to poverty."**

Connie and I always followed this great message, and to this date, we don't owe anything to anyone—except our bodies, which we owe to our parents. People took lots of things from us, which we gave with happiness. Some borrowed loans and other things, yet to this day, no one has called to return those loans, and now I want to forget the debt. We managed (or rather, Connie managed) all the budgets and financial planning so that we never depended upon anyone except the supreme body, which belongs to God.

13. **"Test a servant while in the discharge of his duty, a relative in difficulty, a friend in adversity, and a wife in misfortune."**

Connie and I went through this many times with some friends and relations. We tried to forgive them, as difficult as it was. Connie never expected we would be betrayed after we helped them in every way we could. Now, I don't know if I have the ability to forgive them for their betrayals. I have cut off my relationships with those who were users and disappeared from our lives when they got what they wanted,- especially when Connie was sick. I am extremely bitter and angry because of their neglect. I do not even think about those who betrayed me and my Connie. I do not need users any more. That is one of the great experiences. "A friend in need is a friend indeed" is an old Indian saying.

14. "If one has a good disposition, what other virtue is needed? If a man has fame, what is the value of other ornamentation?"

How true is that? Connie's internal and external beauty truly did not need any other ornaments to show the world her true self. Those people who knew her were amazed with her knowledge and inner beauty. No one I know ever had anything bad to say about Connie; rather, they esteemed her as the best of the best. She was gifted with so much inner beauty, education, knowledge; hospitality, housekeeping, and traveling. It is the truth; I am not trying to brag or exaggerate her goodness.

15. 15. "The one excellent thing that can be learned from a lion is that whatever a man intends doing should be done by him with a whole heart and strenuous effort."

Connie was a lion, and she did follow the above message throughout her. She took on any project—education, housekeeping, hospitality, shopping, bookkeeping, organization, and duty toward her family, husband, friends, and neighbors. She did not lack anything.

16. "Foolishness is indeed painful, and verily so is youth, but more painful by far than either is being obliged in another person's house."

Connie reminded me of this message if I was having a hard time making a decision, or if I was faced with a user who sought to take advantage of our soft hearts.

17. "Do not reveal what you have thought upon doing, but by wise council keep it secret, being determined to carry it into execution."

Connie and I followed this message throughout our lives. We never gave up once our minds were set on a course of action. We were firm believers of this message, no matter how difficult or how impossible our course seemed. We never gave up, except when I lost my battle to save my Connie.

18. "The world's biggest power is the youth and beauty of a woman."

I applied this message to Connie all my life and will continue to do so. She was beautiful both externally and internally. I agree with this message to some extent, but due to lifelong love for Connie, I sometimes don't want to believe the truth of this. Connie was Connie. I cannot find any other person like Connie in my life. We will definitely meet again. There have been movies and stories about rebirth and meetings of couples parted by death. God knows the answer.

19. "Never make friends with people who are above or below you in status. Such friendships will never give you any happiness."

Connie and I never thought of this. We sought friendships with people who were like us in education and intellect. We cared nothing for the income of our friends; we only cared that they contributed something to the world. We had some great and intellectual friends. I don't know whether I will meet them again without Connie. Connie was so special and helped forge those friendships. Even if I meet them, my memories will haunt me, and our friendship will not be the same as it was.

20. "The serpent, the king, the tiger, the stinging wasp, the small child, the dog owned by other people, and the fool: these seven ought not to be awakened from sleep."

21. **"There is no austerity equal to a balanced mind, and there is no happiness equal to contentment; there is no disease like covetousness and no virtue like mercy."**

22. **"As soon as the fear approaches near, attack and destroy it."**

Connie was very successful in this message. She is gone, but my life has become unbearable pain, and I don't know if it will ever end. I do not think it will.

23. **"He who lives in our minds is near, though he may actually be far away; but he who is not in our hearts is far, though he may be nearby."**

24. **"There is poison in the fang of the serpent, in the mouth of the fly, and in the sting of a scorpion; but the wicked man is saturated with it."**

25. **"God is not present in idols. Your feelings are your god. The soul is your temple."**

My Uncle's Advice

My uncle told me the qualities of wife. "Son, a wife is precious, if we truly do the analysis from an educated and intelligent point of view." How true it is. No wonder Connie is always in my heart and soul, and she will remain that way all my life. The world is different, and that is why the divorce rate has gone up tremendously among the younger generations, and even among couples married for decades. I still cannot believe that divorce is healthy for anyone. There is an answer to solve this dilemma. I think marriage is an art, and we have to care for that every day or week, just as we give water to the plants and to the gardens. Our cell phones and new innovations such as the Internet are good for emergency talks and important things. What did we do when we had no cell phone thirty years ago? What did we do when we had no TV or other gadgets eighty years ago? We had simple lives and high thoughts. It is terrible that a sacred marriage is so easily broken. How can we expect the people of the world to be friends when there are fights between couples or within families with kids? Are we progressing or going toward darkness? Gandhi truly stated technology would ruin mankind. Now the world is different. Perhaps newly married couples enjoy intimate relations and fun, entertainment and kids, but then they end in divorce. Why? This is not the case with everyone. There are beautiful marriages that last for lifetimes. I give credit to those couples, and they have my greatest respect.

In our marriage, it was love. To love and care for each other was the most important thing for us. I want to mention openly, without offending anyone, that Connie had the same beautiful body until she got too sick for two years and was getting weaker and weaker, until she found it hard to even walk or do anything. Two doctors spoiled her body with their mistreatment, and I hope God takes care of them. As she grew weak, her body became a god for me. I used to touch her feet and worship her beautiful body. I was not praying to God so much as I was praying for her body. It was and still is my most painful memory. I knew I would have to live for her; her weak body was my God. Perhaps when Buddha left his palace as a child, he saw weak and fragile bodies, death, and other suffering. I was no different, but I did not become Buddha. However, I would serve Connie's wishes for charity, education, and bettering humanity. Although we were from different cultures, I never thought that a wife was secondary to her husband. In my case, Connie was extremely important, and I cared for her as much as she cared for me. Perhaps that is why I am writing this book.

That is why Gandhi said, "I have the highest respect for woman as she is the incarnation of tolerance." I followed that message all my life. He further stated, "Woman can tolerate most of the things her husband does, including drinking, gambling and cheating on her; although she would be extremely hurt, she finally may forgive him. However, if a husband suspects a woman's character, that is death for her."

As I mentioned before, I had forgotten my bad childhood memories once I met Connie. My happiness was Connie. Now, the tragedy of my childhood is nothing, because Connie's death is much more painful and unbearable. This is due to Connie's love, but Connie's death is absolutely unbearable. My biggest loss and unhappiness is the demise of Connie. I don't care for all our wealth and would concentrate on helping humanity and teaching others to follow the path of Connie's honesty, loyalty, ethics, charity, and selfless work. I followed these same principles, but I would do more to get some ray of happiness from her memory. I will never be able to forget her goodness in my life.

Now I feel I understand why the young in India used to consult their elders during crises and when facing problems. The elderly have worldly experience that can't be learned in school. The knowledge of seniors comes from facing a life of problems. Perhaps within my limits, I am getting ready to share what I have learned from my own experiences. I still have to learn more; I can learn from everyone I meet. Education reaches an endpoint, but knowledge keeps going if one seeks it. Knowledge is like an ocean: there is no depth to it. That is what I have always believed.

Beginning of Our Love

As I look back, I cannot believe I came to the United States with seven dollars. I was desperate to go back due to homesickness, regretting I was a well-educated with no long-term plans. I thought, *I am struck on foreign soil. How can I reverse all that? Why did I decide to leave India, my family, and my brother? It's a new life, a different culture.* Looking at the snow and downtown was somewhat depressing, with large, high-rise buildings. Homesickness truly bothered me. I was absolutely desperate to go back, but I did not have the flexibility. I used to count on those who lived in India and who came here for a week or two years and then went back. I was struck till God know when. These things were driving me crazy, and I was having withdrawal by myself.

I started working in one suburb of Chicago while staying in Old Town, not far from Second City I was staying on the second floor of a business building in a five-bedroom apartment with my own bedroom and bathroom. There were three elderly married men who had come on a working visa, leaving their wives and children. We supported each other. I did so many errands for them because they never learned English. That was a short time before I met Connie, my future wife.

The third floor was vacant, and the landlord was trying to get a tenant. The landlord was very fond of me, and at one time he asked me if I wanted to buy the whole building. He was old and was rich, and he wanted to retire after selling his five to six buildings in the neighborhood. It was a great price, which was unbelievable. I am sure he was either feeling sorry for me or liked me. He did say, "Mr. Berry, you are a jam of a kind person and treat me like a father. My own family truly does not care for me and wants to grab my money. I feel I might as well sell you one at a price you can offer me. Further, I am tired of looking after so many buildings, and my health does not permit me, even if I hire a manager."

I was shocked that wealth issues took place in the United States too. I had seen family disputes over money in India. I had no idea how to buy the building at a throwaway price. My goal was to go back to India. His offer would have flourished 500 percent as of today.

However, Connie was the best thing I had. Ever today, I think of all those happy and sad days. I am crushed anyway, with one look at me. If I had that much money, it would never make me happy regardless. I am simply writing about how things are happening, and how my happiness and sadness have taken over my life. I know all human beings have many such stories with happy and sad parts. But who knew my Connie was waiting for me as my destiny? This is the most important point in this biography of my lovely, darling wife. We were born in two different countries, but our meeting and marriage and love were predetermined before our births. I could never had imagined that I would come to America for a very short duration and go back to India because many things were supposed to be happening, including my consulting, marriage with an Indian girl in Delhi, and my brother and I living together with the extended Berry family. These were unknown variables that were difficult to solve. However, I am the happiest man because I had Connie. This small paragraph is my book is the short version of my script for the movies based upon true stories, and many of them have had won Oscars.

When I came to the United States forty-two years ago, it was an extremely difficult decision to make. Back home in India, I had an excellent education, all the comforts of a wealthy family, and the makings of a successful professional career. I did not feel in control of the unknown variables of my life by going to a foreign country, whether for a short or long period. A possible destiny of mine had already failed to come to fruition: I had thought to go to the UK to study chartered accountancy from the Institute of Chartered Accountants of England and Wales. My grandfather, fearing that I would leave India, forbade me to study in England. He wanted our family to stay in India. Some of my friends and my chartered accountant colleagues left for the United States and the UK, which made me think that perhaps my future lay in America. With the encouragement of a friend who was teaching at an elite American university, I considered moving to the United States. I eventually decided to come but postponed my move by six months to rethink my decision.

Finally, I did it. I took a Lufthansa flight to Chicago with a stop in Frankfurt. I had a five-hour layover in Germany. Those five hours waiting for the flight to Chicago were the most troublesome hours of my life. Once the plane was on the runway, I became extremely homesick and depressed, thinking that I was giving up my brother, my maternal grandfather, my aunts, my friends, and my education to restart everything. I would be like a newborn baby in a new place. I got up from my seat and started calling the hostesses, who tried to force me to sit down with my seatbelt on. Their many attempts to force me to sit failed. I was desperate to get down from the aircraft, and eventually the captain came to me to ask me what the matter was. I told him honestly that I wanted to go back to India and to please let me get off the plane in Frankfurt so that I could take another flight for India. He tried to persuade that me it was not possible because the aircraft was on the runway, but my persistent request made him feel compassion for my predicament. (I would have been arrested for this behavior in the present day.) He asked me to show him the return ticket and told me that I had a restricted ticket, so I must stay in Chicago for fourteen days. He asked me how much money I had, and I said seven dollars. His response was that I would be struck in the Frankfurt airport for a long time with no food, no hotel, and no flight. I told him that I could request any airline to take me to India, and upon landing, I would call my brother, who would pay for the ticket. The captain told me it would not happen that way, and he advised me to go to Chicago, spend the fourteen days, and take a return flight back to India.

After landing in Chicago, my relative came to pick me up. I asked him if he could arrange for me to go back to India the next day. He was dumfounded and did not say anything. I stayed with my first cousin that night, and she was surprised by my behavior but calmed me down with scotch and dinner. We talked, and I finally went to sleep at 12:30 p.m. but got up around 5:00 a.m. with a panic attack, feeling depression, homesickness, and terror at finding myself in some other part of the planet. I started thinking desperately of how I would go back to India.

Later, some friends and cousins came to welcome me, thinking I was happy to have arrived in the United States. I was depressed and only thought about going back home. They told me to calm down, because homesickness happened to everyone. I wondered why they were no longer homesick, and why didn't they offer to help me to go back to India.

After ten days, I came to live in an apartment in Old Town, Chicago, right across from Second City. At the same time there was a great pressure placed on me to go back to India by my uncle, for my professional career. He wanted me to help run the family business and commit to an arranged marriage. This pressure caused me great stress. I was living in a very confused state of mind and dealing with homesickness. I started meeting many Americans and Indians who became my friends. Late at night, John Candy from Second City came to a restaurant where I was sitting. I did not know anything about him or Second City at that time. Later, they became my good friends and were a great support to my troubled mind.

Each weekend, a good-looking man would come to one of our beautiful bars for drinks and sit, smoking and drinking by himself. I did not know who he was. One night, an American teacher whom I had known as a part-time waiter asked me if I knew who he was. I told him no, and he told me the man was a famous film critic, Roger Ebert. I introduced myself to him, and he was extremely happy and was full of love and passion for his work. He started coming for long hours to talk to me. He became a good friend of mine and showed me some of his work, and he asked me to come for a movie premier. The people I met—Roger Ebert; John Candy and the Second City cast; Don Ross, the editor of *Readers Magazine* and now a political advisor; Andy Shaw; journalists; and politicians like Honorable John Metcalf—helped cheer me up. Eventually, I fell out of touch with those friends, and I have not seen or met them since 1977.

Students of international languages at the University of Chicago also met me with their full class. Mr. Douglas Goodman, who was studying Indian languages, became my dearest friend, and he started taking me out for recordings to send to my brother in India. Douglas got married to his college girlfriend, and both of them went to India and visited my brother for four days in our huge ancestral house in Old Delhi. The house is still there, but no one is living there anymore because my family is living in different houses today. I have not met Douglas since late 1977, but I would love to try to find him now. He and his wife would be great friends in my life now, although Connie cannot be replaced.

I get panic attacks and feel depressed from the unhappiness I face by writing this book. I cannot imagine that Connie is gone. It is absolutely heartbreaking, and I find myself extremely weak in writing this book. I am of two minds, unsure whether or not I should write. But I also feel that I must write this no matter how difficult it is for me, putting the words on the page. I truly want to restart this life, taking me back to where I was forty years ago. That would be the happiest thing—Connie and Pradeep in this life again.

My Connie met me, and that brought me happiness, a new life and passion. We had lots of conversations regarding my plans to go back to India, and she respected my desire to return but suggested I must see some parts of Chicago before I left. She told me to the Museum of Science and Industry, the Art Institute, Northwestern University, the University of Chicago, the Shedd Aquarium, McCormick Place, Michigan Avenue, Lakeshore Drive, and many restaurants around the city. She also suggested that I enroll at an elite university for another graduate program, this time an MBA, before going back to India. I was reluctant to do so because I already had a superb education from India, but then it struck me that education had no end, and an American MBA would prepare me for more knowledge and advance my career worldwide. Over the past forty-two years, I have had the opportunity to gain more exposure and advancement. Further, Connie suggested that once I returned to India, I might regret it if I did not take advantage of my chance to know American culture and experience European culture on my return trip to India. She suggested that although I was well educated, there was a difference between knowing things and seeing them, meeting people, and exploring. She even told me that I should study foreign languages to advance my career in India, or to benefit me if I decided to come back to the United States after my marriage. She said that it would benefit me in the long run, and I could choose my own destiny with my future wife to see where we would like to settle for our careers. She told me that she had finished her education from Carleton College and the University of Michigan, and she was teaching while doing another master's in Spanish and French. Although she already knew the languages well, she was motivated to study further in order to advance her career.

Meeting her changed my sorrow, sadness, and homesickness. I was a different person with the most joyful life. I felt a new revival of happiness, and so did she. Now I knew why so many obstacles, so much unhappiness had kept me from India. It was my great and happy destiny to meet Connie and begin a new chapter of my life with her. We were two bodies with one soul. That priceless happiness can't be bought at any price on this earth. All of the wealth on the planet could never buy happiness and love like we had.

My Connie also went through great happiness, but her happiness changed, and later she faced the most difficult time due to her sickness in 2013. I am reminded of a true story of Lord Buddha, who came across a lady praying to get back her dead son. Buddha told the woman that if she could bring him a bag of rice from a house where there had been no tragedy for five years, he could bring back her son. After going from house to house day and night, she was unable to find a household that was free of tragedy. That was when Buddha made her realize the suffering of everyone on this planet. But even this story does not lessen my pain.

It is a miracle that our first meeting of one hour was the happiest sixty minutes of my life. That miracle led to forty-two years of life together, and yet it ended with one of my biggest regrets, which I will have to relive the rest of my life. I left Connie's hospital room for one hour, and that cost us both. In my strong opinion, her doctors came in my absence and falsified her medical records, ending Connie's life. I became a lonely person without my Connie. Sixty minutes brought us together for forty years, and then sixty minutes separated us.

I was struggling to make the decision to stay in America or leave, which became a boon, but that was the greatest thing of my life. I met Connie, and immediately we knew we were one. We escaped and got married.

As a young man, I was an extremely qualified professional in Delhi, and I was offered many senior positions in different parts of India, along with other career opportunities. However, when a vey senior school friend of mine, teaching at elite US university, came to Delhi and suggested I come to America, I began to see a possible future there. It took three months for me to decide whether I wanted to go. I decided to come for exposure for two months with a senior job in the restaurant, food, and import and export business, where I was responsible for accounting and cash flow, finance, and running the whole operation with the other employees. Although it was not in my profession, I decided to get some different work experience. I was absolutely ready to go back after two months because I was very home sick, but my employer requested that I work a minimum four to six months. Even that seemed too long. I was about to leave when I met Constance Fuller. It was true love in one meeting, and after meeting for sixty minutes, we got married. It was our first love and our last one. Constance Fuller became Mrs. Constance Berry, and we became an exceptionally strong, devoted, true, pure, and loving couple. I would say our marriage was so much fun, loving and caring for each other. There were lots of people we met who were surprised to see that love, wishing that they had the same rhythm with their own spouses. I knew this special marriage would remain that way as long as we lived. "A great wife and a good friend are only for the lucky ones," says a great quote from Indian culture. I must mention that my first employer did not pay my salary for two months, saying his cash flow was bad, which was not true. Connie spoke with him on my behalf, telling him that no one worked for free and he'd better pay me; otherwise, she would report to the IRS and Labor Department. I was not paid for a week. Connie told him a second time that he had better bring a check with proper tax deductions, or else she would report him to both the departments, and I would quit. I got the check right then and worked another two months with pay.

Connie wanted me to go back to my own professional career and advancement, for which I had the offer before coming to America. I returned to the field of finance, and I was promoted three months after that. I never looked back. My employer paid for my MBA from the elite university, and I was traveling close to half the time all over the United States. During these two years, Connie sacrificed her life for my work and college, and we had very little time to interact because she was also studying to advance her career. I noticed that many of my friends and co-workers were having problems with their spouses, because they were asked to travel and be apart. Some of those co-workers got divorced, which was an eye-opening experience for me. In spite of our time apart, Connie and I were enjoying our lives, taking nice vacations, and having fun experiences that surpassed those of our friends, co-workers, and clients.

I would like to mention a true episode that I experienced. I was extremely depressed when I was leaving for the United States. It was something new, and I truly did not know whether or not I wanted to go. My mind was set on no, but some people told me to try out a new thing. I was on the Lufthansa flight from Delhi to Frankfurt, with a five-hour layover before my flight to Chicago. I could be there for just fourteen days and then come back because I had the round-trip ticket. Those fourteen days became forty years, and now I am delighted that I came, met Connie, and progressed in my profession. Without Connie, I would have come back to India after six months, or maybe even earlier. Sometimes destiny brings you to the most unlikely of fates. Again, I never expected that I, her husband, would have to oversee her cremation and last rites. I still remember my first meeting with Connie and how she brought a new life in me.

I would like to recount a few more true incidents. In 1994, I had to travel in the winter to Michigan to evaluate a new large borrower. I did not want to go alone, because other junior associates working under me were on their Christmas vacations, and some were in different parts of the world. I requested that Connie come with me, and she traveled with me. I did a fantastic evaluation. The same kinds of things happened many times in 1981, 1984, 1993, and 1996. She knew how to entertain herself by seeing different sites, exploring shops, and reading on the hotel balcony. She would pick me up for lunch, and after my work we would go out to dinner. I would work late in the hotel, and she would read her book and watch TV. Where would I find that diamond? I did the same for her mother since 1989, after her father died

On September 1, 2005, I left my career to devote myself to her and traveling all over the world. Although we traveled from the early days of our marriage, she wanted to see the world. With five weeks of vacation a year and my own consulting, we could not work and travel as much as she wanted. During her last three years of treatments, although we traveled some at that time as well, I was with her every moment of her life. It is so painful that she died before her time.

I must mention that our love was unconditional. We immediately knew on our first meeting that we were in love, and there was no need to have a second meeting. We knew that this was a nonstop flight, and we wouldn't think of getting off the plane. Many people have many dates and meetings; sometimes their families inquire about one another or ask the family's permission before couples decide to marry with a huge wedding. We were successful without fighting these hassles and compromising for our families. I am always happy to see those couples who have been married for a lifetime. Our faith and values were that marriage was a lifetime commitment. We are lucky we passed our silver anniversary, but we failed to make it to our gold anniversary—in my strong opinion, because of medical negligence. That negligence was so quick that it did not give us time for me to save my partner. I absolutely failed in my battle and a big war, fighting alone against so many people. I wish I had had a strong army behind me, but I was alone, and the other side had too many fighters. One black belt, no matter how well trained he is, cannot win if he is attacked by many enemies or betrayed by those he trusts. This is what happened to us. What a shame to humanity. Even animals have some principles. Kings many centuries ago had some principles. At the same time, there is an old saying: Never let your enemy go.

I loved it when Purus won many battles against King Alexander and pardoned him. Later, Alexander won, and Purus was brought as a prisoner of war to the palace of Alexander, who asked Purus, "How would you like to be treated?" The brave Purus tells him, "I want to be treated as one king treats another king." During that episode, Alexander's bodyguard wanted to attack Purus. Purus told the guard, "Don't you know how to behave and not interfere when two kings are talking?" King Alexander was very happy and told Purus that he would give him back all of the weapons and wealth he had taken. Purus told him, "It means you are obliging me and then you want me to be obligated to you and always consider that you showed your mercy, and I would still have to respect you as my king."

Alexander immediately told him, "No, Purus. I want you to be my best friend, and now I want to come and shake hands with you as my dearest friend. I am desperate to have a friendship with an extremely brave man, and I would feel honored that Purus is my dear friend."

This true episode reminds me of many things in our life together. We were always best friends, and no differences would come between us. We also thought that if something happened to one partner, the other would not only love but worship the one who was gone, waiting until the next life to meet again. That is what I am doing with great pain, but with hope for this love. I have seen these things in my eighth grade studies of ancient civilizations and the Vedanta, which is an open book for anyone to read and research, and which tells of various true episodes. With the technological advances of the twentieth century, many Indian movies were made as much as one hundred years ago, and they remain hits today for the older generation. It is sad that now the new generation is not taught the principles expressed in those films. As Gandhi-ji stated, "Technology will destroy humanity." Therefore he was not in favor of too much technology. One can see that we have lots of technology, but the destruction of humanity, greed, love of money, and materialism have taken over with technology. The answer is hidden in the above sentences.

It also reminds me of Julius Cesar and how his close friend, Brutus, betrayed him. In Connie's case, in my opinion, medical negligence and betrayal by the doctors during my one-hour absence was a much more serious stabbing to a crippled person like Connie after her cardiac arrest.

She was fighting for her life, and the medical staff and the hospital were supposed to be her parents because this crippled sick person could not speak or move, as if someone had tied her completely in a small cage. Even a tiger or a lion cannot save himself in that cage. If you think you are brave, go alone or with ten people without any weapons, and have a hand fight. I would call those people brave, and the medical staff was no braver than if attacking a helpless, powerless animal with weapons or guns. I was also attacked behind my back when I was gone for an hour. I would have shown my power if they were brave and waited for me to attack me to my face. I would have jumped and attacked them. But cowards attack from behind. A brave person would always come in front, face-to-face, giving a full challenge to see who was powerful. They were worse than Brutus.

Her biological sibling and his family were equal to so many Brutuses, but they would be her friends when they wanted something. There is a saying that some people are givers, and some are takers. This was the case with Connie and her family. People never change. Greed is greed, and as time goes, it keeps increasing just as a wildfire always grows. A fire never says, "It is enough. Let me stop. I have had enough fire, and I am satisfied and want this fire to become cooling rain to help the suffering people in the heat who have no cooling system and are struggling to take shelter." People without air conditioning suffer until some humanitarian gives them a cooling system for their hard work. They are not beggars, and neither do they want to beg. But then the old theory of supply and demand comes into play for the whole population during bad economic times. Let's hope it gets corrected. As man has made the mess, only man can correct it.

I have to mention again that Connie was extremely adventurous, and she left behind the most precious memories of happiness in my life. Yes, there was happiness, but perhaps some punishment was also part of the package, and that was last three years of her sickness. I do not know if I should be thankful to God or call myself grabbing punishment now that she is gone from my life. My hands are asking for mercy to God to grant me one more chance and to give me Connie back. I am absolutely lost.

Before coming to the United States, I used to watch both Hollywood and Indian movies with my brothers, school friends, and my family. Girlfriends were absolutely banned in that era. Forty years ago, it was the same way, and then thirty years ago it was a new way. Twenty years ago, the waves were beginning to move fast. Fifteen years ago, it was moving toward a bronze medal, and ten years back it touched silver. Currently it has exceeded gold medal. With hope, we planned to win the Kohinoor diamond. It would have been impossible for me to think of being without Connie, as if I was falling from the top of the Himalayas. Connie would have saved me from falling. That is not possible, and we both see each other in our dreams. We are desperate souls dying to meet each other. The movie *Who Kaun This* (*Who She Was*) was based on this theme, and I can only see her in my dreams and simply talk to her soul. We are like two desperate souls. I am reminded of the raga-based song "Naina Barse Rim Zim," meaning "eyes and soul falling to meet each other as desperate souls." That is what I am going through now, living the same melody and the scenes of that movie. Why does she not come to me? I try to catch her, but she is gone. Has she taken a new birth, or is her soul still waiting? My heart is breaking. I am seeing Connie everywhere, but I can't touch her, can't talk to her. I am seeing her soul coming to me. My heart and soul are making me go catch her, but in reality I can't get her. Who was she? I am sure it is her soul coming to me, and I am desperate to have her back, but I am upset that I can't even touch her. She was my wife and is still in my heart and brain. I keep seeing her, but I can't believe that she is gone. I see her soul, her face, and I suffer. This movie can be easily seen on YouTube, and I am sure it is on Netflix. It would be listed under international movies or Indian movies.

Another touching Indian movie that I asked Connie to see with me on Netflix was *Anupama*, a love story of husband and wife. The husband has a similar situation to me after the demise of his wife. The movie shows the widowed husband blame his newborn girl as the cause of his wife's death, and he is isolated with all his wealth, servants, and business, losing interest in life. My life has practically the same theme, making me bitter with the family and friends who did not call Connie or me for one year, or even up to six years. They may wonder how many times I called. Should I blame them or myself? My shock is so deep that I want to blame them without realizing that others may have lots of problems too, and they are all justified. However, I am not ever conscious of my fault, because my loss has pierced my every minute of thinking about Connie. I would respect all of them, but nothing can heal my constant thoughts of my wife. I don't talk to them; maybe I don't want to describe the trauma I faced. Even if my family and friends know or come to know, no one would ever be able to understand a fraction of that trauma. I wonder whether even God would be able to evaluate the trauma. But I have to thank the Lord to not punish me for my behavior. I surrender and ask for mercy and forgiveness. I am already going through the suffering of losing Connie, and I ask for forgiveness.

From our very first meeting, we were happy together without even going out on a date. We wanted to spend more and more time together, and we were happy to be alone together. We did not try to cultivate hundreds or thousands of friendships to be happy, and we were extremely happy in each other's company. In spite of this, we were very social, going to parties, dancing, and eating out. We were honest and sincere, and we never let another man or woman come between us. All of our lives, we were pure. We never cheated on or hurt each other, and we were never jealous or attracted to other people. We took an oath to be honest to each other no matter where I had to travel, or if one of us had to work late or go to a work party alone. When I was out of town, Connie would drive alone to events and be sure to return by ten thirty so we could talk before going to bed. We both had to leave early for work the next morning, regardless of how late we stayed up talking the night before.

Connie Was My Destiny

Again, I was happy after meeting Connie. Connie was my destiny and my reason for coming to the United States. She was the greatest thing in my life and helped me to forget all my childhood pain. The true pain of losing Connie is much harder than my childhood pain. I would relive the pain of my childhood to now have Connie's presence. We had so much love for each other, and I am living with a great pain now in the hope that we will meet again. This much faith I have, and the revival of this faith gives me the strength to bear this pain. I know miracles happen, that reincarnations happen. Hope gives life. Never deprive someone of his hope; instead ask God to grant his wish. These are great tools and thoughts that wander through my mind at times. It helps to know that God knows all this and will definitely grant this wish in our next lives to be the same couple. I would be granted this desire of having Connie, even if I have to see hardship mitigating the joy of having Connie. It would be the best thing for both of us, I am sure.

I only had seven dollars when I landed in America. Neither my father nor the rest of the family ever paid me a single penny from our inheritance. Connie and I got married. I was extremely happy and started working hard. I was smart and motivated to show her and my family back in India what I was capable of. After three years, once my family knew that I was doing great in the United States and that we were comfortable with what we had, Connie and I went back to India together. Things were very different with my family. They had always respected me, but now we were treated as if we were kings. That is why I must mention success and winners are always respected. We must play to win no matter what the game is. I do not care for that now, but the loss of Connie is deeper.

I practice many great messages that I have studied and known for years, in memory of Connie and for my own peace.

I thought of what Jesus said: "Father, forgive them, they know not what they do." It is natural for me to undertake self-examination in order to remember and evaluate my past deeds, and to think of the holy preaching of the Bible, the Gita, and the Quran. Soon, the holy sermons came to my mind.

a. Surrender and accept when you are helpless, but keep the mind and body active.

b. Think of my past deeds in order to act correctly in the future.

c. I must prepare for mental and physical hardships if I want to survive and do noble things for humanity, including sharing my knowledge and learning more for myself.

d. Pray for the self, for humanity, and for the world.

e. Keep busy, occupy my mind, and pray for forgiveness from Connie for anything bad I ever did to her. I ask her blessings and will keep doing good things for her sake.

f. Find a purpose in life to do things, which Connie would appreciate.

g. Lead a simple life of high thinking, and deprive myself from the great pleasures we had (traveling, dining out, etc.).

h. I am doing that, and perhaps I will not go to cruises or any trips, except to India to see my brother and my family.

i. Lord Krishna stressed an evenness of mind in all circumstances and situations, skill in action and overcoming the law of opposites, and working without attachment and considerations of returns, rewards, and prizes.

j. They told lies and got ahead in life, and here I am, telling the truth and stagnating.

k. In the Bible, Adam said in a similar vein, "Allow your mind to think and say anything it will, only do not identify with it. Allow your body to do what it needs but do not react, everything would happen on its time and accord."

l. Religion is not a business; it is a mission, a great way of life.

m. Manu said, "The whole world is kept in order by punishment, for a guiltless man is hard to find: through fear of punishment, the whole world yields the enjoyments which it owes."

Some Nice Quotes for Our Daily Life

I'm reminded of wise quotations from my late uncle, Dr. P. N. Behl. The following are things he told me.

Darts, barbed wire, and heated spears, however deep they penetrate the flesh, may be extracted. A cutting speech pierces like a javelin to the heart, and none can remove; it lies and rankles. Bad language used in anger or otherwise hurts the person. The wound of the dagger heals, but the hurt caused by the speech leaves a permanent scar on the heart. Hence, control of the tongue and speech are very important. Never hurt others with your words. I strongly recommend austerity in speech, body, and mind. A man's job is to help one another and not to hurt each other. The latter is an animal instinct and not a human one. A good, cheerful word can win the hearts of others; a bad word makes enemies. Similarly, a dirty look can be killing. A cheerful smile is always appreciated. Women can seduce with a winsome look and a sweet word. Self-restraint is very important and essential in all walks of life; restraint in speech is important. If you hurt or abuse somebody with foul words, you hurt him. He becomes an enemy and vows to take revenge. Further, if he returns your foul language, it shall hurt you as well. One can put knives and arrows in somebody's heart, but it can be taken away with medical treatment. A bad deed and a bad word from the mouth rattles the whole life, and the person sometimes has a tendency for revenge.

I will try to follow his great messages.

Further, Per Khalil Gibran in one of his books,

> My soul is my friend who consoles me in the misery and distress of life. He who does not befriend his soul is an enemy of humanity, and he who does not find human guidance within himself will perish desperately. Life emerges from within, and derives not from environs.
>
> I came to say a word and I shall say it now. But if death prevents in uttering, it will be said by tomorrow, for tomorrow never leaves a secret in the book of eternity.
>
> I came to live in the glory of love and the light of Beauty, which are the reflections of God. I am here living. and the people are unable to exile me from the domain of life for they know. I will live in death. If they pluck my eyes I will hearken to the murmurs of Love and the songs of beauty.
>
> I came here to be for all and with all, and I do today in my solitude will be echoed by tomorrow to the people.
>
> What I say now with one heart will be said tomorrow by many hearts.

Prayers have a very soothing effect on troubled mind. But sometimes that fails, depending upon our love and devotion. I am going through that pain every moment of my life. My suffering is worse than ever I thought after Connie's demise. I am aware that we all have to go one day, but I am not able to accept that now, because of my deep love for Connie.

Gandhi Ji—His Messages and His Teachings

I think about Mahatma Gandhi, father of the nation of India. His sacrifice and fight for India's independence from British rule succeeded on August 15, 1947. He was a barrister by profession, and he fought for equal rights in India and in South Africa. A small-built man can get freedom for all. Why, then, can't I get peace of mind and the power to bear the loss of Connie? However, this is a personal loss, and I cannot use this example. Gandhi said things like:

"My life is my message."

"Truth always remains forever."

"Nonviolence."

"My uniform experiences have convinced me that there is no other God than Truth."

"God can never be realized by one who is not pure of heart. Self-purification therefore must mean purification in all the walks of life."

"But the path of self- purification is hard and steep. To attain to perfect purity one has to become absolutely Passionate in thought—free, speech and actions: to rise above the opposing currents of love and hatred, attachment and repulsion."

"I am bidding farewell to all the readers, for the time being at any rate. I ask them to join with me in prayers to the God of Truth that He may grant me the boon of Ahimsa in mind, word and deed."

"I have nothing new to teach the world, Truth and nonviolence are as old as the hills."

These are some of his messages, and they were extracted from *The Story of My Experiments with Truth*, an excellent book for all readers.

The first lesson, nonviolence, is mentioned for my readers, and it is excellent.

Gandhi was married at the tender age of twelve or fourteen. His wife, Kasturba Bhai, was twelve. During the marriage and after, his friends told Gandhi that he must do something to prove that he was the boss of his wife and the head of the family. They said, "Your wife must follow you." He was innocent and told his wife, "You will not go anywhere without my permission, because I am the head of the family now." Kasturba kept quiet but started going out every day for two to four hours without Gandhi's permission. It was happening every day. Gandhi reminded her of this twice, She kept quiet and did not utter anything, Gandhi was upset, and again he told her after few days, "How dare you go out daily without my permission!" Again his wife ignored him. After two days, he lost his temper and yelled, "Why did you not follow my orders?"

This time, Kasturba told Gandhi, "Do you want to say that you are the head of the family? Should I listen to you or your mother, whom I consider the head of the family? Your mother ask me every day to take her to the temple, and that's what I have been doing since we married. Now, my husband, tell me who is the head of the family—you or your mother. Do I take your order or listen to the respected mother of yours?"

After listening to these words, Gandhi realized that he was too aggressive and violent, and now he had to act as a nonviolent husband. That was what brought a new revolution to Gandhi for nonviolence in his whole life.

Nelson Mandela

President Nelson Mandela was a big follower of Gandhi, and he practiced nonviolence—and suffered for years in jail. But he forgave everyone, and his truth and sacrifices made him the president of South Africa. He was a world-renowned figure. He mentioned when Gandhi was going back to India, "India gave us Mohan Dass Karam Chand Gandhi, and we returned to India Mahatma." The same Mahatma became Bapu and Father of the Nation. In 1984, a great movie, *Gandhi*, was released, where Ben Kinglsey played the role of Gandhi. This film and Mr. Kingsley won Oscar awards. It's a wonderful, true movie that helps elevate the mind to find inner peace. I might see it again to get more enlightenment, and to reduce some of the pain from losing Connie. How much peace I will get, I am not sure.

Also, the great Dr. Luther Martin King Jr. was a follower of Gandhi, and he fought for freedom and practiced nonviolence. He too left behind a legacy for the world.

Swami Vivekananda

Swami Vivekananda attended the first world religious congress on Michigan Avenue, in Chicago, in 1893. He said, "If you forget and forgive, that ends everything." He was the first person in history to say "My dear brothers and sisters of America" before his long speech. People were in tears. There is a street on Michigan Avenue where the world religious congress took place, in a hotel. It has been given the name Swami Vivekananda Marg. He stressed, "Strength is life—weakness is death. However long this life is, do something different, so that world can remember you- otherwise, where is the difference between you and trees and stones. They also live die, and decay."

Marg is a Hindi word that means showing the right directions to youngsters, to students, to men, and to ladies; to help people for humanity; to show new rays of hope when stressed; to show a way to go in the path where they can realize their bad deeds; to show new ways of living to the criminals who are ready to remorse their crimes; and to show a new way to all the purpose of life leading them to become good citizens.

I suggest that readers do further research on Swami Vivekananda.

These messages are great and were very meaningful to me when I was young and helped others, but it does not provide any comfort to me now that I have lost Connie. I hope I find some ray of hope, and that is reincarnation. It is my true and solid faith that if there is any supreme power, he could listen to our love. This hope allows me to have some peace once in a while. Further, if I have done any good karma, the Lord will fulfill my desire in my next life. Also, my pain will be heard by the Lord for sure, and that great hope is a power in my life now.

In memory of Connie, I want to share some thoughts on the great poet Tulsidas; we had to study his work in sixth grade. Tulsidas's poems can be read on the Internet or in books. I remember he was one of the most learned poets and scholars of the sixteenth century. He was too obsessed with his wife, and her absence was like his death. One night she had to go to see her sick parents. Tulsidas was not able to stand missing her, and he walked through the night in the rain to see her. Because it was late and raining, he used a rope to climb up to her room. His wife was very upset, telling him, "It is 2:00 a.m., and you foolishly climbed my window." She told him that he was lucky to be alive; the rope he used was actually a huge python. Perhaps the snake was not hungry and was enjoying the rain; otherwise, he would have attacked and killed Tulsidas. She then told him to devote his obsession to God so that he could learn and become something in the world. That was his enlightenment, and he surrendered to God and wrote many chapters on spirituality and education, which are known throughout the world in the Sanskrit language and have great meaning for soothing the mind.

The Education and Career of Connie

Connie went to one of the best high schools. She went to Carleton College in Minnesota, one of the finest liberal arts colleges in the United States, for her undergraduate degree. She later transferred to the University of Michigan, another top college. After graduating, she taught junior and senior high school for few years. Later, to advance her career, she went for her master's in Spanish and French. She studied at top colleges in Mexico and Spain, and then she taught Spanish and French to the children at US military bases in Germany, England, and Spain for five years. She taught in California, and later, she moved back to her hometown, Chicago. That is how I met her, and she became the true love of my life.

Connie exposed me to American culture, dressing and polishing me to advance my career. As such, we both had professional careers, but that didn't interfere with our love and understanding. Even though I was traveling all over the country, I was home for the weekend and sometimes more. We were in touch four or five times a day over the phone while traveling apart. From Friday through Sunday night, we were always together, and depending upon the reports I was writing, I was in my Chicago office for weeks and at home each night. It was a great life combined with our professional senior positions. Connie taught for thirty-four years and took early retirement, but she continued substitute teaching to keep her teaching license, and she was in great demand for Spanish and French. She got offers of full-time teaching positions with different school districts, but she turned those down. I told her to forget work, enjoy life, travel with me, and have fun. She enjoyed teaching and had very close teacher friends, with whom we had wonderful times. I give great respect to my wife as a teacher who did her duty.

Also, in honor Connie's character and memories, I would like to mention some quotes I learned from my uncle, Dr. P. N. Behl, and his book *The Lord Of Darkness*.

Wisdom leads to freedom,
Education to Character,
Culture to perfection,
Humanism to joyous living
In a sense, human beings sometimes are crueler than the animals, when greed comes.
Our thoughts wander in all the directions
And many are the ways of Man,
The Cartwright hopes for accidents,
And the physician for the cripple
And the priest for the rich patron
The blacksmith seeks day after day
The customers endowed with gold
Our thoughts all run towards profit
For the sake of spirit, of mind
Let go all these wondering thoughts.

Character: Man is what his character is. A man of good character makes his life good, while a man with a bad character usually ruins his life and mankind. Character means goodness of heart, tenacity, truth, living by your words, discipline, respect for others and elders and for the weaker sections of the society, respect for the teachers and wise. A man without character is considered to be worse than a beast. People with weak character are usually feeble, meek and easily changeable.

Here are some nice knowledge things in memory of my Connie.

Dark Age or Our Values

My true tributes to Connie. I want share knowledge that Connie knew that would be good for my readers and for myself.

In my opinion, the medical profession is truly passing through a difficult phase, and the noble cause and image is tarnished. Adherence to the Hippocratic Oath is questionable. Press, media, hospitals, nursing homes, pharmaceutical companies, and the greed to make billions of dollars means the system of medicine is not suitable to all. Many seniors and younger generations are going through the big trauma of surviving, which is a necessity of life, forgetting the extra fun activities of vacations or travel. There's very uneven distribution of wealth all over the world. In developed countries like the United States, there is also very uneven distribution of wealth, where the richer are getting richer and others are just surviving. Have humanity and passion in mankind improved? That is a question I think on most of the time. The great kings, presidents, leaders, and wealthy were born alone, empty-handed, and they died the same way. I still have hope that this great county sees shining rays in the future. That would be a new era, "Satyug," bringing crime-free streets and improved economy for human beings and for the world. This is in contrast much better than the current Kalyug, which has crime, corruption, and suffering from the necessity of life and jobs.

Zen in the art of archery, culture, and flower arrangement have provided the inspiration in this paragraph. The call of Shri Krishan in the Gita, the holy book of India, showed the shining lamp of wisdom.

Eugen Harrigel's only focus on the spirituality in archery is very appealing and subtle in this noble profession. Like medicine, spirituality and its need are undeniable. The human physicians have to approach the mind and body for healing. In the same way, the desire for egolessness, selfishness, and self-regard for Zen is equally, if not more, applicable to the art of medicine.

According to John Ruskin, the good of the individual is contained in the good of all. Also, in *Unto This Last*, he contends that man can be happy only if he obeys the moral laws. He also says that there are five great intellectual professions in every civilized nation.

1. The pastors, to teach it.
2. The soldiers, to defend it.
3. The lawyers, to enforce justice in it.
4. The physicians, to keep in it health.
5. The merchants, to provide for it.

Einstein has rightly said, "Concern for man himself and his fate must always form the chief interest in all technical endeavors. Never forget this in the midst of your diagrams and quotations."

Regarding the way to beatitude through the medical profession, Ali Ridwan points out that to reach beatitude (which of all men, the physician is best able to do), he should do the following: "Use part of the day to practice medicine, the remainder devoted to reflections about doing what is right to uphold the priceless value of our work: to dedicate all our time to keep abreast with new developments, innovation, research, to contemplate despite all pressures."

Medicine requires three *D*s—duty, discipline, and devotion. It is not a nice niche for the business. If medicine becomes business, the whole purpose of the noble cause vanishes, and greed, sickening, and suffering (along with financial burden) begin taking many people into poverty and death. Sickness breeds poverty, and poverty breeds sickness. The old Chinese system involved paying the doctors as long as the family is in good health, and stopping paying him when any member falls ill. Then the petty jealousies were also far too common. I hope my readers would like all that regarding the different messages I read and shared with Connie, and my uncle, Dr. Behl, told her all that too. He specially gave what he was writing with his signature, "With love to Connie and Pradeep." He too was very fond of spirituality, and he believed in reading and following the message of Gita, the holy book. That was instrumental in many serious things that happened in his life, which saved him from a few tragedies. He therefore decided to share, and he told us it was ours to read and share with everyone on this world.

After retiring, Connie would go for weekly lunches with her teacher friends, and I was very happy. I used to go with them because it was like a close family. Although she kept substitute teaching, she had more time to travel with me when I was traveling, and that made my life great. I combined working and traveling to have fun. I remember her going many places with me, and her company gave me comfort. The most important time that I needed her was when I had to go to Germany in 1996 for two weeks, and then to France for another two weeks. During my career, we went to California, Dallas, Michigan, and many small towns. I think it was a great help that she was able to travel with me so that I would not be lonely. I would have never dreamed that loneliness was tolerable, but her demise has crushed me, and I will never see her except in my mind. All the forty years of memories are painful. They include:

1. Daily diary with beautiful, handwritten notes of things we did
2. Household notes of bills in folders
3. Receipts of cash and credit cards
4. Names of all the vendors and suppliers, with telephone numbers
5. What day services such as painting, carpet cleaning, car services, and other utilities were done, with notes of how much was paid
6. Her different drawers of clothing, with lists of the contents
7. Her drawers of important documents
8. Her makeup kits with date, expiry, and all other details
9. Our pictures of traveling, and at the back, when and where and sometimes names of friends
10. Her letters from my family, her family, and our friends

11. Important certificates and pictures for the future, just in case

12. Years and years of our marriage anniversary, birthday, and Valentine's Day cards

13. Separate books for household inventory, with date of purchase and prices

14. She would read different designs for ladies and man and accordingly would order new clothes for her and for me

15. Appraisal values of our paintings and actual cost

16. Medical reports and all the payments

17. Medical reports and medical history for both of us

18. Our business and pleasure trips

19. Old, cancelled checks for future references

20. Folders of her parents' pictures and their important documents

21. Folders of her grandparents and their pictures and letters.

22. Most important wedding cards from friends and relatives in special decorative plates

23. Kept special napkins, for different occasions

24. Kept different greeting cards

25. Special thank-you notes and quality diaries for different purposes, with notes in her beautiful handwriting

26. Variety of coasters, table mats, table cloths, special candles, silver, plates, and glasses for different occasions

27. Her beautiful writing for forty years, well organized, with perfection in all aspects is one of the most painful things besides losing her.

28. All the brochures and itinerary of the cruises to Crotona, Italy, Ireland, Norwegian, Budapest, Amsterdam, Caribbean, Alaska, Spain, London, France, Germany, Seven times to India, Palace on Wheels in India, Jaipur, Agra, Khajoraho, Bombay, our stay in Hotel Ambassador, Berlin, France, Vienna, Switzerland, and fifty to sixty more. All are individuals and are in the files, intact in the separate folders in her big cabinets.

I was curious to clean some of the files on August 14, and was very upset to see how smart she was. Now all that fun we had is now over. I see all those and get upset. I think and look and think and put them back nicely in the cabinets. I do not want to throw them away, and neither do I want to give them to any foundation or library. It has our diplomas where we were studying the culture and food, along with history of these places. The last day, all the people in the group had to prepare and present on stage. If you have done your homework and write those in the exam, you are honored with the diploma. Those diplomas do not have much credit, but at least they get us into the door for some position if we have a postgraduate degree. It is a very tricky diploma, and we never even tried to do anything with it. However, it was nice to show to our friends. Now, Connie is gone. It's a monument for me, for my own happiness or sadness. I am going to keep them.

29. I found ten books of the world's best cuisines and recipes that Connie had been reading in the papers and magazines, nicely cut and pasted in the books. I am sure restaurants, libraries, and educational institutions would be delighted to have them. I am sure they are antiques. I will see what I can do with them.

Connie also started doing volunteer work in Wilmette Library two to four hours every Wednesday, even when she was sick. She took that very seriously, as much I told her not to go when she was sick. Later, I started dropping her off and spending time reading and buying books for donations. Everything we did was wonderful. She was my obsession and my love.

My Connie: The Blessed Lady

Connie was highly intelligent and intellectual, and I am only mentioning a very few of her philosophies, otherwise I would have to write another book with all the beliefs she applied in her life.

Connie always had Irish blessings in her book as a book marker.

> May the road rise to meet you. May the wind be always at your back. May the sun shine warm upon your face, the rain fall soft upon your fields. Until we meet again, may God hold you in the hollow of his hand.

Here is a quotes from St. Francis De Sales in her bookmarks.

> Make yourself familiar with the Angels, and behold then frequently in spirit: for without being seen, they are present with you. God grant me the serenity to accept the things I cannot change—the courage to change the things I can and the wisdom to know the difference.

> Remember your debts of gratitude. Live in a way that leaves no regrets. Everything people say or do is ultimately noted in the belief that those actions will lead them to happiness. Your dream is possible. Never seek happiness outside yourself. Seek to understand your mistakes so that you may never repeat them. (Quotations from *Open Your Mind, Open Your Life* by Taro Gold)

Connie's Passion for Reading

Connie was a born reader, reading the *Wall Street Journal*, *New York Times*, *Chicago Tribune*, *Barron's Financial Rimes,* and many other magazines and books. Her influence to read other magazines and books is one of her intellectual gifts to me. I wasn't fond of fiction, and she suggested I read true stories and books, which I always enjoyed. We were readers, however now I miss her for doing all that. I have cut my reading but want to write books too.

Connie was a great reader. She used to read different magazines to get the most popular news and best-rated appliances, cars, TVs, and anything related to the home. She would let others know the information she found. It was a great humanitarian cause. She loved exploring different cuisines and restaurants, attending Broadway plays and symphonies, and doing other things. She loved these cultural events and made me see them with her. I would have a very simple and plain life with all the withdrawal symptoms of my grief. The more I think, the more I want to write on each and every topic of her life. I am convinced that I will never find another diamond like that in my life. I hope and pray that God grants me Connie as a wife in my next life. I have a strong feeling that we will both meet in our next lives. This belief is the only thing that gives me happiness, as well upsetting my life due to the loss of Connie. After her loss, I began to read articles that she had suggested but that I was not originally too interested in. After reading them, I wanted to read the same articles many times over. Her awareness, intelligence, and common sense were beyond approach, and she was super smart and busy all day long. I am blessed to have such a gem in my life, and no one else can ever replace her. She was absolutely amazing and beautiful in my forty years of life with her, and she was always writing and building her knowledge of different topics. Connie was a super reader. Her average daily time spent reading was ten to fifteen hours a day when she took early retirement, and before that she read five to six hours each day.

Connie used to read many intellectual books; she must have read over eight thousand books during our marriage. She was very fond of the authors Susan Vreeland, Elizabeth Phillips, Jane Robinson, Woody Allen, Shakespeare, Ruth Rendell, Tom Wolfe, and Jon Krakauer, to name a few. Besides that, Connie also loved all cookbooks, health-related books about symptoms and their causes, and different recipes of world cuisines. She loved to read *Time, Consumer Reports*, travel books for destinations around the world, and world history. Connie loved cutting recipes and trying them for me and for her friends, listening to old classical records, watching Oscar-winning movies and European movies, and listening to different music genres (including Elvis, the Beatles, the Bee Gees, Frank Sinatra, Mozart, and hundreds more). Like I mentioned, we saw practically all the Broadway shows, including *Joseph and the Amazing Technicolor Dreamcoat, Mama Mia, Miss Saigon, Elephant Man*, Frank Sinatra, and Irish songs and plays. I would have to write two hundred pages to write all of these down.

This time, while I am writing, I have pain in my heart and soul, feeling that Connie was truly one in a million and this diamond has left me totally alone. I am going to miss reading all that, depriving myself of the world, including plays and Mozart, which was my passion with her. I was just reading about Turkey and its ancient heritage, where King Alexander and Cleopatra visited. I would be depressed and would get a panic attack if I ever decided to go alone or with any family member. I can't even think of going. The only thing I like now is to go to the health club, do important household work, and stay home. I can think of going to see my brother and his family in Delhi, India, but that is all. I now have realized that every author has written books in memory of someone, showing that authors write about their loved ones. That is wonderful; otherwise, such a book is not perfect.

Reading Passion—Her Intellectual Mind

The other day, I was thinking about Connie's reading habits and her interest in diversified magazines and knowledge. Our whole family, including the entire Berry family, consists of about two hundred people, three generations of my grandfather's sisters' and brothers' families included. Some of them, about fifty to sixty, have settled in the United States, and some of them are smart. Some are computer engineers, and some of them have graduate degrees. There are about one hundred people on my mother's side. Overall, if we consider a population of three to four hundred people, including some of her friends, I can prove it statistically that out of the whole population, Connie was the most intellectual person of all and the most well-read. I don't think anyone in the group can compete with her as far as intellect on every subject. The people I am talking about are very successful in their businesses and are intelligent; one of them is a medical doctor. I can even compare Connie with her, and she is a medical doctor who studied in America; her husband is also a doctor. I don't know why people think medical doctors are like gods, but this is the way they think, and this is the way they are. I think these doctors may be very good in their own fields, but they have no knowledge about any subject other than medicine. In my opinion and experience, I spoke to my family members who are medical practitioners, and I found that they don't read anything other than their medical books. I don't think they know anything about the world, or about ancient civilizations, or about the histories of different countries. Their knowledge is limited to the medical field.

I would say that Connie was a gold medalist in her knowledge. Businesspeople, like doctors, are very good at what they do, but they know nothing else. It all boils down to the intellectual level of a person—what they can discuss, what they know about diverse topics. I feel that an intellectual person should be able to discuss world languages and cultures. Connie knew every state in India, as well as their languages, foods, and cultures. At the same time, she was familiar with most world cultures. For example, she knew how different countries in Europe such as Ireland, France, Denmark, Germany, Norway, Italy, and Spain progressed; what they did; and whether they were Communists. I don't think I have ever seen anyone else with this kind of vast knowledge in my lifetime. When I think about it, I realize that Connie was brilliant. In this particular area, she exceeded me a million times. She even knew the history of India, however she sometimes questioned whether the Mahabharata or the Ramayana really happened. Some Indians believe that the histories recounted in these epics truly occurred, but some are skeptical. Some are confused, but most Indians, including me, believe that those events really occurred. When we have a question about these things—such as yesterday when I was watching Ramleela in Delhi—we Indians ask ourselves what we believe. Most of my fellow moviegoers believe in the story of Ramleela, but some people don't believe in it and claim it was a show and is considered mythology. If I have my own doubts, I don't think we should single out anyone else.

Having said all that, Connie would put across her point in a brief moment and be done. Those who speak less and read more are often more intellectual than those who speak often and don't read. I mentioned this before, and I am repeating it now: listening is golden. Connie's intelligence was internal and external. I was very lucky to have Connie in my life. Her loss has really rattled me, and I don't have any peace of mind, even eight months after her death. People want to see me become normal, but I feel it will take me years to overcome my grief. The only happiness I get is from meeting new people. The people I met when I went to collect her medical reports were much nicer to me than anyone else, even better than my friends. Our real estate agent, whom I spoke to for a couple of hours recently, showed great compassion, and it was mental stimulation for me. I am seeking this kind of interaction.

I just want to say this about Connie's reading: her knowledge was immense. I want to give you one more example. I did not know that while she was reading about twenty magazines, she was also giving copies to our neighbor, because the woman was a widow and could not afford to pay for the subscription while she looked after her family. Connie was already a member of those magazines, she subscribed to the magazines for our neighbor. The other day when I was talking to the widow, she told me that she knew I was going to India, and like always, I would get her a gift from there. She asked me not to get anything from India, but instead to subscribe for her to the magazines that Connie would read. I was very happy to hear that. I had not known about this selfless charity of Connie's. I will continue her legacy of helping people. This gives me immense happiness, but at the same time, it makes me sad.

I was not sure that I would actually travel to India until I got on the plane on October 17, 2015. On the night of the sixteenth, having only had two hours of sleep, I packed all of my papers into my briefcase and carry-on bag. I now had to spend hours in Delhi sorting these papers and making copies. I would leave these documents in Delhi and take copies back to the United States. Connie knew about all of the documents, and dealing with them made me very tense. Connie always helped me organize my documents when I traveled. That was her greatness; she was the whole world to me.

She could read very fast, and she would always find time in the night to read. She would carry books with her on the plane and take them with her wherever she went. Sometimes I would get sick of her reading! I couldn't believe she read so much, and she wouldn't even talk to me. She would tell me that there was nothing to talk about. She would then put the book down, only to start reading again after a while. I would get irritated, and then she would get irritated and ask me why I couldn't pick up a novel and read. I would tell her that I liked to read the business section of the local papers and the *Wall Street Journal*. She would tell me that I needed to develop a habit of reading other things, like novels. She would say that instead of depending on her to explain why world events like wars took place, I should read about them on my own. Although I knew these things, I wanted to refresh my knowledge. Once Connie read something, she never forgot it. That was the difference between us. I want to reiterate that of all the people in my entire extended family, she was the most intelligent.

Connie's Love for Music and Arts

Connie loved classic songs from many singers, such as Frank Sinatra, the Beatles, Elvis, Abba, Christmas music, Mozart, many symphonies, Broadway plays, classic masters, and at least two hundred more singers. She used to have two gramophones and old records of singers like Cliff Richard, Tony Christie, and Ray Charles. I was extremely fond of all that, and our shared interest was a plus. I loved Broadway plays, and so did she. Of all the plays we attended, we never left early.

Regarding art, Connie used to collect many artistic pieces for the house. She had special baskets for different places, like for her newspapers and magazines, as well as small, decorative art objects for the house, kitchen, study room, and bedroom. She collected several historical paintings. She took me to see many art and cultural shows. She was a member of the Museum of Art and Science and donated money to Channel 11, which was supported by the public and provides absolutely great programs. Channel 11 airs music, history, Christmas programs, and symphony shows. It is truly difficult for me to write everything about her interests. Beatles, Carol Burnett shows, Jones, Frank Sinatra, and Original Masters Classical Bewind—many series of these are sitting brand-new. She ordered them specially to watch. She ordered new speakers, and I was lazy or slightly concerned that I would call a professional to install those nice speakers for her to listen. I cried that I could not do it due to my own fault. It took me over a year, and even on August 24, 2016, I wondered why I did not do such a small thing for her. I got her a new phone, a new jacket, and many new shoes February 2015. Who knew what Connie would open and see? This all happened as I was single-handedly looking after Connie.

I recall one incident in April 1999. We were taking a trip to Crotona and Tuscany in Italy with the University of Michigan. Connie's mother was nervous, and we used to go and stay with her. I used to work from her house. She was into a lot of mischief, calling the police during the night and claiming that someone was drowning or playing music. Connie brought her to our home after we spent a month in her home. We had practically cancelled our trip to Italy. It was lots of money, and we did not buy the travel insurance, it was still in our mind that we may or may not go. That was Connie; that was her character. She mailed her sibling and children and grandchildren their marriage anniversary and Christmas cards in 2014 and 2015, with checks to all of them. For Christmas, birthday, and anniversary cards, as well as gifts for Christmas in 2014 and 2015, she sent them two months before her demise. What a duty she performed. On top of that, Connie left some funds for them. Do I have a right to write this or not? I let the readers judge. I'm her loving and crushed husband. It's a very painful love for my Connie, and she was such a great person

Connie was curious about the subjects covered by different magazines and TV channels. She would read reviews and ratings of the channels and shows, and she knew which shows were popular. She also knew which program was going to end and when, when a new show was coming along, and the ratings of films in theaters. She would watch award shows like the Oscars and the Emmys, as well as the country music awards. She enjoyed programs like *Night Line* and *20-20*.

Connie also loved to travel to cities with important artistic events. Connie took me to Santa Fe, New Mexico, in September 1993, and I loved it. She knew that during September, craftsmen come from all over the world. She enjoyed shopping for herself and for me in Santa Fe. I still have all those objects. Connie also took me to Austin and to Dallas for different culture shows. She took me to a very exclusive furniture store in Florida in 2002 to get new furniture, and to Wisconsin for different handmade watches. We went to Germany and to a German market in Milwaukee to purchase nutcrackers. Connie had season tickets to the North Lake Club for stage plays and Marriot stage plays, and we often went to Las Vegas, where we must have seen over seventy beautiful shows. We saw *Mama Mia!* twice, in Chicago and in Las Vegas. We also saw *Jersey Boys* twice at different places. Each city has its own cast, but the show is the same.

Her Exposure to World Travel

Connie exposed me to world travel, which I truly enjoyed. She used to study and plan the best cruises and other trips. I am extremely grateful and obligated to her for the beautiful cruises and other trips we shared both in the United States and in some of the most exclusive places in the world. Without her, I would not have traveled the world for pleasure. She often told me that I didn't take any initiative to plan anything other than trips to India. She came to India with me seven times, and she made me travel to the most beautiful places in India, including the Palace on Wheels. It was a treat, and I recommend this trip to everyone. It is a princely trip designed for kings during the British Empire. The Palace on Wheels runs from October through May, as well as in the first week of January. We went in 1995, and the Palace on Wheels is one of the best and finest trips in India. My readers can find more information on the Internet if they would like to take this trip, which goes from Delhi to Rajasthan. Connie was amazingly happy during our trip, and she mentioned it for the rest of her life.

Writing about this is difficult because my mind is 100 percent on Connie, who is in my soul. I focus on her death and seeing her dying, thinking that I am dreaming that she is gone. I am thinking of her grave. The most painful thing is her ashes under the green grass on which I have to stand to touch her beautiful granite stone. That kills me even if I am not there. I am seven thousand miles away from our home and from her grave in M. P. Cemetery. When I think of Connie, the green grass that has ashes kills me: under that grass is my Connie. Her body is under that grass, and I am walking over the beautiful and intelligent Connie. Although her body in that casket was put in with the help of four professionals, I was a part of that. Body and casket were together, hiding Connie inside. How can I do such a thing, burning my Connie in that? How do I know she is dead? It's very much possible that she was alive and weeping, crying, "Pradeep, why do you put me inside? Please let me get out from this covered thing. I am suffocating." It was one of the most painful things I ever did.

When I came to the United States, Connie must have been waiting for me, and I know with 100 percent certainty that Connie was my destiny. Maybe God put us on the earth so that I could meet her and marry her. Maybe both of us had some past relationships that was incomplete, and God gave us a chance to be together again for forty years.

We traveled to the Taj Mahal, Jaipur, Kashmir, Khujuraho, and other places in India during her seven trips. I also traveled frequently throughout America for my professional career, and if Connie was on vacation, she would accompany me. I was very happy and had a ball while I was working. Sometimes I would work long hours, and she was very capable of exploring and finding the best places by herself. Later, she would talk about her adventures and would take me to see all that she discovered. If I had been alone, I would not have done anything. All these made me curious to explore more about travel and shopping. All these experiences made us compulsive shoppers for clothes and gifts, and we had a great collection of the best pens, picture frames, shoes, clothes, and other items for the house, as well as for our family and friends. We were very social for a while, and later we both were so happy that we didn't care whether or not we were alone. We used to have a few evenings every week when we would go out for dinner, and for visiting or inviting over friends and family, but we preferred being by ourselves to share our love and company. We talked of different things, sharing our knowledge and reading, and we spent our time together writing, dining out, shopping, traveling, driving, going to the health club, and attending small gatherings of friends. We were inseparable and used to feel lonely without each other. I think it was a great time and love, and even if we were sitting in the same room doing different things, as long as we could see each other, we were happy. I know that sometimes this kind of love is very painful, because spouses who feel this way cannot go on if something happens to one of them. But we have no control.

As we traveled together, we saw practically half of the most important parts of the world, in addition to our travels all over the United States. We saw Broadway and Las Vegas shows, as well as symphonies in different parts of the world, including Vienna. Dining out in the best restaurants to experience new cuisine was a powerful part of our lives. Connie wanted the best but was financially conservative at the same time. She took me to Spain in 1987 for two weeks. We went on an Alaskan cruise in 1988 and visited Alaska a second time in 1989. We went on a Caribbean cruise in 1989.We also went to New Orleans in 1989 and spent time in the French Quarter. We went to New Mexico in 1990. We also took many mini vacations over long weekends, traveling to Santa Fe and even to England. We took Michigan University alumni trips to Tuscany, Ireland, Denmark, and Norway.

One of our greatest memories, especially for Connie, was my sense of humor and laughing when our friends of thirty years started calling me Doctor. Because of them, a cruise ship of fourteen hundred people truly believed I was a medical doctor. The older ladies on the cruise in particular spread the word to all the ship that Dr. Berry was on board, and so they should not be afraid to climb historic buildings. I told them not to worry, to breathe deeply and climb slowly, and they complimented me as the best medical doctor. Other senior ladies told me they loved sweets and asked if they were harmful. I didn't want a lawsuit, and I had to improvise. I asked, "Are you diabetic?" When they said no, I told them to keep eating and not to worry. They stuffed themselves with sweets, and I began to worry that if anything happened to them, I would be in trouble. But God is grateful, and I started getting letters from many people who were cured by Ayurveda medicine and yoga. I decided that I would never do that again, and we no longer traveled with our friends, except to Spain. Connie and I decided to focus on each other and began to drop the friends who were not close to us. Now they want me to join back in that group of friends, thinking that will help what I am going through without Connie.

Later, we took trips with Vantage Cruise, a two-week trip in Norway, and another river cruise of seventeen days from Budapest to Amsterdam. We took a Christmas tree cruise for twelve days in England during the winter, and we went to the French Riviera, Germany, France, and India. I went home almost every year for two weeks to see my brother in India. But from 2011 until 2015, I did not even think of going back to India due to Connie's health. In fact, I did not think of leaving her for one day when she was sick. I left my high-powered senior position in 2006 to be with her, and I have no regrets at all. Rather, I am happy that I could serve her, and that gives me the greatest satisfaction, but I cannot bear the pain of losing her. She wanted to go to Australia, New Zealand, and China, but some way or another, we could not go. I will regret this all my life. We went to Door County three times, as well as many other beautiful places in Wisconsin, Lake Geneva, Crystal Lake, many cities of California (including Palm Springs, where she found the standing table she had been seeking for two years). She was a perfectionist. We also want to cities in Texas, North Carolina, and Nevada. While living in Chicago, we saw all of the Broadway shows that came there. Later, we went to Sanibel Island for five weeks and also to Marco Island, staying for three weeks at the Hilton Marco Island Resort to escape the cold and snow of Evanston. It was nothing but fun, love, and billions of dollars' worth of our happiness, which money cannot buy at any cost.

Connie was very conservative and was not concerned with high society. She never wanted to impress the world, because she was very modest and was not a showy person. She enjoyed meeting interesting and intelligent people. We both shared the same rhythm, and we respected every human being, whether educated or not, because we had always been down-to-earth all our lives. Now I have lost that momentum and will not enjoy the same life without her. Many family members and friends tell me that life keeps going, but there is a big stop for me after seeing the way our lives together was.

Connie: Her Charm and Beauty

Connie was charming, ethical, honest, giving, faithful, and extremely intelligent. She was a great reader in addition to being an incarnation of tolerance and strong will. She was exceptionally beautiful, both externally and internally, and was a wonderful wife and best friend. In addition to being well-rounded and bright in every aspect, she was the darling of my family and friends. Whoever met her became her fan and friend, and so they became our friends too. Connie was born in Glenview, a very affluent suburb of Chicago. She loved her parents, was very faithful, and always offered help at any time. She used to invite them to our house every week. I also enjoyed having them, and we were all very fond of Indian food, which we cooked for them.

In their old age, Connie took care of them. I was involved in helping Connie care for them. Her father got sick first, and we were there every moment for his help and support, including doctor appointments and trips to the hospital. We were there when he died in December 1989. We asked her mother to stay with us after his death, but she refused. Let me make it clear: her mother was crazy, and after becoming a widow, her life revolved around her four grandkids from her other child. She wanted to stay with them, but they refused to have her. She kept trying but in vain. I think it was a pathetic and dirty thing not to fulfill her wishes but they had their own lives. We brought her mother to live in our house for months when she was sick, but otherwise she was living in her own house. Later, Connie's sibling took her to Wisconsin, a three-hour drive from our home, and put her in a nursing home.

We used to visit her mother every month, sometimes twice a month. We'd stay in a hotel for two nights and take her out for lunch. We had some satisfaction and happiness, knowing that we made her old age and her last fifteen years of life extremely happy, even after her husband's death. We both were instrumental in arranging her cremation and service in the chapel of peace, and in putting her ashes in her plot next to her husband.

Connie was extremely upset after the loss of her parents and did much charitable work, which gave her happiness. "It is extremely important for me to mention that Connie and I would have brought her mother back from the nursing home, if Connie had not been suffering from a rare skin disease, pityriasis rubra pilaris (PRP), in 1999–2000. The disease was more painful than her fight with other diseases, except in 2014 and 2015 when she suffered from the advanced stage of spreading cancer. Connie was extremely hurt that her mother was in the nursing home, and it was a tragic thing for me to see Connie' agony during this time. I would mention more about more painful episodes in a later chapter.

Connie's Character and Thinking

There is no end to the greatness of Connie's thinking and her character. She was loyal and honest, never lied, always forgave, gave without taking, had great work ethic, and maintained our household without asking me for help. She never depended on anyone but always found a way to cope. She was very brave and bold. If someone was in error, she would tell him to his face and make him realize his mistake. Connie did not care if someone was wealthy, and she was friendly with all intelligent people. She did not run after wealth or social power; that was not in her blood, or in mine. We cared about what people were and not what they had.

I give my tributes to Connie by quoting the following messages from Swami Vivekananda. Swami Vivekananda quoted the following messages. These sometimes give me strength, but still they do not heal my pain.

1. "Have faith that you are all brave lads, born to do great things. Let not the barks of puppies frighten you; no, not even the thunderbolts of heaven, but stand up and work."
2. "Your country requires heroes; be heroes. Stand firm like a rock. Truth always triumphs. A country wants is anew electric fire to stir up a fresh vigor in the national veins. Be brave."
3. "Trust not the so-called rich; they are more dead than alive. The hope lies in you—in the meek, the lowly, but the faithful. Have faith in the Lord. Give me a genuine man; I do not care for anybody to help you. Is not the Lord infinitely greater than all human help? Be holy—trust in the Lord, depend on Him always and you are on the right track; nothing can prevail against you."

4. "Faith, faith, faith in ourselves, faith in God—this is the secret of greatness. If you have faith in three hundred and thirty millions of your mythological gods, and in all the gods which foreigners have introduced into your midst, and still have no faith in yourselves, there is no salvation for you. Have faith in yourselves and stand upon that faith and be strong."

5. "All truth is eternal. Truth is nobody's property; no race, no individual can lay exclusive claim to it. Truth is the nature of all souls. Who can lay special claim to it."

6. "Look upon every man, woman, and everyone as God. You cannot help anyone, you can only serve. Serve the children of the Lord Himself, if you have the privilege. If the Lord grants that you can help any one of His children, blessed you are."

We both applied these messages throughout our lives, and I will continue doing so for the sake of Connie. My message to all my readers: Please have a bond of love, care, and respect for each other. Have full trust and honesty. Plant your relations as we give water to the plants. Connie and I did all that; however without Connie, I am suffering as a fish without water, the pain an animal feels when slaughtered, or the pain of human beings and animals that are killed by others. Gandhi-ji was right when he started his movement of nonviolence: fighting never brings peace. Living by the code of an eye for an eye would destroy the world. Please try to understand how sensitive the relation of a woman and her husband is when they are married. The majority of wives only want love, care, respect, security, a faithful and caring husband, comfortable living, and a nice family who cares for her. Wives can sacrifice many luxuries and material things in return for their husbands' love, but they must have that love. Yes, there are exceptions, but in my opinion it holds true. Husband and wife must admit and say to each other three words. "I love you."

Connie's Character, Part Two

I want to write more regarding Connie's character. I think you can tell we were made for each other. I was raised in an environment with very strong values and with an emphasis on character. Our grandparents were very strict about focusing on studies, sports, and other activities like Boy Scouts and the National Cadet Corps (NCC). I was extremely good in Boy Scouts; I was the NCC battalion sergeant and had a lot of other extracurricular qualifications. We were given the strongest foundation possible to build our character. That also meant not having any relationships or attachments to the opposite gender. The priority was to get educated first; all other things could happen after one was well settled in life. In reality, because we were brought up in this way, we never really even thought of having any female friends. It wasn't unlike today, where it is very common for people to have boyfriends or girlfriends who might or might not marry each other. In any case, that was a different era.

Connie was brought up in exactly the same way. Her focus was only on her education and her research. She was keen only on her studies, and she was not interested in parties or meeting men. She was very happy with her closely knit family and girlfriends. Her mother was very strict, and Connie herself had a moral code that meant she was not interested in parties that involved drinking and dancing. In addition to her education and her intellectual nature, we found this to be a common aspect among us. I think this is one of the contributing factors behind us getting together. Ordinarily, I would have gone back to India for an arranged marriage, because there were a lot of proposals from rich families that had come my way. Perhaps God wanted me not to go because I was destined to meet

Connie, who was beautiful from the outside and from within. Connie liked to say that I was her first boyfriend and she was my first girlfriend, although we really started out as friends.

To this day, I don't know how I gained the confidence to talk to a woman. If you are from India, talking to a woman is the most fearful and dangerous thing. Of course, after I came to America and met ladies in my corporate life, I developed the courage and faith to form friendships with women. The reason is that in America, men and women have been raised in a different environment; they have been brought up full of confidence throughout their childhood. I remember that when I first came to this country, one of my colleagues who was working under me told me, "Pradeep, let me tell you one thing. In this country, children are given the maximum freedom." I was astonished to hear that because in our era, even though we were given freedom, we were also watched like hawks. We were always kept track of regarding our activities and where we went. I noticed a big difference in our cultures. If you talk to people over here, you notice how confident they are irrespective of their age, because they have been brought up in such an environment. I'm not trying to criticize or hurt anybody's feelings; I'm simply sharing my own experience and knowledge without offending anybody. When I go to the health club or to shops, or even in my professional life, women talk to me as if we have known each other for years. There is a lot of joking around, and our conversations are full of fun.

I have not seen that kind of atmosphere with Indian ladies, whether they are married or otherwise. They tend to be very reserved, and it is a big cultural difference that I find very interesting. Once again, it is not a reflection on these cultural ways of communicating. I have traveled all over the world, whether in America or Europe, and I find that outside of India, people are friendlier and more open with strangers. It is not as if people in India are not like that—in fact, they are very wonderful and hospitable. But there is definitely some kind of rhythm that's missing. I find that sometimes even young Indians are reluctant to talk. In America, I meet many Indian school and college students, and often they don't say hello. At times if I ask them if they are from India, they mumble yes and claim that they need to get back to their work. This has happened several times, and to some degree it has upset me, but then I decided that this is a culture difference. But that is not answer. A simple smile and a little hello are always good.

Connie Told Me, "Make Good Use of Your Time

During the late seventies and early eighties, Connie and I were working very hard to build our careers. On Saturdays, although it was not mandatory for me to do any work, I would get up in the morning and work on my reports because I wanted to increase my knowledge and advance my career. I used to put in that extra effort, and Connie would do the same. The only difference between the two of us was that while working, I would turn on an Indian program called *Chitrahaar*. I used to watch that program from eight to nine o'clock while I worked. Connie would let me watch it and not say anything. She was very selfless and probably thought that because I enjoyed it, she should not interfere. Those were very interesting days for both of us.

One day in 1979, my uncle, Dr. Behl, came to our home when I was watching *Chitrahaar*. He turned it off and said to me, "Why on earth are you wasting your time watching this useless program? I know that you are working, but instead of this junk, why don't you watch some financial programs so that you can do like I do? I listened to some lectures while writing my book, and this is way you teach yourself."

His wife, who was British, told him, "Pran, leave him alone. Let him enjoy his program."

He replied to her, "Listen, Marge, you don't know. This is about his career. He is my favorite nephew, and I love him like a son. I want him to shine, and I want that Connie should be proud of him. So he should stop watching *Chitrahaar*." He turned to me and said, "Pradeep, you forget about this lousy program and concentrate on your work." I enjoyed watching it for one hour, and I thought at that time that my uncle was being very tough on me. Later, at the age of fifty-five, I realized what he was trying to say then. Now I don't enjoy those kinds of programs.

In 1984–85 I got into the habit of watching Indian movies. Connie was initially happy that I enjoyed watching the movies. Later on, when she saw that the habit was increasing, after about a year she told me, "You waste your time watching movies that have no theme. Girls are dancing and boys are running. These are not intellectual movies. If you really want to watch interesting movies, watch movies based on true stories that make sense. Those movies have some sort of intellectual ending. You are not learning anything from Indian movies. It is the same plot: a hero fights with a hundred people, the hero can do anything, a villain comes, they have a flight, the villain hurts the hero, and finally the hero meets the heroine. The actresses are gorgeous, and I love their dresses and sarees, but they are lip-singing the songs, unlike the actresses in a Broadway show who are properly trained to sing. These Indian actresses no doubt are beautiful, but the background dancers are not so beautiful because they want to show the contrast between the background dancers and heroines. Our American movies are not like that."

I used to watch a lot of American movies when I was in India. After coming to the United States, maybe because I was homesick and was away from my family, I started watching all the Indian movies we used to see in the theaters in India. That habit persisted for a year or two. Connie told me, "If you use the time you spend watching movies to read your reports, business documents, the *New York Times*, the *Wall Street Journal,* or even novels, you will get knowledge."

I said, "I don't like to read any novels; they are useless fictions. I like reading the autobiographies of people like Nelson Mandela, John F. Kennedy, Mahatma Gandhi, Dr. Rajendra Prasadin, Mark Twain, US presidents, and people who did research in different fields. But mostly I prefer reading business books relating to my profession."

She said, "Read whatever you want, but keep the habit because it will give you a hobby, will keep you occupied, and will stimulate you. You will become an intelligent person." Her average reading time was four to six hours a day when she was working. When she took early retirement, her average reading was fourteen hours a day. She used to read magazines, books, newspapers, and very selective and intellectual books and articles. I used to read during the days that I was working, but after I took time off, I started writing articles for MBA students and for many institutions. I would write on my passion, my subject area, which was commercial lending, mergers, and acquisition. People used to ask me questions on the Internet. There were questions from all sorts of people about banking, Internet banking, and the commercial loans sector. There would be questions about hostile mergers, how to buy companies, how to run a company, how to start a company, how to leverage it, and many other things, including improving sales. I used to write because I had lots of knowledge.

This knowledge did not come because I was a special man of God, but because I worked hard for it. I went to an elite US university for my MBA. I passed over eighty professional development courses while working for different finance companies and banks, which were mandatory in order to be promoted and build knowledge. Without bragging, I can talk about any subject or topic, whether it is about my career, spirituality, ancient Indian civilization, Buddha, Shakespeare, the Bible, the Koran, Indian classical music, Mozart, or Broadway shows. Thus I developed my personality a lot, and all the credit goes to Connie. If Connie had not been there and if she had not helped me, I would not have changed myself. I started feeling embarrassed that Connie may see me as the same person who was not well cultured. Thus I ended up shining for both of us.

I don't mean to offend anyone, but I see certain people in my distant family— there are about fifty of them—who don't do anything on weekends. They don't read or research papers; the only thing they do is gossip and waste their time. I am surprised that some of them are born in the United States but have not adopted any elements of American culture. Their knowledge is limited to their jobs. Some of them have been fired ten to fifteen times despite their qualifications. I wonder why that happened; I think it was because they were doing their job half-heartedly from nine to five, and not doing much to enhance their career. For the last ten to fifteen years, they have been begging me to find them jobs. Often I helped them find one, only to learn that they were fired because they did not know the subject.

Nothing is easy in life. The only thing that pays is hard and smart work, and innovation. Education is a constant, daily habit. Degrees have finite points of completion, but education and systems and technology keep on changing, whether it is in banking, finance, or computers. For example, in banking, different structures have been developed for different kinds of lending. I know all these new systems because I am interested in learning. This is because I want to be proud of myself, and I was also doing it for my wife, so that she could say I was an intellectual person. That was the reason why, when we were going on different trips all over the world, I used to interact with people more than she would. She was sort of quiet. When the final exam at the end of the trip would come, Connie would answer the questions because I was not well prepared. She did a fantastic job, and she used to tell me, "You should also take some initiative." Then I would stand in front of up to one hundred people and talk about the subject. I worked very hard for that. These incidents I am narrating would not have happened unless Connie was there.

That is why I feel that Connie was special, and I will never find someone like again, except in my next birth. I pray every day that I get Connie again in my life. This is very important to me, and I am willing to sacrifice anything for that. As I have repeatedly mentioned, her loss has been the most painful thing in my life, and no one else will ever understand what I am going through. Our love was one out of million people. When I say this, I want to ask for forgiveness, because people will think I am talking nonsense; they will say that their own loves were also the same. I agree that their loves were maybe the same, but I don't know their stories. Our love was great because we were known as Connie and Pradeep everywhere. At least fifty thousand people must have told us over the last forty years that we were too attached to each other and that God would bless us. Many people used to tell us that both of us were special.

I Want to Feel the Presence of Connie in One Form or Another

My love for Connie was very deep and pure. We had the greatest love for each other. I sometimes feel guilty or selfish about my grief, but I have seen many tragedies. Those tragedies also affected me very badly; regardless of on whom the tragedy had befallen. I always thought about these tragedies. Why did they take place, and why did such things happen? After the death of Connie, I don't want to think of all those tragedies. All those tragedies are mitigated by Connie's death. I don't want to remember them. How has Connie's death changed my way of thinking? I don't want to say it is selfish, but you really only understand the grief when it happens to you, when someone very close passes away. Connie and I were inseparable. I don't think I should feel guilty about it. Even if I feel guilty about it, I don't want someone pointing it out because it is solely my point of view.

God forgive me for what I want to say, but if something happens to someone, unless it is someone whom I really truly care about, I do not feel sad or sorry. Connie's death has made me bitter and angry, so perhaps I will not care deeply for the grief of others; I will probably only feel sorry for their pain. The new realization in my life is that there is a difference between feeling sorry for people and truly feeling their pain. I know that we all have to die. If someone is older than me and my relative, and if something happens to him, I do not know how I would react. Even if I go his funeral or last rites, I am not going to say a whole lot of things. I will stand quietly in the corner thinking about it, and maybe at that time, my tragedy will be with me. I will be there like a bystander without any emotions. The reason behind this is that so many people who I thought were close to me did not care during my three years of pain, so I will not feel for them. Even if it someone is very close to me, I will feel sorrow but nothing more.

Nobody will be able to match my love and the depth of the feelings I have for Connie. What I'm writing is very difficult to put down on paper, but this is how I feel. Some people will hate me; some people will think it's good that I'm being honest; still others will think I'm correct and say that I was very much in love. Some people will think I'm selfish and have a one-track mind, but I'm not going to worry about them. If someone says something to me after reading this, my only response will be to say that I'm sorry. No one can compare my loss with any other person's. Connie was very special to me and will remain so.

Today, September 29, 2015, I went to visit her at the cemetery. I used to go there two or three times a week, and I decided to go again. I think I was there for thirty to forty-five minutes. Whenever I go there, I have noted that I get some peace of mind. Maybe what I feel is not peace of mind exactly, but a shadow of letting go of the grief. I feel that I am with her when I go there. The pain inside is deeper because I had never expected that I would have to live to see this situation. She was alive six months ago with no inkling that she was going to die so soon, and today she is no more. It was just yesterday that I used to take her to the hospital and doctors, I remember how we used to sit together and chat. Suddenly in one second, everything is gone. Going to the cemetery makes me feel that. I think that mentally I'm ready to live near her headstone. People will think that I've gone mad, but I'm not crazy. I have seen how people used to live with dead people in some parts of the world where I have traveled, such as in Egypt. I think if I had a choice, and if they allowed me (which I think is next to impossible), I would live in a small house near her. Even if that life would be very hard for me, I would still take it. I have never had that experience, and neither will I ever have it. It might look like the stupidest thing to do, but every individual has a different way of expressing grief. Many people don't think like I do about this subject.

I want to write every single thing coming from the core of my heart that I have already conveyed. I have thought many times and have shared this with my brother and everybody, when I went to India and spent two months with my family. When I think of going back to India for a month to have a change of scenery and get some work done, I will see how I feel. When I leave the house for an extended period, the things I used to do with her, like preparing her meals during the day and praying in her room, to her picture, and at her cemetery will haunt me. I will feel that her soul is still around. I know that her soul is in peace, but my mind is not at peace. I think it is going to be very difficult for me. In India the girls weep and cry when they are leaving their parents' home after marriage, because they will miss their families. Similarly, I weep whenever I have to go anywhere. The girls cry for maybe one day, but I am grief-stricken whenever I go out of the house for more than a few hours, except when I go to the store or health club and know I'm coming back home shortly. If I have to go anywhere for an extended period of time, or if my relatives come to visit me and I go out with them, at least I will be in the United States, so the gravity of the pain will be a little less, but I will still be thinking about her.

However, if I go overseas, then the gravity of the pain will be a million times stronger because my mind will be at home. After I reach my destination, maybe I will handle it for a few days, but after that I will get restless and return home. Many times I think that I should go for one week or a couple of weeks, but then I realize that it is not a small journey and takes a lot of time to reach India. It is not always easy to go for a week or ten days. It was a different era when we were working, and Connie and I would both go, or I would go alone to India, but I would never be gone more than two weeks, including travel. Later on, I cut it down further to twelve days including travel, because then I knew that I was responsible for my work and for Connie. Now there are no responsibilities. I have left my senior position, I am not working anymore, and Connie is no more. The attachment to home has caught me in a different way, and it is very difficult to get out.

I don't think my grief will lessen; rather, it will become worse as time passes. Many people told me that it would take me six months to one year to overcome this, but I feel it is going to take much longer than that. It is a sign of my love for Connie. I don't know what Connie must have gone through when she was sick with cardiac arrest, and how she was holding my hand and wanted to say something. I don't know what she wanted to say, and that bothers me. This would not have happened if she had passed away in the house, without any mistakes by the doctors. I would have been very affected, no doubt, but the trauma I saw—the medical negligence by the doctors, the way they delayed their response to her cardiac arrest, and the three weeks I spent fighting with them—is worse than anybody can go through. I pray to God that no one else goes through it. I am very upset about it and cannot believe it happened in America. Things like this happen; some people say it was destiny, and some say her time on earth was finished. I don't buy that. I used to believe that when the time comes, you pass away. I refuse to accept this kind of death, which comes after so much suffering and negligence by doctors. I now say that the end-time is in our hands.

I think I am being naïve, but my love for Connie is still there. I'm being very honest. Some people will appreciate this, some people will say I am stupid, and others will say that they realize it was true love. Hopefully, they will learn something from this. This is how I feel, and I think I am going to put in the heading "Realizations of My Pain and the Pain of Others." The only way I keep myself very happy is by talking to people I meet. They listen to me, especially young ladies over here, and are touched by my story. Then I casually ask them if they want to tell me about themselves, if they are comfortable enough to do so. I think that they are very honest, and once they trust me, they share their stories. They say that they wish they had a marriage like ours. They wish their husbands were like me and say that they are still searching for the kind of love Connie and I shared. I think that in that respect, I am extremely lucky. Many people in stores and restaurants who don't know me have told me that I am lucky. When I make phone calls to various companies and talk to various people, I have observed that 98 percent of people are touched by my story. Maybe 2 percent people say that I should get on with my life, but I don't think I want to hear that. I think I need sympathy all the time for this incident. I know that whenever you ask for sympathy, you show your weak points, but I don't care now.

I am going to write what I really feel. I think that when you read something written from the core of the heart without worrying about what people will think, it becomes a gem of a book. That is how true stories are written, and it's how so many movies are made about real-life incidents. I ask that people listen to me, and I hope that they will understand my emotions at this time. It is five o'clock in the morning, and I am now going to sleep. In the past, I would wake up at this time and go to the health club. Yesterday, I was awake until 7:30 a.m. writing, but I didn't have to worry because it was a weekend. Tomorrow is a working day, and I know I have to do a lot of work. Even then, I could not help writing her biography because I want to get it published as soon as possible. One day, when this book is published, I will go back to my original routine of sleeping by midnight and waking up by 9:00 a.m.

Connie Is Still with Me

For the last eight months, I have noticed that Connie has gone away. However, while I am at my house seeing her pictures, I feel as if Connie is still with me and talking to me. Yes, it's a good feeling, but more than that, it's a very sad and upsetting feeling that is stronger than the good feelings. The other thing I have noticed is that for the last four months, from July 2015 onward, when I turn on the lights if I wake up in the middle of the night, I worry that Connie will be disturbed by the lights, because my first thought is that she is asleep. I then feel a shock and realize the truth, and that is like an arrow in my heart. It takes me than more than an hour to go back to sleep. In the morning, it's the same arrow. One can see better in the morning because the house is empty. I leave the lights on in her office until eight thirty in the evening, and at eight thirty in the morning, automatic lights come on until 10:30 a.m., when there is enough natural light.

These days, my sleeping hours are extended well beyond the usual 1:00 a.m. I go to sleep at 4:30–5:00 a.m., and even on occasion as late as 8:00 a.m. That was when I had written an e-mail to some legal advisors because they were already at work at eight thirty. When I was working, I was in office by seven, and at other times I was at airports at 5:00 a.m. or at the pool by that time of the day. This shows how life has changed. There are people I know who are older than me and maintain certain daily habits. They get up at four in the morning to go for a walk, and then they go to work at 8:00 a.m. This is not a universal fact, and daily routines and waking hours change from person to person. Not everybody is same, and people are different. I am simply relating my experience. The other day at 6:30 a.m., I was preparing to sleep, and when I went over to my balcony, I saw people walking dogs on the sidewalk. It was bright and early, and people were going to work. That reminded me of my earlier life back in college, and with Connie. We both used to get up at 6:30 a.m., and Connie would leave by seven forty. I would leave by seven forty-five or earlier. I had to travel in my great profession, so I used to start my car or take a train depending on where I was going, perhaps at 5:00–6:30 a.m. My limo was waiting for me to take me to the airport.

Later, when Connie took early retirement after teaching for thirty-six years and doing volunteer work at the library, she kept the same schedule until 2006, when I also left my career to be with her for traveling, enjoying life, going to her medical appointments, dining out, shopping, and more. We were together all day and night. Yes, I used to visit India for two weeks every year, and my last trip was on November 6–20, 2011. My next trip was on May 17, 2015, after her demise and when my world was over.

Time changes, the economy changes, and nobody can predict nature and its changes. Morning is followed by night, and that leads to morning the next day. Nobody can control rain, snow, or sunshine. These days, I feel as if Connie is around. I can feel the vibrations, and these days the vibrations are increasing in intensity. I feel sometimes that I should wake up Connie because she will be late for work. When I realise she isn't there, I still tell myself that perhaps she's in the bathroom, or maybe she is in her room watching TV and reading her books. But when I am lying down, I suddenly realise, *What am I thinking? Connie is gone—she's no more!* It takes me twenty minutes to one hour to digest this, and it is the most painful experience one can go through. These are the experiences I am going through right now. I am in Delhi today, and last night I woke up unsure as to where I was. I thought later that I was sleeping at home. I eventually realized that I was in India, and it was surprising for me that I dreamed of Connie, thinking I was at home. I think it will take me days to understand that I am in Delhi. But my mind is somewhat happy to be in Delhi. I am happy to be with my nephews, grandnieces, and brother. Other than them, I have no desire to meet anybody else or to do anything else. I'm slightly tired right now, but I go out with my brother and nephew to the market to get some snacks or go somewhere for a couple of hours. I might go to the health club, but other than that, I am in no mood to meet or be friends with anybody, or to attend parties and gatherings. These are all sad occasions for me.

People tell me, "It's okay, Pradeep. It is your grieving period." I'm not sure how long the grieving period is going to last. Perhaps it will last forever and will become part of my life for as long as I am alive. It is possible that this is why I am so keen to arrange things in such a way that that after I am gone, my house, art, furniture, rugs, and other expensive collections are taken care of. It often worries me what will happen to all of those things. People tell me to look after my health instead of worrying about material things. They don't understand that I am not talking about material things; Connie's soul is in every one of those items, which have been collected over years. It's not just about the material possessions, and I am not crazy to not want to sell them and get money in return. These have Connie's life and soul in them—how could I possibly ever get rid of them? This is the tremendous hardship that I am facing, and it is worse than anything else I've experienced. I have faced many other tragedies, but I have forgotten about them or at least tried to. I will never be able to forget Connie's loss.

There are two kinds of losses according. One is related to money and property, and there are disputes over them leading to lawsuits and overall bad feelings. But I am not talking about money. Money is nothing to me now; it is just a way to live. It is a way to maintain myself and my lifestyle of simple living and high thinking. I am content that way. Even if I suddenly get millions of dollars, they are not going to bring back my happiness or Connie. If there was some kind of means whereby if you donate all your money somewhere and get your loved ones back, I would get Connie back. There are countries where you can donate money and get into schools and colleges; this is mainly for the private institutions, not necessarily for the good institutions. There are good places in India, and of course America has one of the best educational systems in the world. So there are a lot of vocational courses where you can get a degree, but you have to donate a lot of money. It is not possible that I can donate money and get Connie back, because if it was possible, I would have given away all of my money. I was watching the Ram Lila, which is an episode from Indian history, and my brother and his daughter-in-law were discussing it with me. They mentioned that the characters in it have the ability to curse others and take back their lives. I wish I could find some of those people so that Connie might come back. They said it was not possible because they had done a lot of sacrifices for a very long time to achieve that ability. I agreed that their sacrifices were more than mine. However, as I have said in other chapters about the story of Savitri and Satyavan, if they could do it, why can't I?

The answer was given to me by my brother's daughter-in-law. She said those people were different in that time, and they had special powers because they had never done anything wrong in their lives. She said I must have good karma, but it is possible that without necessarily intending to, I may have done something wrong. I agreed with her; perhaps sometimes I'd lied, and at other times I did not listen to Connie. She used to ask me to develop new things, because she was very interested in my progress in life. Maybe I have sinned, but it is definitely true that she tolerated a lot of things from me. I don't know the answer. Only God knows the answer, but it is also true that there is nobody who can bring back Connie, and that is very painful.

I marked that I should keep talking about this chapter for as long as I can, but at the same time more is not always good. "More is not always better," Connie said to me. I know there is a lot of repetition in my story, but it's all right to repeat things, especially because people will be reminded of things once they read again. Also, I don't use words like "my wife" or "her," which sounds impersonal. That is why I use her name, Connie, again and again. Perhaps it is not the best way to write, but for me it is the best way. Those other words don't carry the same weight as her name. I don't expect that everybody will like my writing, or that I will be a bestseller, or that this will be the best book in the world. I am only writing and expressing myself, and hoping that even if only one person can understand my pain, I will be very happy. I won't say there is only one, because many people have already requested a copy of the book. In fact, most of the people who are asking for a copy are unknown to me. There are people from technical support, or computer technicians, or customer service representatives for different airlines. Some of them are employees of call centers where I used to call for my banking needs. They listen to me because I have to tell them honestly that Mrs. Berry is no longer here. The other day I spoke to this person from *Consumer Report* for almost an hour and a half! He was almost in tears, and he gave me a prize for the subscription. I promised him that I would begin reading all the magazines that Connie used to subscribe to, which are very instrumental in building knowledge. There is another book called *Health and Nutrition,* as well as another to do with wellness and health. There is a magazine called *Men's Health.* There are magazines to do with women's health and nutrition, and I don't want anything to do with the magazine for women, because I don't want any other woman in my life. Maybe I will subscribe to the others because they'll give me happiness when I read them. This is a new experience for me. I will also give away some of the other magazines that others have requested, because I will never turn down any request that has anything to do with Connie, except of course a request for some of her personal possessions.

The other day she wore a jacket and asked me how she looked. That picture makes me cry, and I have had it framed because it shows Connie laughing. That was true love. I remember she'd gotten a brand-new jacket and was very weak. She always worried whether she looked nice or bad. She looked pretty and kept looking at me. That picture goes through my heart like a sword or arrow and makes me break down. Before I came to India, I carried that picture with me, a small one in my pocket and one in my briefcase. I am going to keep looking at that picture; it has become the most important part of my life. People will think I am talking about emotions and mental issues. I don't care, but I know I am still able to do many constructive things, especially relating to Connie. These are not just emotions but are facts of my life.

The other day, I went to the store to return some things I had thought we would enjoy. As per their policy, they took them back, but the man asked why I was returning them. When I explained, the man was really touched and went out of his way to help me. The other thing was that on the October 19, 2015, before departing from the United States, I went to the cemetery. I had decided on the flowers that I intended to buy. I went into the store and told the young man what I needed. I showed him Connie's picture, and he was really bothered by the story. He complimented Connie, saying she was beautiful, and he refused to charge me for the flowers. He said that out of two different colours, one flower would be from the store in Connie's memory. The young man said that because I was a regular customer, the store wanted to give me something as a token of appreciation to the memory of my wife. It was only $6.50, and I took the two different flowers. I went to the cemetery, and it was very dark. I took pictures and sought Connie's blessings so that I could go to India in the morning. I slept for barely two hours, and now I am here in Delhi. I hope the day will come that I will be in my own house back in America. I'm really confused because if I stay there, I am very unhappy, and if I'm here in Delhi, there is some happiness but some sadness as well. I am living in those four parts of the world, with happiness mixed together with sadness. I have no idea when it'll get better, but I have to take it one day at a time.

Her Home Was Her Life

To Connie, it was very important that her house be decorated with the best of things. Her taste was much better than any professional. She was very selective in choosing the right items and matching things—furniture, decorative items, paintings, carpets, kitchen and bathroom appliances, floor, and tiles. We got many compliments for her decor, the cleanliness of our house, and the quality of our home. Friends used to wait for the invitation to come to our house to see the soothing atmosphere and have great food. We were extremely happy for our hospitality. She was extremely organized, and would keep lists of everything. She kept the carpets and windows clean, and she kept a careful schedule of what to clean when. I have to say our house has always been neat and clean. Perfection, quality, cleanliness, and changing styles on certain things were in her blood. I have not seen anyone else like that.

I remember that when she renovated the kitchen with granite stone and tiles in 2006, it took both of us over two months before she chose her matching materials and fixtures. Later, she hired the best company to put tiles on the floor, granite stone on the kitchen counter, tiles on walls, and appliances in the sink and kitchen. Friends gave her many compliments on the renovation. She invited all of our neighbors and friends for drinks and snacks. They said that our house was the best house they had ever seen. These were our American friends. We received the same complimentary remarks from thirty Indian families when they came to visit. In addition, they asked us to invite them back again and again. The same thing is applicable for her furniture, tables, lamps, chairs, and other things. A few years ago, she wanted a walk-in shower, and she hired the best company and the best materials. It took one month to finish, and we had to live with just one bathroom. After that, she replaced the air conditioners and other appliances, which I likely would never have replaced. I was extremely helpful and happy for her to get the best. She was my life, and so I got the greatest happiness to see that she is happy. Serving her, making her happy and healthy, and not depriving her of anything was my only happiness. It gave me the most powerful motivation to deal with the world and other human beings.

My happiness was to teach the new generation and share knowledge. Guiding new professionals was a great time, and I was extremely happy because Connie was with me, either at home or out together. I am not going to enjoy all that now. I will explain why that is later, however I would like to teach and share my knowledge, education, and the experiences of our life, which might take away my loss and pain for my happy days.

Later, I am lost again. Temporary happiness and sadness is going to be my life from now on. I have seen the suffering of spouses married for a long time after the death of one, or after divorce. How effective that pain is, I now know. I am suffering from that pain and from withdrawal symptoms, which are incorporated into my mind and heart. This book is a little happiness, but the sadness is much more with me. I don't know what I can do, and I am waiting for what life I will have to face. I would live to fulfill Connie's wishes, which is still painful because I can't see her. In ancient Egypt, mummies are a great example of how people dealt with the loss of their loved ones. I think it was right for those people; at least they could still see the body, which might have given them a feeling that their loved ones were still with them. I don't know whether I could have done that, because she wanted to be cremated. I never thought that her husband and her love would have to go through the pain of handling her cremation and other things. How much pain and suffering I went through, I don't know. I would like to know why I had to experience that. Her pictures, our pictures in their many frames around the house, and the paintings on the wall in our house are my life. My life is a combination of happiness and sadness, and I cannot choose which emotion I feel. I will have to go through my whole life to find the answer, if I am meant to find that answer. Now, my pain and withdrawal symptoms are incorporated in my mind and heart.

Cleanliness and Housekeeping
Was in Her Blood

While talking about Connie, I must say how neat and clean she was in the house. She kept our house like a museum. She used to take a keen interest in the house, and her collection was unique. Sometimes it used to take her years before she could make a decision about the fabric she wanted, the kind of covers to use, the kind of kitchen design she wanted, and the kind of granite she wanted to use. She was very selective in the house. I would say that her taste, her thinking, and the way she used to perceive things were better than any interior decorator. She was emphatic about cleanliness in the house. She could not tolerate dust in the house.

She was very particular about the laundry, so she would change bed sheets every couple of days. She was so efficient and organized that cleanliness was ingrained in her. No matter what time it was, whether night or day, she would take a shower and change her clothes. She would wash laundry every two days, including my clothes. She was very particular that I wear a shirt for only one day, and she would say, "No! It is more than enough!"

Sometimes I used to argue, "I just wore it for one day. I can use it for one more day!"

She would say, "No! Look at the collar at the back! You have a professional job. People notice the small things, like your collar."

I would say, "I don't think so, because I wear a three-piece suit."

She would reply, "You are not going to compromise. It is better that you buy—or I will buy for you—one dozen white T-shirts. You will not wear them for more than one day."

Then I would ask her, "Is it not too much work for you to do the laundry?"

She would say, "I can handle it. It's not that difficult. Doing laundry in the house is very simple. You just have to put it in the laundry room, and then you have enough time. I do two loads every other day. It makes no difference."

She was very organized. She would iron my shirts, T-shirts, socks, and handkerchiefs. I think these things show how dedicated she was to me, and she would make such an effort to see that her husband looked great all the time in his professional job. She used to feel very proud about me. I got a lot of compliments from my office. They would say, "Mr. Berry, we see you as the most fashionable person in our whole organization. How do you do that?"

I would say, "Well, my wife, Connie, is very particular about my suit, and what kind of tie, scarf, and pen match it."

"Well, she has made you a model. I think you should be in the model industry."

I would reply, "Well, it's not like that, but I like being well dressed." I got many awards for the best dressed person of the year. I dressed like that from childhood, wearing three-piece suits, so I carried on that legacy.

When I think about it now, I realize how much energy she spent caring for me, and how much pain she had to bear. God bless her! I don't think I could have done all that with so much affection. Sometimes I would be upset that she would even polish my shoes. I used to feel like a criminal because my wife was polishing my shoes. I did not polish my shoes because I thought it was just dusting. Here, shoes didn't get dirty. But she would say, "No, I think the first thing people notice is shoes, and a well-dressed person is always liked. You have so much intelligence and personality.

Being well dressed will be like the icing on the cake." I think that attitude really put a sparkle in me. I used to take pride in it. Regarding her clothing, she would rather buy two clothing pieces that were expensive and pretty, rather than buying several cheap ones. She always emphasized, "Pradeep, I think it is better to buy quality and buy less. Whenever you buy, get the best quality because they will last long and look good."

We had friends who held good positions, and they would wear polyester shirts and cheap suits and ties. She used to be surprised that they could thrive in the corporate sector. Eventually, she could not tolerate it any longer, and she told them, "I hope you won't mind my saying this, but I think in your profession, when you are holding a good position, you should not wear those polyester shirts and polyester jackets. I think you should try to learn how to dress in a professional way. This is not a blue-collar job."

I remember one year, when we did inventory accounts, we would be delighted that we wouldn't have to wear a suit. We could wear casual clothes. Most people came in jeans. She told me, "Jeans are unprofessional." She never allowed me to wear a pair of jeans. She was very particular even for casual clothing. She bought me so many different kinds of pants and shirts. I think I must have over one hundred shirts, and they are sitting with me. Some I never wore, and some I wore maybe a couple of times. I am never going to give away those shirts because those are memories and great gifts from my dear wife. I think I can go on writing about clothing. I have lovely pairs of socks by Nautica and Pierre Cardin.

She was very classy, and I think all the Italian ties she bought were lovely. She used to buy one or two ties for me every month. Whenever she went out, she would buy something for me. She would never ask me to pay for anything. I used to tell her, "Well, you are spending so much money."

She used to say, "No, it is my love for you." I used to reciprocate that. I used to travel, and wherever I went, I would bring a lot of things. She was so considerate and would say, "No, I think I want to pay."

I would say, "That is not right. You spend so much money on me, and when I want to give it to you, you want to pay."

She would reply, "No, this is the way I am. I generally feel bad."

I would say, "No, please. In the future, don't ever say to me that you have to pay me, because this is my love for you. The way you love me, I love you."

So she would say, "I will accept it, but don't buy too much. If I ask you to buy one sweater or two bracelets, you get so many!" She was very fond of silver. She would say, "Okay, you can buy me one necklace and one bracelet." I would buy maybe ten bracelets and ten different kinds of necklaces for her. She would say, "You know what? You don't know the difference between two and ten! What a collection I have!"

I would reply, "Just keep it. Or give them to your friends, or your nieces."

She would say, "I think next time when we go, we will try to return them."

Just as she was very considerate about my money, she was also conservative. She would use coupons and save money. Regarding our house, she used to say, "I would rather travel all over the world and be house poor." That's how we started enjoying life, and we went all over the world on different cruises. I can name hundreds of them. We went with the University of Michigan, with Carleton, with different alumni, and with professors. It was all intellectual, and there were lectures, studies, and sightseeing. The cruises gave a lot of intellectual input in every area of our lives. This is one of the great qualities that she would combine in her house. She used to combine housekeeping with my dressing.

These were some of the qualities she had. I am going to write in more detail about many episodes and stories where she excelled. We went to Ireland, and she said, "You have to dance this Irish dance, because it is a cultural activity. Irish culture will ask you to wear these green clothes, and the girl will ask you to dance with her." She was not jealous that some young girl would dance with me, because it was a part of the Irish culture. She was very happy to see me dancing. She took pride that her husband was dancing in the Irish style.

I want to mention these things. I want to continue writing, so that we can leave a legacy about how much we love her, and how much love she could give. I always consider my Connie as not only my wife but also my best friend, sister, and mother. I think in Indian culture, in 500 BC, Chanakya wrote about the same four qualities of women, and how they can play these different roles. It is also written in Sanskrit, in our Vedanta, that a woman has four qualities, which I already mentioned. There were times when her love was like a mother, and her advice was like a sister and friend. As a wife, she was a great companion. These kinds of qualities are very rare. I am lucky that I had this opportunity. It was my destiny. There were a lot of girls that my family had chosen as prospects for me, and if I had gone back, perhaps I would have been married to one of them. Then I would never have seen Connie again.

I lived all these years because Connie was with me. Now after her demise, everything is over. This is most painful, and I pray to God that He can take anything from me, but He should give my wife back, give my Connie back. I really hope that in our next life, we will be together again as husband and wife. I would say if there is any power, if there is a miracle, we keep on taking new life every time and are always husband and wife, enjoying the same kind of life. If that happens, I am going to get over my anger. After a few years, we will meet again. This is a great hope. You should never deprive someone of his hope, because hope may be the only thing he has.

Her Love for the Best Cuisine

Connie was extremely selective about the food we ate. She liked to cook and eat the highest quality food, both at home and in restaurants. She was an amazing cook and made different varieties of food and homemade desserts which I would never have had in my life without her. They were fresh, not fat, healthy, and organic. She took me out to the best of the restaurants for excellent food. Her selection was great, and she didn't care about the prices, although she was very conservative in many ways and knew to save for old age and rainy days. Cutting coupons to save money was her great hobby. Her passion for reading about new restaurants and recipes, and trying different foods from all over the world, was unique. I enjoyed all of that.

At the same time, she looked after the house—shopping, cleaning, doing laundry, and taking care of my professional clothing and accessories. This was a gift from God to me. At the same time, her choice for casual and traveling clothing was another unforgettable gift of my life. She truly loved me, to do all that for me. I had never before been blessed with that kind of love, except from my elder brother, who took care of me when I was in India. I would have to write a whole new book on every subject that I am writing about to cover each of her qualities.

I helped her with everything, because she was busy and we were partners in cooking and shopping. It was only due to my love for her that I learned excellent cooking and shopping. When I came to the United States in January 1976, I didn't know anything about cooking except how to make tea. It took lots of self-teaching, and I can say that now I am an excellent cook. Now, I doubt I will cook because I have lost interest in food due to her absence.

Morels are one of the finest foods in the world. They are very expensive, even as dried mushrooms. India is one of the world's most important producers of morels. Even in India, they are considered a delicacy, and during my grandfather's time, they would be served at every marriage and major function. Guests expected to be served morels, and a host who couldn't afford them would have to apologize. I may ask my niece, Mona, to bring some for me when she visits, and I am sure she knows how to use morels to prepare vegetable dishes and rice pulao. I used to bring some for Connie, and she also used to buy them from Whole Foods or Spice House. Another healthy delicacy that we loved was saffron rice. Saffron rice was a favorite dish of ours, and like morels, it is a rare delicacy.

Great Deeds and Ethical Values of Connie

Connie Darling did so many great deeds of karma. That includes, but is not limited to, charity for different organizations, schools, colleges, low income families, hospitals, the Red Cross, the Salvation Army, the USA Olympics, and foundations for children and for education. She was instrumental in looking after her parents, taking them for doctors' appointments, buying groceries, cooking for them, and bringing them to our home for dinner.

After the death of Connie's father on December 20, 1989, we insisted her mother stay with us permanently. We would have been very happy to look after her. But her mother refused, hoping to be near her grandchildren, whom she adored and got the biggest joy from while sacrificing many things. In reality, she cared and loved them much more than she loved Connie and me. It bothered us, and we felt betrayed. However, we both decided that if it gave her happiness, let it be. We used to do whatever she wanted us to do, whenever she asked. Many times she behaved badly with us, taking the side of Connie's sibling and his family and being nasty to us. We tolerated that for her happiness. Later, Connie told her mother, "Mom, you'd better be nice to Pradeep, because when you are old, Pradeep and I will come to rescue you. He has been brought up to always respect elderly people." Connie's mother still had one hobby, and that was her grandchildren.

Right from the beginning, when Connie came in my life, it was a mind-blowing experience for me. Connie told me that her mother was extreme, and I didn't understand this, because my elder brother and I were brought up by our grandparents; and I came from a joint family system. Connie was so right, and after Connie's father died, Connie was in tears. Connie and I made the decision that we would do anything to make her mother's final years happy, and it truly happened. Connie and I were instrumental in looking after her mother. It was great to serve the elderly. True love should be selfless, and we should sacrifice to see others happy. I have seen many examples of these kinds of sacrifices.

When Connie and I met, it was true love on the first meeting. We both wanted to be together and marry. Connie frankly asked me if I had some other person in the United States or in India, because arranged marriages were common in India. I said that my parents and family had selected many girls and their families for me to marry; however I didn't know if I had that desire. She told me, "I don't want you to regret anything later, and I am willing to sacrifice my love if you have someone waiting for you in India." She also stated that she would never marry anyone except me. I immediately told her the same thing. I would only marry Connie.

It breaks my heart and upsets me that I am writing this after forty years. Where is my Connie? Where did she go? Why I am left alone, and when will I meet her? I will forgive everyone in my life and start all over if Connie comes back. I know that is naïve thinking, but I want to think for my happiness. I tried to forget all that and started to give Connie the maximum support and love to help her overcome her troubled mind. Further, I would have never written this if Connie was alive. Her demise has brought to light many hidden, painful episodes. Now, all these things are new wounds in my life. Connie used to bring her mother to our home to stay for months. I was very happy to see that Connie was happy, and Connie's happiness was my happiness; it gave me joy to see them both happy. Most of the crimes in the world have many reasons, however in my opinion, the majority of them are due to money. Greed, property, love, and jealousy are pretty common.

Connie was the most ethical, honest, selfless, charitable, and giving person I have ever met. I truly mean this. I might have lacked somewhere, but Connie was perfect. She looked after her mother without expecting anything in return. Rather, she used to buy her what she needed. Connie told me that her parents had put her through school and college, and that was enough. I am extremely grateful to them for spending money for her education. Further, due to them, I can make my own living. It is absolutely amazing and true that she never took a penny from her parents. Instead, she worked part-time jobs to pay for her master's and other education. I was new in the United States and was surprised to see that. In India, we were used to asking for everything from our parents or grandparents. It was a new wave for me, and it took me few years to learn about it. I am now the same kind of a person, a giver who doesn't expect anything from others. Neither would I take anything from anyone. In the past, many people wanted to give me a token, but I couldn't accept it.

Our Love Destiny Would Continue, but with Unhappiness for Me

Our life was a true story of pure love. It was wonderful to feel and vibrant to enjoy each moment, even while we both worked on highly professional senior positions. Everything looks different now that she is gone and I am lost. I will not go to the places where we went; it will haunt me like Dracula, making me go through more pain and suffering. I wonder whether I will find an answer to my loss. In memory of Connie, I might start humanitarian acts and teaching undergraduate and MBA students, as well as professionals in the field of commercial financing, mergers and acquisitions, buyouts, crisis management, spirituality, or world economy.

Sharing knowledge is the best way for me to survive, and she always loved to share her knowledge with others. I will always seek her blessings and forgiveness for any mistakes I made. Her life was to live for me, and mine was to live for her. I am thankful that with a broken heart, I was able to do her cremation in two days and inter her ashes in her plot, next to her parents. My happiness and unhappiness were a combination that was necessary. I wanted the best cremation done in two days to cut my pain. She was special, and God kept me alive to do that. It tears me up to think of what would have happened otherwise. She was very special and was not a charity case. Peace comes and pain starts after seeing and praying to her. For thirty-nine and a half years, our lives were ingrained in the house. It is full of her memory: our pictures going to different places, her cemetery, and the maintenance of her designed house with very selective furniture. Living here is a double-edged sword. However, these are my lifelong possessions. I am sure we will meet again in our next lives.

Currently, though physically she is not with me, spiritually she is here and still guiding me.

While she was going through medical care, I left my high-powered income and professional career. I truly enjoyed every moment with her, including taking her to the doctors, shopping with her, and doing other things. Serving her was a great joy. Although I was very upset about her health, and for the last two years it was painful for both of us, sitting and looking at her and the satisfaction of being with her was happiness enough, and I was devoted to her. I was extremely hopeful that Connie would be alive for another ten to fifteen years, and I always used to worry about her and pray to God to keep me alive to take care of her. I never thought she would go so fast, and I was shattered and practically broken down. I didn't think I could survive my loss. But I prayed to God to keep me alive in order to do her cremation and chapel of peace ceremony, and to bury her ashes in the plot next to her parents. I told the funeral home and crematorium that I wanted the best of everything for her last rites, and that I would not compromise with the cost and the quality. It has given me happiness as well as lots of pain, which I will experience as long as I am alive. Each and every moment, Connie is in my mind, and my heart is broken when I think of the last few months. I start shaking and lose all my happiness. I don't think I will be at peace anytime soon. I have no desire to remarry or have a great social life. I get both peace and sadness at our house. Even when I am visiting my family in India, my peace of mind is not there. My brother and his family give me all their love, but Connie still remains in my mind, body, and soul, and I don't enjoy anything. Yes, my brother and his family, and my two grandnieces, are keeping me happy, but inside I think of Connie. Now I realize why people enjoy their grandchildren. Still, I have seen many relatives and friends who were missing their spouses and not gaining much happiness from their grandkids. To each his own.

Some people immediately go for a second or third marriage after the death of their spouse. It is an individual choice, depending upon the love they shared and other factors. There is no universal law governing the choice to remarry. In my case, I took the demise of Connie extremely hard, and

I have known for years that true love happens only once. This is the way I feel, and I don't expect everyone to agree with me. I am not perfect, and I think of many things I should have done but could not do for her due to circumstances. At the same time, we did so much that others can't even imagine.

Connie and Her Devotion to My Professional Help in Many Places

The experience of traveling was her great gift to me. Her exposure to American culture and the development of my personality was a precious gift for my career and advancement. Connie bought so many things for me to make sure that I always looked great. She never lied, cheated, or hurt anyone. She did so many selfless things to help me and others. If I start writing all the other things she did, I would have to write another book. In reality, there is no end to her good karma and deeds.

My mind is blank, and I can't wait to write that Connie was extremely exciting and fun. I have never seen such a great person. She was a wonderful human being and was super bright and beautiful. I also had good karma. That would justify why I am upset that God didn't save her when there was a hope that she would live and do more in the world. Why didn't God save her from death?

I truly believe that my success and advancement was only because of Connie. Last night around 3:00 a.m. on July 29, I was sharing the childhood lie of my elder brother and me. I had not joined my family's booming business, as my father's elder brother had offered; he desperately needed me to join with a 25 percent share. In the beginning of 1975, after the death of our eighty-five-year-old employee, the 25 percent share that my grandfather had given him because of his devotion and intelligence (despite his lack of higher education) became available. I was told that he was a six-year-old kid when he was hired by my grandfather to work with him in the business, because he had no one to feed him. Later, he was trained and was the engine and right hand of our business. My uncles were neither educated nor bright, and that's why my grandfather gave him a 25 percent share. I was offered the opportunity to take his spot.

My father didn't encourage me, saying, "Son, you are exceptionally bright and should go for your own career." The truth was he wanted that share to be given to my half-brother. I refused because many variables were uncertain. How would my father and his young brother treat me? Then I decided to go to the United States. Had my darling Connie not met me, I would have been back to India, and everyone would have been badmouthing me. I am sure I would not have been a failure because getting a great job was not difficult, but Connie was my destiny. I am sure I would have been extremely unhappy in India without her. I thank Connie for my success and destiny, and I know that we were meant to be husband and wife. She was a special reward and gift from God.

I would like to write about an incident that occurred when Connie and I were traveling toward Palm Springs, and we came across the most powerful sight one can imagine. We were driving in the mountains, and the roads were very curvy. I asked Connie, "Do you think there is any problem in driving? Do you think people take that many chances in driving?"

She was familiar with the surroundings and told me, "Oh, no! I don't think you have to worry about it, because it is pretty safe. It is not like in underdeveloped countries, where people worry about driving. It is just this time of the year, unfortunately, you are not finding too many cars. Don't worry and just relax! If you are uncomfortable, then I can drive, and you can just watch."

But I told her, "No, let me gain some confidence." It took us about two hours, and then we finally reached Orange County. That was one of my most difficult driving experiences in the United States. When I came back, I said, "Oh, my God! That was a piece of cake!"

Connie told me, "I told you that!"

I think the reason I am mentioning this incident is to point out how Connie helped me gain confidence about driving. When we came back from where we stayed, I was ready to drive anywhere, especially in California and San Diego. It's worth mentioning how much Connie helped me in every aspect of life.

One time, my friend who lived in New York invited me to visit him at his house. I was forty miles away and was scared to drive there at 8:00 p.m. for dinner. Connie, who was in Chicago, asked me to not go, because I was driving a rental Lincoln, and New York could be dangerous if one got lost. I thought I had good directions, but I didn't arrive until nine fifteen, and they were waiting for me with ten dishes on the table. I could hardly eat because I was worried about the return trip. I was such an idiot on this occasion. I did not have the telephone number or address for the hotel in which I was staying. I was lost for hours and drove until 2:00 a.m., and I was convinced that I would never reach the hotel. The only choice I had was to call my friend to come rescue me, but then I worried that he would think me an ignorant fool if I called him for help. He was extremely rich because of his inheritance from India and his large, wealthy family, but he respected me because I had no inheritance and the best education.

I have not talked to Palli since Connie died. He used to call once or twice a week to check on me and Connie. Perhaps I should fly to New Jersey and surprise him with a call, asking him to meet me at the airport. He would never let me stay in a hotel; he would have me stay in his house. He was a childhood friend of Arun Berry, and thus he was my friend. I have thousands of friends all over the world who loved Connie and respect me, but I do not want to have to tell the whole story about her illness and the negligence that led to her death. I would get very upset. That is why I am happier living in isolation for now.

We were trying to find different places to go, and Connie told me, "You know, the best way is to call the hotel people, or let me get the magazine." She was very good at reading and finding out directions. We stayed for two weeks in Palm Springs, Orange County, and San Diego, and we enjoyed every part of it. I must say Connie had an intelligent brain. Later on, we went to Carlsbad, which Connie knew and had read about. We made many trips like that. After that, she told me, "Next time, next year, we should go to Santa Fe."

Santa Fe is one of the most charming places. It is the third largest place on earth as far as the art and crafts are concerned. Number one and two are France and New York. In Santa Fe, people and artists come from all over the world. I was amazed at the art I saw in Santa Fe!

The other great experience she gave me was taking me to French Quarter, and that was magnificent. We stayed in the French Quarter, and the food and the culture there was totally different. We had a ball, and she showed me everything because she was very adventurous. I must say that I was not adventurous, but Connie was very adventurous. As a result of that, I was able to enjoy many new experiences because of her spirit. A similar incident happened later, when I was working in San Antonio. My employers told me, "Pradeep, do you want to come back, or do you want to stay there?"

I said, "Well, I don't know."

They offered, "If you want, you can have Connie fly over. Just put it on the expense report." I called Connie, and she flew over. I picked her up, and we stayed there for one week. We had a ball! I was working, and she would drop me off at the office, pick me up for lunch, and then she go do her shopping. In the evening, we would go back to the hotel, and I would work for half an hour or an hour on my report. Then we would have fun. When we came back at night, she would watch TV, and I would do my reports. Connie was a great contributor in traveling with me so that I was not lonely.

Connie told me, "Pradeep, having the best clothes that show you to be a well-dressed person is extremely important, especially in the United States, for people in professional careers." I knew all of that, however she taught me much more. Connie and I were involved in gaining knowledge and sharing with the world. According to Chinese and Indian philosophy, it is a sin to not share knowledge. It is our primary duty to share knowledge with those who want to learn; otherwise, you waste your time and theirs. People who think they know everything are the most ignorant. Connie and I have come across many of them, and they want to gossip and tell useless lies that they are overqualified for jobs; they try to fool other people. They do not realize that others are smart and that they have made fools of themselves with their bragging and lies. Such people are left without respect and with only a handful of family and friends, often depending on their parents.

These circumstances can ruin marriages. A wife wants her husband to no longer be a mama's boy, and mothers should make their sons realize that their wives come first and mothers come second. Some mothers provoke discord, telling their sons that they are henpecked, and these small things may break a marriage. No wife can tolerate a husband who ignores her and is always with his family. Why did he marry her, then? It would have been better to stay a bachelor, live with his parents, and lead a miserable and lonely life. Even then, only a desperate woman would marry such a man, and that too would be according to her conditions. It might be a marriage without love.

I could write an entire book on this chapter, based on the research of Connie and me. With our work and travels, we never thought of publishing, especially when Connie began to fall ill. We decided that youth and time would ebb. I am glad we did, and the results are this: My Connie died unexpectedly on February 28, 2015. No more travel and dining out for me. I will have to go on living in pain, although I may make jokes and pretend to be happy when I am with someone. Sometimes I am extremely happy, especially when I am having an intelligent conversation with intelligent people. I like to talk to everyone, regardless of education or wealth. I love people and animals, and I respect every human being as part of the planet. I am not so great myself that I have to decide about people. I must have many faults, and I want to teach everyone from my faults and weaknesses.

Sympathy and Empathy—But Pain

I would like to add in my memories that I am trying to understand the pain of some of the people I have met in my professional life. They have gone through more tragedy than one can imagine. Even at that time, I understood how much pain there was. After the demise of my darling wife, Connie, I can understand the gravity of the pain that they went through.

I will give an example that I must narrate. I think it was sometime in 1983. I had flown to Charleston, Virginia, for some work. I flew on Sunday night because of Connie. She had gone with her students to show them the political system in this country. In those days, she was teaching Spanish, French, and political science. She had to leave on Friday and was supposed to come back on Monday. They were to visit White House, among other places. I was not doing anything, and so I left on Sunday afternoon.

My clients, the borrowers, were the second largest trucking company in the United States. They were desperate to get a loan at that time because the trucking industry was deregulated. This company was struggling in their business, although they were very wealthy. To expand their business, it was important for them to show certain credits in their financial statements. When I arrived, the borrowers picked me up and took me out for dinner, and then I stayed in the hotel. The next day, one of the senior partners took me to his house and treated me to dinner.

Here is the real story that I wish to share. On Wednesday, one of the main owners, who was extremely wealthy, took me to his house. He said, "Mr. Berry, I want you to have dinner with me, and then maybe you can sleep in my house." It is very rare that a borrower who was not known to me would take me to his house. I think he must have liked me very much—my professional approach, my conduct, and my behavior. He was highly impressed. He said, "Mr. Berry, let's go out tonight, and I will show you something." It was pitch dark when he took me to a place, and he stopped his Audi car. Then he got out of the car and said, "Mr. Berry, please walk with me to this place." As I walked, he said, "You know, this place where I have brought you is where my young son, who was twenty-four years old, was killed in an accident. As a result of that, I have really lost everything. I cannot function because of this tragedy. My son was going to take over my business. All my hopes have gone. My daughter, though she's working, is not capable. She is not highly educated. My younger son has no desire to do anything except to become a truck driver. I have bought him a truck worth $250,000." We were chatting in the night, and he said to me, "I don't know, Mr. Berry. Somehow or other, I feel that you should join me. I will pay you double the salary, or even three times the salary you earn now. Plus I will pay for your wife's salary, and I will buy you a house and will give you 30–40 percent stock in my company. Finally, I will give over this company to you because I cannot work anymore due to the tragedy of my son." He was practically begging me, and he said, "Please listen to my pain, and please move to Charleston. I can assure you that you will be very happy, and because of you, I will get a new life."

I felt very sorry for him and was confused. It was a good offer but at the same time I thought of Connie's career and of the repercussions of leaving Evanston, her parents, and everything else. I declined the offer.

It continued to bother me that this person had gone through such a tragedy. I've been trying to contact him, and I found out later that he closed his company due to his shock and grief; then he sold it and simply disappeared. For the past twenty-five years, I have been looking for him, but I cannot find him and I have no idea where he is. I would love to share his tragedy and my tragedy.

Now I can understand what he was going through at that time. It is something you understand only when it happens to you. This is what I want to add. I have many other stories that I will mention and that relate to pain. When some other person is in pain, that pain does not seem that deep to you as an outsider. But when the same thing happens to you, you realize how painful it is. I will never forget this realization, which relates to me and is affecting me deeply.

Cruises—Part of Her World Travel

Once again, I want to say that Connie was instrumental in putting a love for travel in my blood. I went on many cruise trips with Connie, and she was very adventurous. She took me along and gave me the opportunity of going to different parts of the world. She used to take interest in reading about which cruises were available from the University of Michigan, which was supposed to have some of the best cruises. Recently, I heard Carleton has also started offering cruises. We also made some trips that were not cruises; for example, we went to the Black Mountains in Germany and France. We also made trips related to my business. During one of our trips to the Rhine, Connie had a desire to take another trip, which was from France and would go through many countries, all the way up to Amsterdam. From Amsterdam, it would go to Switzerland and then to one more country, where we would rest overnight in a hotel and return to United States of America the next morning by flight. They also provided the option of adding extra stops if we wished, like we did in Norway. We flew with them, and because we were part of the Advantage group, we stayed four days in Bergen. It was such a wonderful thing, and it's a beautiful country. Connie and I stayed in the hotel with about thirty people. On the final day, when we had to depart from Bergen in a ship, ninety-eight more people joined us.

All these trips that I have mentioned were not the kind of trips ordinary people make. The people who came on these trips with us were interested in learning, and they were intellectual people. These trips were not just ordinary trips, and there would be many lectures given at each stop by professors speaking about various topics. For example, on one trip, they spoke about different lakes. They would explain how the dams on the lakes were constructed, how the water is controlled in the Daniel and Rayan Rivers, and how they have to match and control the water. It is a magnificent thing to see how the York men have controlled the water system. In addition to these lectures, there would also be beautiful sightseeing excursions in small boats that carry up to 130 passengers. The tourists on these trips were intellectual people from sponsoring universities; they'd graduated in different years and were mostly seniors. There were no kids on these cruises, only very bright people and professors. There were doctors, professors, banking and finance professionals, and teachers.

We would share common tables during breakfast. We would sit with different people for every meal, so we could have stimulating conversations with different people. Sightseeing would also be done with different groups. In the buses, the drivers, coaches, and guides would guide us and tell us the history of the places we visited. As a result of that, we learned so much about the country and its history. We would also visit different schools and colleges, meet the professors there, and listen to them speak. Finally, there would be a small exam, which we had to pass. I don't mean to say that they would give grades so we could get a degree, but it meant a lot because nobody wanted to fail those exams. We really had to study for the exam!

Cultural activities would also be included in the program. For example, we would have to dance according to the particular culture. When we were in Ireland, it was part of their custom that girls as young as seventeen years old would ask the guests to dance with them. I was sort of embarrassed when one girl just grabbed me and said, "Come, man. We have to dance!" I had to dance with her for half an hour in the Irish way. Connie was watching me, but she didn't feel jealous. She didn't think, "Oh, my God! My husband is dancing with a young girl!" It was acceptable to her because Connie had a lot of faith in my character, and I had a lot of faith in her character. However, it is not very popular in Irish, German, or French culture for men to ask ladies who are not their wives to dance with them.

When we had to dance in France, it was mandatory for me to dance with Connie, and we were very well dressed for the occasion. I knew the different kinds of dance steps to some degree, but Connie taught me a lot of them. She also told me, "Pradeep, you should take some dancing classes." I did so. Look at how many cultural things she exposed me to, and how she cultivated in me a love for dancing and experiencing different cultures. This added to the experience for me. I think with so much experience now, I can talk about it in schools and colleges for hours. I can explain different points of the cultures from Ireland, Germany, England, Norway, and America. This world is a magnificent place if you know where to go. However, there are people who will go on the buses, and they don't get that same experience because they are not educated. They don't have professors and coaches to guide them.

I recently got mail from Carleton College announcing that they are taking a trip to the Rhine and Switzerland. We have already been on this trip, although they are covering slightly different cities this time. I would love to go with Connie, if she was alive. We would never have thought twice about it, and we would have made the reservations. The trip will start in November, but I don't think I want to go because I know I will be depressed. I also received a brochure from the Carleton Alumni Association about a cruise that is going to Sri Lanka for nineteen days. I thought that in case I'm already in India, I can take a flight to Sri Lanka and join them there. I'm not going to go on my own accord without approval from Carleton. Carleton would love to take me because it is not really a business but is also based on feelings for their former students.

Connie's connection with Carleton will give me the power to say that Connie is with me, and she would be happy that I'm attending a cruise. I know that I will not meet Connie, and neither will I be able to meet Connie's match. However, I'm sure there will be a younger batch of people. I will feel like there is some sort of a bond in our conversations during lunch, dinner, and other times. I will have some sort of a background, a great tool and power to talk about Carleton, and why I came to the cruise. Then I can talk about my wife, Constance Berry, and how she was part of Carleton. People are so compassionate, and they will definitely respect me for this. They will give me moral support and will say, "Oh, Pradeep! I think you should do this more. It's a good tribute to your wife Connie, and it will be the greatest thing you can do." They might encourage me to travel more; otherwise, I will be sitting in the same big hole.

Connie went to went to top universities in the United States, Mexico, and Spain. She finished her postgraduation and her advanced courses in different languages, mostly Spanish.

Connie used to tell me that when I met some Indian friends, it felt as if we were glued to each other, like brother and sister. I'd say to her that it may seem like that, but in reality I felt as if I was imposing on them, because it was I who made an effort to go talk to them, whereas they were reluctant.

Our interactions were full of such exchanges because we were of such innocent character. Possibly because of this, I told her that we should get married. Connie thought about this for a while, but she was not sure. She wanted to know how long I intended to stay on in the United States, and whether I'd leave her high and dry. She said to me, "Pradeep, you know I like you and care for you. I love you. But I don't want the possibility that you may leave me alone. If you do so, I will not be able to bear the loss. I think I will go crazy if you leave me, and you never know what I can do because I am not one of those who can remarry again. To me, marriage is sacred."

She said I should take a few months to think about it. Even when we were about to get married, she asked me ten times if I was serious. She did not want to be betrayed. She asked me repeatedly if I had any doubt whatsoever, or if I was marrying her under some kind of pressure, because then we were better off remaining friends. I remember reassuring her that I would never leave her under any circumstances. I will treasure the memory of Connie in her bridal gown as she said all these things and "Till the day I die." When I think of those days, I really feel hurt, and it reminds me of what a wonderful gem my Connie was.

The Truth Always Wins

The last position I held in an organization was as the head of the Midwest region, general manager (or one can say head of the division) for leverage funding. Before that, I had my own consulting firm. When their offer came, Connie told me, "Pradeep, I think you are making a big mistake by joining this large company. They are offering a very good package. However, you are doing much better in your consulting and already have projects lined up for the next six months to one year. I think that you shouldn't get tempted because it will be very hard for you. Just think about it. Right now you have your own consulting firm, and you travel when needed and then come back home. You have a choice whether to go to the office or work from home. You are only looking for benefits. These benefits are mitigated by the fact that your freedom will be compromised. Your consulting allows you to spend more time at home if you don't want to work for a few months. This sort of thing will not be possible once you join."

She was totally against me joining, but this company was persuading me, and I was confused because it was a difficult decision to make. It was in December 2002, and I remember not being able to sleep for the whole night. Connie was so upset with me in the morning, and she said, "I don't think you ever want to listen to me, and you will regret it." I think Connie was right. It was a forty-five-minute drive to the office. We always had two cars. One car was for Connie, and I hardly drove the other because I was flying most of the time. After that, Connie told me, "I think considering the amount of money you spend for parking and maintenance, and the fact that you hardly drive, you should get rid of this car. We have one car, and if you are working in the Chicago area, your company allows you to rent a car. You can always rent a car." In my consulting work, it was not mandatory to have a car, because they would pay for mileage. It was my idea that I wanted to have a car in case Connie drove the other one. She said, "Where do I go alone? Wherever we go, we both go together!" Finally I listened to her and sold my car.

When I got this job, we had to buy a second car. Connie decided she would pay for the car. Look at her sacrifice! She told me, "It is your duty to buy your own car, but don't worry. You have been very kind to me, so I'll buy you a new car." She bought a new car in two days and she would drive her car, which was also brand-new. Again we were stuck with two cars. On the first day, I wore my suit and drove the new car to reach the office about twenty minutes early. I was standing in the parking lot and thinking, "Should I go inside or not?"

I was just about to leave when suddenly the vice chairman, who had hired me, saw me, and said, "Pradeep, what is happening? We are all waiting for you, and we have hired ten new graduates. They are all waiting because you are going to be responsible for starting a new division. Please come inside, and we are going to welcome you." I think for a minute, I felt happiness.

In the office, I met everybody, and they were all excited and happy. They told me, "Now that you are here, we are going to learn from you, and we are going to grow." The first day was totally enjoyable.

But on the way back home, I thought, "Oh, my God! Now I will have to start going back and forth every day." It meant getting up early. I was used to my independence, and now I had lost it. I went into a serious depression in January 2002 that lasted about six months.

Connie told me, "I told you! You might as well quit the job." I talked to my other consulting clients, and they told me, "Pradeep, people make this mistake. Don't worry about it. If you want to quit, quit right away and start our projects." I think I should have listened to Connie and started on my projects right away. I was independent and was getting paid more. If you compare the benefits between working for an organization and self-employment, they are equal. Overall, even if they were giving the benefit of Medicare, I think with my own practice, I was still ahead. But I was committed and did not quit. As much as I wanted to, and as much as Connie wanted me to quit, she sacrificed her wants for my decision. I was miserable. Later on, I started liking the job because training all those young people was the only thing that gave me happiness. Looking back, I think God wanted me to train them in three years compared to the ten years it would have taken them otherwise.

There was another person working there as a senior, but surprisingly he did not know anything. He used to think that he was my boss, and I told him, "Listen. I am not working for you. Rather, you are going to be working for me."

There were a lot of politics involved, so when I mentioned this incident to my senior boss, who was the chairman, he told me, "I hired you, so you are reporting directly to me, and the staff of twenty people will be reporting to you. You are their boss." This man still thought that he was my boss, so I was unhappy and was about to quit. Then they told me that they warned this guy and told him, "If you don't behave with Mr. Berry, we will get rid of you immediately." Finally he apologized to me.

I am mentioning this because I don't know how political connections work. I left that position in 2005 when Connie became sick. After that, I took an oath that I would not work at all and would dedicate myself to Connie.

Now I will recount an incident that shows the dedication of Connie. I had left the job I described above, and I had to find new medical insurance. My old company offered me coverage for eighteen months. I said, "I will take it." I was in a senior position, so they gave me insurance called COBRA, and I had to pay more than what they were paying. I was paying the full cost because the program was very good, so when it ended after eighteen months, I was fiddling around and getting quotes from different insurance companies. I found out that there were a lot of loopholes with these policies. Sometimes they can say, "We don't cover you for this, and we don't cover you for that." Medically, I was totally fit, I didn't have a problem, but I took precautions. When these companies had to pay a buck, they were very careful and said, "Oh, it was a precondition." That way, they don't have to pay out. I had heard that from many people. My insurance company was very clear, and they had sent their policy in writing.

Connie told me, "Listen to me. My insurance from the Education Board System and Illinois Teachers Association is very large. You'd better take my insurance because my insurance is the best in the country." Of course, they used to subsidize her insurance coverage. She said, "I will pay." It was very expensive; almost double the amount I was paying. I was paying $300 and it was about $750.

I said, "Why pay $750 when I am not sick?" She said, "You never know. If God wills that you be sick, and you have to claim, then they will say that you have a precondition. Don't get involved with all this nonsense. I will pay."

I insisted, "No, I will pay."

She said, "If you wanted to pay $350, you pay only that much, and the rest I will pay from my own pocket." I declined, but it was greatness on her part. How much she loved me, and how much she cared for me. I have not seen anyone offering that. She truly loved me, and she paid for part of my insurance for several years. Later on, I think she was not getting the government Medicare. Medicare is a system where everyone has to pay when they are working as Social Security, where they pay 50 percent. It's the same way with FICA: the revenue from the taxes goes to the government. We all have to pay, and it is the law here. Only if you pay do you get a check. In my case, I had to pay for every single thing on my own.

I used to get a 1099 form, which is only issued in the United States; other countries don't issue it. They send you a statement showing how much you have earned, and whether you have a foreign account or something like that. I was getting my 1099, and I filed my taxes very promptly. Connie would tell me, "I don't want you to ever miss any income because if the other company has not sent you the 1099 form, then it is your responsibility to pay." I said I knew that. She said, "Otherwise, if we get caught by the IRS, there will be lot of trouble, and I don't want to get into trouble." I knew that both of us were ethical so I told her she didn't have to worry about it."

One time, one of my clients told me, "Mr. Berry, we are not going to file the 1099 form. As far as we know in human resources, we don't report that."

I said, "It's not possible. Someone must be reporting it, because you have to report this as part of your P&L. You are wrong. I will not take any chances. Either you send it, because someone might find out electronically, or there will be problems. I want to be honest, and I want to sleep well." We were both ethical, and everything was going fine. The time came when I decided to take my earlier benefits, which is called social security. Connie was paying into the Education Board System, where she was not qualified to get Medicare. She was missing maybe ten credits, and maybe one year of teaching. She had worked very hard at a private institution, which was taking care of her social security and Medicare.

I made a big mistake that I regret in my consulting: she used to do a lot of work for me. When I was so overwhelmed with the reports, she used to edit my reports. She used to print them out and make folders for me. She used to e-mail my borrowers and do a lot of other work. I should have been paying her some money as a secretary, and I would have put it as an expense and would have saved on my income tax. During this time, she would have got those credits for her Medicare. She would have been independent to get in a year or a year and a half for what she did free of cost to me. I wish to God that I would have paid her enough money, because it would have helped my taxes and would have helped her get Medicare. She was so nice and never asked me to pay her. Where can you find a rare person like Connie?

Something was bothering me today while I was swimming. I thought about what a big mistake I'd made with that precious diamond. I was very upset, and I said, "I pray to God that Connie will forgive me. She did so much work for free, selfless work, but I did not realize her worth." Later on when I got the rest of my social security, she was definitely eligible to go into Medicare. But there was also a problem, because there was also a time factor we did not expect. The Medicare people told us, "Once you get your benefit, Mrs. Berry will also be entitled to social security and Medicare right away." I have a full record of all those people. But they refused to pay, and I decided to fight. They said no. They were charging her more premiums, and they would not give her the benefits for another two years. Finally I appealed, I had to fight for the right thing.

Connie told me to forget it, but I said, "No. You have done so much for me. Now I'm going to do the same thing for you." I filed for appeal. They say that in the appeal, you generally lose. I thought if we have some good karma, we would definitely win. There were two choices: either we could go for trial in front of the judge, or we could have it over the phone. We thought that if God was there to help, we would win regardless. So we got a letter that on a certain date, at exactly 11:30 a.m., the judge would call us.

Luckily on that date, the telephone rang, and the secretary said, "Are you Mr. Berry? Is Mrs. Berry with you on the line?" I said yes. Then the judge came on the line and said, "Mr. Berry, Mrs. Berry, how are you?"

We replied, "Honorable Judge, we are fine. How are you doing, sir?"

He said, "I am fine. I understand you have been appealing. It has been the most difficult thing, and I think the final verdict was already given to you. I do not know why there is so much confusion, and I don't think I can do anything for you or reverse it for you, because the final judgment has already come."

I told him, "If you listen to us for twenty minutes, both of us will be very grateful to you." Then I told him that we were both very ethical people, we had been paying our taxes for the last forty years, and we were good citizens of this country. We always paid our taxes in time, and we were not involved in crime. My wife had been a teacher and professor for thirty-four years. She had gone to the top schools, and I had many degrees. I told the judge, "My petition is this. We will never tell lies. I have the names and dates of these people."

He said, "I got all that in written letters. How do you prove it?"

I said, "Well, I told you under oath. You earlier asked us to take the oath. I said all this under oath. This in itself is a big thing in the United States of America, that we are saying this to you on the phone under oath. I don't think you need a better explanation than that. I have my handwritten note, which I can mail to you or fax it, whichever way you want. But it's a little amount. We are not going to lie to you, sir. This is definitely the mistake of this person. She was very rude to us, and she was jealous that Mrs. Berry was making more money in her retirement than she will. She was spiteful, because she asked me why Mrs. Berry needed Medicare if her income was so much, and she could pay any amount for a premium. She had no business to be so rude, and we are entitled to our rights. We have paid our taxes. It is not as if United States of America is paying us for free; it is our money we have contributed into this system. My wife contributed into a different system, and she is only getting the pension. But she is not getting any benefits and is maybe short of one credit of one full year. I think you should reconsider."

The judge listened to all that and said, "Both of you are very ethical people. You people definitely deserve it, and I will have to look into further investigation. I will make calls and talk to those people. I will give you my answer in the next three or four weeks. Good luck to both of you. It was nice talking to both of you. Let's see what happens."

We were still in confusion, but from the message, I could understand that hopefully we would receive a positive answer because, he mentioned it when ending the phone call. We were convinced that we were going to get a positive reply. With great help from God, in two weeks we got a letter that we had won the case, and it was written that given the extra Mrs. Berry had paid in premium, whatever was not covered, they had to send us a check. The amount which we lost, Mrs. Berry got everything back from the hospital and from the Medicare system. This is karma. That is why we should be honest, because honesty always stays through the life of the person. Dishonesty is caught very soon, and people lose trust.

Especially in America, there are two things people don't like: lying, and not asking for an apology or not showing remorse. If you apologize right away, people will forgive you, and this is why this country has an advantage. I'm sure in every country this is the way, but it is especially true in this country. Whenever there is a trial, and a murderer says, 'I am very sorry. I think I made a big mistake, and I apologize to the family members of the people whom I killed. I hope that they will forgive me,' if he shows remorse like that, the judge will give him a lesser sentence. If the murderer says, "I am not going to apologize. I have done the right thing," then the judge will increase the sentence. I think people who are reading my book and are in the United States will not take much interest because they already know. If someone is in India or another place, I think this will be a great example. I'm sure even in India, people are very intelligent, and they will know. But still I think it is important for me to write this incident, which is a tribute to my wife. It is because of the beautiful things she did that we got the rewards.

Unfortunately, despite all these things I'm saying, the truth is that Connie is no longer with me. That is the biggest thing. No matter how much I praise her, it is not going to bring her back. My hope is that I become her husband in my next life, so that my purpose will be successful. I pray to God all the time, "God, give me Connie, *the* Connie, the same beautiful Connie so that she can be with me. In fact, in our next lives, we should meet when we are very young, as young as kindergarten." That would be a wonderful thing to happen to us, so that our lives together start as little children, and later grow up and then fall in love. And if that happens, I think I will be the happiest person. I don't have any other wish, like being born into a millionaire's family. I only want Connie to be my sweetheart from a very young age. If that happens, my sorrow and my pain will go away. Today if I hear God telling me, "Pradeep, I grant you that after your death, when you are reborn and Connie is already there, she may be elder to you by a couple of years, and you are able to meet her," I will accept it, however much older she is to me. I will accept that if I hear a voice coming in the next life that she may be elder to me, but she will still be my wife. I don't care if I'm sixteen years old and she is thirty years old, I will accept it—I love her that much. Miracles do happen, and I'm ready for anything.

Even if she meets me like a sister, or she becomes my mother, I would still take it. That is why Chanakya quoted, "A wife can be your wife if she can be your best friend, sister, and mother." The same thing is written in the Vedanta about the duty of the wife. This is my pain, and it doesn't lessen if I go to a support group or read. Connie is on my mind all the time.

Realization and Enlightenment of Pain after Connie's Death

Memories of My Paternal Grandfather

I wanted to share one more thing, and that is about my paternal grandfather. He was very learned, very spiritual, and very knowledgeable. He had four sons and several grandchildren, and we were his first grandchildren. We all lived together in a very big house in Delhi. My grandfather was pretty wealthy, and he was supporting everybody. His sons were working in the business too. We were students then and were just about to finish our education.

When my grandmother died, I remember he did not go to the cremation, but he asked his elder son and everybody in the family to take her away. He managed to say some sort of good-bye. It was clear then that he was very upset, but I still fail to understand why he did not perform the last rites or even attend the cremation. After the cremation, he asked if everything was done properly, which we confirmed. He used to stay alone on the ground floor, and the rest of us stayed on the other four floors of the house. I think we were all ignorant at that time, but he was by himself in a dark, lonely house with many rooms. I remember asking him if I should stay in the same room that my grandmother used to be in, but he declined. He said that he was fine, and he was very knowledgeable, adding, "You people have to study, and as a result of that, I don't want to do things that ruin your studies." I think I asked him a couple of times, but perhaps I did not mean it very seriously. I doubt I had thought of the pain he was enduring then, because I believed he was very knowledgeable and capable of handling it.

He was the one who told us about the inevitability of death, and I felt that such a learned man would cope.

However, to my surprise within no time he started deteriorating rapidly. He had the support of his family, but he was not himself, and despite being surrounded by so many people, he was very lonely inside. I think he especially struggled at night, when people are alone with their thoughts. We never thought it would happen, but quite unbelievably, he passed away after two months. When I think about it now, I realize he went through a lot of pain before he died. I feel that he must have suffered terribly, but he never said a word to anybody and silently bore the pain. He did not write a biography or share his feelings with anybody. I am sharing this to tell everybody that one should not be silent and should share one's pain so that one can let others know that they should be prepared to face this kind of unexpected tragedy.

That is why I think I am feeling more pain. Although I have seen these kinds of painful moments, I had not imagined how difficult it would be. I thought that I would suffer perhaps 50–60 percent but not 100 percent. Now that it is happening to me, I am enduring it with lot of pain.

I saw the same thing happen with another family member who was living in the United States with his children and grandchildren. He was also very close to his wife, and I think he was close to his grandchildren as well, because he was happiest when talking about them. When his wife died, however, he turned around and felt very lonely. I don't think he had any great love for his own sons, and I doubt he was crazy about his grandchildren. Additionally, I think there was a dispute about money among his children, and it gradually became worse because his children wanted to grab his money. As a result of this, there was deep enmity among his daughters-in-law. It was around this time that he moved out of the home. Sometimes he was living back in India with his daughters, or with some friends in the United States, and at other times he was in a hotel. I doubt if that made much of a difference. I remember a time when I called him at the hotel. I spoke with an Indian Gujarati gentleman attending to him, and he said to me, "Mr. Berry, I want to worship you and touch your feet. Why don't you come over here?" When I wondered why I should do that, he told me that my uncle thought of me every minute. He told me my uncle used to wait for my call from the moment he got up in the morning. When I called again the next day, the gentleman said, "Why don't you come here? I want to meet you, because you are really something. You have the power to heal his wounds."

He told me my uncle looked forward to my call in the morning at eight thirty. I used to call him from my office, and we would speak for half an hour. I used to call him in the afternoon and at night as well. I was doing it out of love and compassion, because at that time I felt very sorry that he was missing his wife. I had no idea as to how much he was suffering, and because it was twenty years ago, I can only guess.

The difference between these two examples and mine is that they were still occupied with their families. That was not the case in our lives, because we had decided not to have that kind of extended family. Thus, in our case our love was split between Connie and me. We had time only for each other.

Their love could be 50 percent toward the wife, or 70 percent toward the children. There was surely a distribution of love between them and their children and grandchildren. His wife was extremely fond of their son, so much so that sometimes she used to fight with her husband over them. I think they suffered so much despite there being a division of love.

Sometimes I compare that with my situation, and I wonder how much suffering there can be if one is 100 percent devoted to someone, as Connie and I were to each other. Even in the other cases, if there was a 100 percent devotion to the other person, it's just not possible. For example, if you travel with your grandchildren, your wife is alone at home. Similarly, if the grandmother leaves her husband alone for months while she is with her grandchildren, there cannot be 100 percent devotion to each other. It is not an apple to apples comparison, but I can see that he still suffered after his wife passed away, despite there not being a 100 percent commitment.

I have seen at least twenty cases where the couples were married for up to fifty years with children and had extremely close relations. In the majority of those cases, fifteen wives were sick, and the husbands were taking good care of them. After the wives' deaths, those widowers were upset for one year or a maximum of two years. After that, we found out all the widowers married again, some with kids and some without kids. All the love and devotion they had with their children and grandchildren were gone, and they were by themselves, having their second honeymoon and traveling. One of them moved to Hawaii, another went to Florida, another moved to Denver, and some went to different parts of California. Connie and I talked about how come their loves with their wives and kids disappeared. We hardly saw them, and they never contacted us except when they got married, and they sent a Christmas cards informing us of their address. Connie was mailing them gifts and best wishes, and later everything stopped. It has been over seventeen years ago.

I could never even think of doing this; no way would I want to remarry. Connie was my wife, and she will remain my wife till I am dead. These experiences and old memories are coming back to me, haunting me. We never interfered in anyone's life, and we were very happy. Now, those memories are part of this book. It's not a great thing to write, but when I pour my heart and soul in this book, things flow from the heart and soul. Spirituality is also based upon some of its versions. Otherwise, why can I not get any peace of mind in any church or temple? My soul is my God, and my peace of mind with Connie is attached to me until now. I talk about four out of twenty, where husbands were married for thirty-eight to forty-three years. These husbands were upset but were not sincere after their wives died. They only missed the wives. They were not crushed as I would have expected. When we both went to see them for condolences and funerals. We found them upset and at the same time a little social. They told us, "Connie and Pradeep, thanks for coming. Let's keep in touch."

We invited two of them over because the other two were traveling with their children and were remarried. These two widowers and their sisters came to our house, and both said, "Oh, Connie, and Pradeep, it is fine. Our wives were great, but now we may think of doing some business. Could you help us get money from the banks for a new venture?"

I told them, "We do not fund new companies because we are commercial and secured lenders, not venture capitalists." They insisted, but I could not. Later, they told us that we both would start looking for widows in Florida, and marry them to get their money and have fun while enjoying our lives. Connie wanted to throw them out, but you cannot do that. It truly bothered us that these two were so different. They were educated people, but their thoughts and mind had changed. We politely told them, "Sorry for your loss. Do whatever makes you happy."

They were gracious and said, "You both are lovebirds. What a wonderful marriage you have." After that, we went down to see them off, and they were totally gone from lives. I was happy with my Connie.

There was another person who was married, and who supposedly could not live without his wife. This woman was so sincere to him, and Connie and I were shocked when we found out she'd died. Four years later, he brought another younger bride. He thought he would be happy, but the new wife with her four children came to the United States. He applied for her US citizenship, and immediately after that, she started controlling him and his money. After a few years, she emptied his bank accounts, took over his business, took power of attorney of his house, and grabbed over 70 percent of his wealth. This caused so much stress to him, along with his two children. He had a nervous breakdown and died after a few months. That is the fun of money. We knew him and his previous wife well, but we never tried to meet him after he remarried. Connie and I were put off by his loyalty and his devotion. He used to sing his song. By the way, his wife died of cancer.

One Indian girl had parents who were big businesspeople, and they had one daughter and one son. The girl was in love with one man making a small amount, and he took lots and lots of dowry as per the Indian tradition, including an expensive house on the lake, a boat, and a luxury car. What a lovely marriage it was. After nine months, he left her. There was a big lawsuit, and he would not return anything to his wife or her parents. He was very aggressive, and the case lasted four years, ending up in his favor.

Later, the same girl left for India and married some man who she thought was a doctor. The new husband and bride had a very expensive marriage in India and a reception in the United States. All were very happy. They had two children, and her parents bought them a bigger house. After five years, there was some suspicious thing his wife noticed. She kept asking him about it, but in vain. One day she got the shock of her life. She found out that he had married an American girl after coming to the United States, and within four years he had three children from his American wife. This husband, who was supposed to be a doctor, was not a qualified doctor. He was a premedical student and was not working as a doctor but as a technician in the hospital. Six children, three from his Indian wife and three from his US wife. He already had grabbed a nice house, nice car, nice bank balance, and nice gold jewelry, as well as a free house and luxury car from his father-in-law. This was a second shock for that girl and her parents. They tried to get him arrested and filled a lawsuit, but later they gave up because their reputation in the family was spreading. They hushed up the case. We never asked them about it, and it has been twenty years since I have even seen any of them. The same thing happened to their son, their niece, and other family members. This book would be full of these incidences, if I wrote many more. Heaven for the scheming husband was hell for the girl and her parents. Just imagine: this girl had two marriages and three children, but her husband got all the material things and houses. Later, the whole family went through the tension, and all the love and wealth was gone to different people. This is the beauty of too much money. We have seen this in the United States and India.

Whenever I go to the swimming pool and whirlpool, I think of one nice lady who told me her daughter married a boy from her own country, her neighbor. He showed them his medical certificate, and the family was very happy. He used to go in his medical jacket with full medical equipment, convincing them that he went to different hospitals. They had two children, a house, and nice cars. Her parents were rich and were a big support. The wife never worked in order to take care of her children. Connie never appreciated that because she never wanted to depend upon anyone but herself. I always loved her advice for years.

After six years, a man approached the girl and the mother; he was some relation of theirs. He told them that he knew the son-in-law well. The girl and the mother were curious as to how he knew the son-in-law. He then told them to meet him in downtown Chicago outside a five-star hotel. The girl, the mother, and the children went there, and a shock was waiting for them. They found out the husband had honesty or loyalty. We have forgotten these qualities.

After Connie's demise, these things are going through my mind regarding how happy, honest, and faithful we were. Why did God have to take my lovely Connie? These old incidents are coming to mind, and I miss Connie and think about what a gem, what a sincere and lovely wife she was. Our love and marriage were out of this world. There was love and love only. Some small arguments did take place, and those were for a very small period. Now when I think of those arguments, I feel devastated and get upset for hours or even days as to why I did that or why certain things happened. I want to say, "Connie, please forgive me, no matter if it was my or your fault. I feel that we should have had nothing but love and not even a five-minute argument or any negative discussions."

There's a saying that we do not care for loved ones when they are alive, but after their deaths, we feel devastated. Why? The world is that way. Many poets, singers, music producers, actors, and great people are not cared when they are alive. But after death, we regret it and cry. We are sorry and upset. I now believe for the coming generation, they should love while others are alive. In my life, and I have lost one gem. I do not want to write more on these stories. I want to concentrate on my Connie and our life together. These stories make me not want to socialize anybody. Let people do what they want.

There are different variations of life, and people go on with their own things. I can give you a thousand examples, but that is not the purpose of my biography. Although I saw the pain of many people, their pain is irrelevant to me. My biography is meant only for my wife. I would say to some degree, pain is always there from your dear loved ones, whether it is your wife or your children. It is a different kind of pain, but it is difficult nevertheless. Some people have overcome the pain of their losses, or perhaps they are just acting. Some manage to keep on going. I spoke to one friend of mine who lost his son to suicide, and he did not want to talk to me, saying it was a topic he wanted to avoid. I respected his wishes, but he called me the next day, apologizing about his rude behavior. He said his son was his darling, and he shared a little bit of his feelings. Thereafter, I was careful not to bring up the topic unless he wanted to talk about it. I suppose everybody is different, and people handle their grief differently. Some start giving to charity; others marry again, and some start doing humanitarian work. That's the way it is.

In my case, I don't think I will do anything in a haphazard way. For example, during the last couple of days, I have kept busy writing articles, meeting people about important matters, and talking to attorneys. There are some diversions, but the moment I leave the office, the pain starts right away. According to psychologists and psychiatrists, sometimes when you start thinking about one thing, that stops you from thinking about other things. In my case, I do not even want to go to those places where I used to go with Connie. I have written that I have stopped reading the newspaper and stopped watching TV. Whenever I read the name Constance Berry on the magazines we receive, it truly bothers me. I begin to think I should start reading them, but I don't think I'm ready right now. However, I am determined about one thing: whenever I receive a letter from MCR and other organizations in her name, I will definitely donate some money. Connie passed away at HH Hospital, close to our home. Connie had given good donations to HH Hospital, and that is the same hospital where, in my opinion, medical negligence took place. I am sure she would not have given a penny if she had known that. I still get letters for Connie asking for charity. I do not want to give a penny to HH Hospital. Reading her name, going through her drawer, going to her room, and not finding her is the most painful thing in my life.

The other day, I was sitting at my desk and looking for certain papers. I found her degrees. I could see how much love she got from her students, how much appreciation she got from the dean, and how many prizes she had won. I knew about these things, but at that time I was not appreciative about their value. Now, all those things are like a monument to her. Last night, I saved all those things in her room and got busy organizing all of them. I sorted out all the degrees, gifts, and letters from her students and school authorities. I look through all the tributes that Connie received from her college and the dean, noting how she was highly regarded. When I read these things, I lose control and wonder, "Isn't all the knowledge and education that one has futile? All of us have to go one day; none of us is special."

I think the doctors made a mistake with Connie. If the doctors had acted differently, Connie would still be with me today. The main problem with me is that Connie did not die of natural causes—her life was snatched away by these doctors.

Different Reactions to Grief

I have seen many painful circumstances, and that is why I want to understand how people who have lost their spouses react to their painful situations. This is what I am trying to find out for my own knowledge, but their experiences are not going to help me. People tell me to read books about Buddha, where he asks disciples to get rice from any house that has not seen death. I have read it, and I know all those things. People tell me there is no house where tragedy has not taken place, I know that, but because of my overattachment and my total love for Connie, all my knowledge has vanished. I don't want to compare events that happen to different people to my own circumstances, but at the same time, I am curious about people who lost their spouses and how they dealt with it.

I know some people dealt with it very positively. I have some friends and relatives who accepted that now their spouse was gone, they had to carry on. I was really surprised because they were very close to each other. I don't know if these people were really close to their spouses, or they simply pretended to be. Sometimes people pretend they are close, but they are not very close. When the wife of one man I know died, I don't think it made much difference in his life. He was very upset, but at the same time he carried on without mentioning her to me. We met many times after that because he was my distant relative, but I don't think he ever mentioned her to me. I used to ask him how he felt without his wife, and he used to say, "I'm okay. She had to go." I was surprised that he was regularly going to parties, drinking, and going wherever there was a function. I don't think he was in any pain.

People challenge me and say, "How do you know he was not in pain? Maybe he was suffering but did not say anything!" I would probably reply that if the person is suffering, or if that person is in pain, he would not be mixing up with people and acting normal. In my judgment, I did not see any remorse that he'd lost his wife. Sometimes a reaction brings action, and an action brings reaction. The whole family told me that he had adjusted and was not missing his wife much. That was very surprising to me.

I also want to share our trips to Sanibel and Captiva Islands, some of the most beautiful islands in the United States, south of Fort Myers, Florida. The islands are very small, less than ten miles in length, and there are beautiful resorts that preserve some of the natural setting, with beachfront views of the Gulf of Mexico. It's beautiful, and they don't allow any fast food, large buildings, or commercial shopping centers. It's a very isolated place for people to relax, and it is mostly a second home for the rich. It's a very rich place, and people who have gone there love it. It is one of the world's most important places for collecting sea. People come there from all over, and I think it is beautiful. We went there, spending five weeks on Sanibel and then three weeks on Marco Island.

On one of our trips, we were having lunch at a famous place, and it was very special to Connie. There is a special kind of fish called grouper, which is available only in Florida, especially around Sanibel and Captiva. It is a special delicacy. This grouper fish cannot be acquired fresh from anywhere else in the United States, just like salmon comes only from Alaska. We had the best grouper when we were there in 1987 and then again in 1989. They catch the fish in the ocean and immediately prepare it, and it is out of this world. Similarly, in New Orleans, they have a white fish that is absolutely delicious. Going back to our incident in Captiva, there is restaurant called the Bubble Boy. They make their fish in a brown paper bag and grill it. It is magnificent, and perhaps one cannot get that taste anywhere. It is absolutely fresh, like fresh coffee in Hawaii.

When we went to the big island of Kona, Hawaii, in 2006 and 2007, we visited many Kona coffee and chocolate farms, where we got to taste different types of coffee and chocolate. We bought both coffee and dark chocolate of different types that are only grown on Kona Island. Similarly, Kona has other delicacies that are super.

In India, mangoes are the best in the world during the summer. India also has many different fruits and vegetables that are seasonal. Nature and God have been very kind to India. I think India is the second largest producer of fruits and vegetables in the world. It is the largest producer of potatoes, milk, fiber, jute, cotton, silk, jumbo shrimp, leather hides, iron ore, and basmati rice. The South Indian coffee has a completely different, gorgeous taste.

I know every country has regional differences in climate and food habits. The economist Thomas Malthus mentioned that every twenty miles, the language, food, and culture of people are different. We are living in a global society, and so the distance probably might have gone up to thirty miles. If I go forty miles from where we live, people over there have a different ways of living. The houses are different, and the standard of living is different. If I go one hundred miles away, then local life is completely different. I think Malthus was absolutely right when he said that India is a rich country inhabited by the poor.

I want narrate an incident. We met a person who was sitting by himself in a restaurant in Captiva Island in 2010. I'm sure he was close to eighty years old, but he was handsome. He had maintained himself very well and looked educated. He was sitting next to us, and we kept looking at each other. Finally I decided to talk to him. He asked us, "Why don't we sit together for lunch?" Connie and I started talking. When we asked where he lived, he stated Spain, but he came to Captiva every year for three months, living in a small house by himself. After I asked him if he had family, he said that he had two daughters and six grandchildren, and they all lived in Spain. When he's with them, he enjoys them. However, he lives alone. I asked him about his wife, and he said, "I lost my wife twenty years ago and did not remarry. She was my darling, she was my love, and I would never remarry. I am alone, and I am fine."

I was taken aback, so I said, "Pardon me for asking, but what was your profession?"

He looked at me and said, "Do you remember seeing my face in the fifties and sixties?" Then I remembered he was one of the most popular journalists, and he used to cover India, China, and Asia. He was one of the most intellectual journalists and TV personalities, and he would announce the world news. He told me he had met Prime Minister Nehru and Dr. Rajendra Prasad. Later, he also met Prime Minister Shastri and many other politicians. He knew everyone.

I said, "Yes! My God! What an accomplishment for you!"

said he replied, "No. I don't do anything now. I used to travel extensively and was very happy. But after the loss of my wife, my darling who was my baby, I don't travel so much anymore." I did not have the experience of losing a spouse at that time, and hence I couldn't sympathize. Now, I recollect that incident and imagine what he must have gone through. I am going through the same myself after losing Connie.

Connie and I talked about that many times. He was being looked after by the young waitresses, who treated him like their father and helped him if he needed something. I don't know whether these kinds of experiences make me strong or weak. I am not going to compare his life with my life. That is my message to people: we should not compare our situations to others. It is good to compare to get some knowledge, but if you think that you can follow the same principle as another, and if you follow a particular person because he is your idol, it does not work. If someone says, "Look at him, and take that example," you cannot be that person. The doctors gave me examples of people who worked their way out of grief. I am not ready for that, because their pain may be different. I think people should not compare losses, and when people are grieving, other people should not say a whole lot except, "Please look after your health. Do whatever you want to do, whatever makes you happy." One should not dictate how people should lead their lives, because one cannot understand the pain others have gone through.

I want to let people know this important message: Do not play with somebody's sentiments by giving them false hope. Some people recommend that I read some biography of some person. I have read these, and I am still reading them, but it has made no difference to me. That is an indication that our love was unique. Perhaps many people have never had this kind of love, this kind of feeling we had for each other. I don't want to make this a very negative book; I don't want people to feel that I am talking about my pain. I think in this kind of hidden pain, there is a hidden message as well. The hidden message is that one should try to understand the grieving person's mind. People should appreciate what I have been through rather than telling me, "This is God and life. Forget about the past; life goes on." I don't want to hear all that. I don't have any other choice but to go on, but I want my own very simple life, and I don't want to go anywhere except India, because it gives me some happiness to be with my brother, his family, and my grand-nieces. After five or six years, I may be able to travel somewhere. Right now, I'm still getting so much mail from Viking, Vantage, University of Michigan, Carleton and other elite colleges whose sponsored trips we went on. I will not go on these trips, because Connie's memory would make me more depressed and upset, and I might have panic attacks when I remember our trips. I would remember how Connie used to be with me every minute, and how we used to take the taxi, get out at the airport, and fly by ourselves. When we were with the Michigan University tour, how happy we were! We would be picked up and stay in the hotel, and then we'd go on a cruise or sometimes a land tour. I won't go to the places I have been with Connie. I might go to places where I have not gone before, like Turkey, Egypt, Saudi Arabia, or Dubai—places where we wanted to go but did not. People behave according to what they believe, but I hope they will understand the message I am conveying.

There are other incidents I remember. There was a neighbor who was very close to us. After his divorced wife married a man, he looked after his two stepchildren like his own. He was very nice to his wife because it was his first marriage. Life and human beings are selfish and greedy. His wife left all her wealth, including their house, to his children, and this man was left with no house. However, he was not too poor and had his own business. After the death of his wife, he was lonely and would call us every day to see if he could come over to spend time in our home. We allowed him to do so, except when I was traveling. I did travel extensively on my professional career, and many times I took Connie with me. We allowed this man to come practically every weekend when I was in town. He was lonely. Connie wondered how come a man in his late sixties could entertain himself and call us daily. She was concerned for my travel and my time.

It went on till his grown stepchildren told him to move out of the house or buy it. He was served with papers to leave the house. That was a very upsetting thing, and he shared all his pain with Connie and me. We both were very upset. After a year, he died. All his relatives and friends came and grabbed whatever they could. His one sister was a leader in taking over his money, car, and other things. The house went to his one son, and the other did not want anything, though he was not too well settled in his life. I have seen two other incidences that much like this one.

I Can See Connie Everywhere

I would like to mention the many practical things about the sadness I feel. For a long time after Connie's death, her caretakers and other people did the laundry. I didn't do it because I was doing other things. Today, I wanted to change the sheets and wash the few clothes that I had, so I was waiting for our helper to come. But she was not coming until next week, and so I decided to do it myself. Today, September 20, 2015, I started doing laundry. I think it is one of the most emotionally difficult things I did today. It was intolerable, especially when I changed the sheets. The sheets are very clean, and the side on which Connie used to sleep hasn't been touched. It was very painful for me to have this experience.

This is same kind of heartache I feel when I see that she is not in the bedroom, her study room, the living room, or the kitchen. She no longer shops with me or rides in my car. I remember when we had just met each other forty years ago: she had so much stamina to take care of everything. She was full of energy. She would change the sheets two to three times a week, do the cleaning, do all the laundry, iron our clothes, and put them neatly in the cupboard. She was a perfectionist. When she got sick later on, in the last two to three years, only then did I do a lot of household chores. I was not a perfectionist like her; I would put my garments here and there and not hang them properly. So many times she would see the way I had arranged her clothes, and she would say to me, "Is this the way you want to put away my clothes? Haven't you seen how I would do it?" I would tell her these things were not important anymore and that we would have to change our priorities. By then, she did not have much energy and was not very argumentative. Remembering such small things are very painful for me. I thought I must write about this experience, and right away I started writing. It's around 2:00 a.m., and I decided that I had to write this so that I would not forget. I think these kinds of things are the true rhythm of pain.

Another thing has just popped up in my mind. Maybe I should write another book, or change the title of the book to *Living in Pain for Three Years*, so that I can describe how suddenly our health can deteriorate. I think the doctors ruined her body, Otherwise I never would have imagined that she would go downhill so fast.

I avoid going to her shower room, which has a walk-in shower that she had specially built for her. In one of our bathrooms, we had a tub, and when she couldn't use it for the last two to three years, she spent a lot of money and got a walk-in shower built so that she could enjoy her baths. Sadly, she did not have enough time to enjoy the new shower. I cannot believe that when she got sick for about eighteen months, she was not capable of taking a shower herself. She was on the oxygen tank, and she would sit on the walker; I would make her comfortable so that she could enter the shower. She was very modest and independent. She would ask me to pass her the towel and leave the shower. I would later help with the drying after she was done with the shower.

Her legs were swollen, and I used to massage her legs with cream for a few minutes every day. It used to bring tears to my eyes that she was retaining so much water. I thought her doctors were not very concerned, so I reprimanded them. I would tell them that they saw Connie only for a few minutes, and they were so busy. If they were forced to see what she was going through for twenty-four hours a day, they would realize the damage they had done to her. I said this to the doctors so many times. One of her doctors was very good in the beginning, and when the case went out of control, he was willing to listen to anything and would not answer back, although I'm sure he didn't like listening to criticism. If he had argued with me then, maybe we would have had more complicated problems. I was ready to fight with him in court. The most important thing for me was Connie, and I had decided that if the doctor said anything or argued with me, I was ready for a battle. I think I did not pursue that more because I did not want to get distracted from paying attention to Connie.

One of the other things I face every day when I go to check my mailbox, or if I am coming in from the front door, is that I imagine I can see her sitting in the balcony with her walker, along with her oxygen. I remember how I would bring my car outside and help her into the car, and she would sit with me on one of our numerous trips to the hospital. I know it was the most difficult thing for me and for her, but even then, it gave me some happiness as well as sadness. I used to feel more sadness but also feel a little bit of happiness that she was still alive and we were together. Even if I had to carry her wheelchair, I would be very happy, and I had never felt such happiness earlier, when we were taking trips all over the world. I think this is true love.

When we were young and were having a lot of fun all the time, that was also love. But later in our lives, our love was like worship to God. Just like one surrenders and becomes a saint, like one has renounced the world, I had left the whole world and practically my whole life in order to be with Connie. Her weak body had become my place of worship. Instead of praying to God in the temple, I would offer my prayers in the form of my devotion to her. Whenever I would see her sitting, sleeping, or uncomfortable, I would pray to God that if there was good karma, to please give her strength and make her better. This was the way I worshipped her.

Even now, it is very difficult for me to take a shower in her walk-in shower. To avoid that, I go to the health club almost every day; I swim and exercise, and I then take a shower there. These are the lengths I go to in order to avoid the pain. I am not saying that this is the reaction of every human being, because although everyone has gone through grief; perhaps they may have had some different experience. I am not trying to compare myself to them, and neither am I trying to say that I am the only person who has seen suffering. Every individual on this planet has gone through some kind of suffering, and everyone's suffering is different. I consider happiness and unhappiness as sisters, and my philosophy is that a candle has less light and more darkness. With a candle, only a few people can study, but if you move away from the candle, there is darkness.

I think it is very difficult, and I don't want to be ungrateful to the mighty Lord, but I am certainly in a lot of agony. I cannot describe this agony. It is very easy for people to say that Connie was sick for a long time, and that everyone has to pass away. But I have not only seen her death—I have also seen her suffering. I'm sure many people have seen that. I'm sure there are people who are all alone like me, and there are people who have suffered by themselves. I'm not making any comparative statement, and neither do I have any statistics, but I think in my life, I might have seen very few people who were alone. Even in those cases, they found children, a spouse, friends, and relatives to come help. Some of the widow ladies used to use volunteer with Northwestern University. I'm not sick right now, but if I ask faculty there for help, then students there, who have a program that helps seniors who live alone, will surely come to help. I don't want to ask for their help right now, because I want to be active. I should keep on moving all the time.

The things I am describing right now are very painful, and I don't know how long it will take me to overcome the grief. People who thought they understood my pain do not understand it 1 percent. I think it is very hard for me when they say that they are sorry she is gone. If they had seen the kind of suffering I saw, then perhaps it would have stayed with them for their whole lives. This suffering will stay with me until the day I die. Every single incident has stuck in my brain, mind, soul, and heart like a movie.

It may be a good message, or it may be a depressing message for people. I have no idea how readers will perceive it, but at least they will know how to plan and be prepared so that they don't have to go through this. I have seen many people who had no plan, and they suffered in the end. However, there is no guarantee that even if you plan something, things will work according to that plan. Connie had planned long-term care, but look at what happened. If I have offended anyone, I want to ask for forgiveness, because this is my personal experience and has no relevance to anyone else.

I remember seeing a hit Indian movie during my teenage years, *Woh Kaun Thi*, meaning *Who Was She*. It can be easily seen on YouTube even now, and I am sure with Netflix. It is an excellent movie and has super songs. After Connie's demise, I am always thinking about her, and I keep her beautiful face in my mind everywhere I go. For most of her life, if she was available to pick me up from the airport (and she focused on being available to pick her Pradeep), she would. This was in spite of my saying, "Please don't," because it was a four-minute walk from the Amtrak to my office, especially if I was working until late in the evening. Of course, going to the airport was a different aspect of her love, to meet her husband as quickly as possible. I was desperate to run from the plane with my carry-on. There was a great love in that carry-on and how Connie used to pack and empty it. Then she'd do the laundry and would never allow me to wear anything but Ralph Lauren or Christian Dior shirts, and Nautica socks to match each outfit. I wondered all my life how my wife was like my mother, getting me up early and making sure that I dressed properly and according the season of the year. How much love was involved in that? She was always thinking of going to Marshall Field's (now Macy's) to buy these things for me.

Her clothing, my ties and suits, and those carry-on suitcases are still with me. Though I may have to spend money to get the carry-on fixed, I would do so, along with two of her suitcases. I am talking about suitcases she bought me thirty years ago. I have preserved them and will continue to preserve them. That is a source of Connie's memories with me. Who she was is now like two desperate, lost souls waiting to meet each other. That is what the *Who Kaun Thi* and the beautiful songs and lyrics are about. I would try to translate the lyrics into English and would compose my own songs. If possible, I would work hard and get an album with professional musical instruments and directions, calling it *My Tribute to My Love*.

My Emotions and India

I must mention that Connie was and will be special for all my life. Our first trip to India was in July 1979, three years after our marriage. We were both thrilled to go and spent seven weeks in India. It was great for us, our family, and our friends. We stayed with my brother, and every day, from morning till night, family and friends would walk in, because the tradition for visiting was to walk in without calling beforehand. At that time, people in India offered true hospitality. Now, a small percentage of friends and family members call before visiting. I think I prefer that to surprise visits. Nowadays, people have less time to visit due to working and the traffic in India. In Delhi, some families live far away, and traffic has become a big problem. I don't want to travel far in the city to see people because of traffic.

Connie and I went to Kashmir, Taj, and Jaipur. We went sightseeing in Delhi and saw historical and ancient places. Some of the most beautiful places in Delhi are Chandni Chowk and Connaught Place. The shopping is excellent and lots of fun. One can find handicrafts and things that are exported all over the world. For lunch we would have picnics or go to the houses of friends and relatives. We went to dinner every night with relatives. We started going to the home of my uncle, Dr. Behl, and his wife, Marjorie. I was extremely close to them. Connie and Marjorie became best friends, and after we returned the United States, Uncle Behl and Aunt Marjorie visited us in Evanston, along with their daughter Vanita, who was like a daughter to me. We had lots of good times, and my uncle refused that I take any time off work because he was a devoted to his medical profession, writing books, attending conferences at different universities, and presenting his thesis. He mixed his business trips with vacations. Connie was also working, and we did our best to provide them hospitality.

I learned a great lesson that I have been following ever since, except for later when we were getting comfortable life. Uncle told me, "Son, I want to stay with you to spend time with both of you, and to pick up our three years we spent apart, missing each other. While I am here, I would like to contribute to your bills for food, gas, telephone, and electricity." I told him that it wasn't necessary, because we could easily afford to house them, and I would not take a penny. He said, "If you don't take my offer, I will stay in a hotel. Son, I can very easily afford to help out, and you are both working people. Unless I contribute, I would rather stay in the hotel, and you will have to come meet me, and have lunch and dinner with us." I did not argue anymore and told him that he would never stay in a hotel when I could house him. I would accept the cost of the phone calls to India, because it was three dollars per minute compared to thirty cents now. He agreed, and the consideration he showed me enlightened me. Connie and I did not stay anywhere in India except with my brother and at Dr. Behl's house.

I then started getting emotional about India. I wanted to come every year to India for my vacation. Connie started to join me, however after four annual vacations, Connie told me, "Pradeep, can't you go every two years or eighteen months? That way we can visit Australia, New Zealand, China, and Egypt, or we can do a few more cruises with the University of Michigan." I never said no. We both were confused that it was a long flight to Australia and suggested that we could stop for week in India and take a flight from Delhi, because it was not that long from Delhi to Australia, China, and Russia. I regret that she truly wanted to see Australia and New Zealand, but we never made it there. Later on, she was not ready for China, Egypt, and Turkey, or even India, due to the long flights. I regret missing Australia and New Zealand. I know that she was most interested in those two places.

I must mention that I had four Indian friends who were professionals, and we had worked together in the same profession and lived in Chicago. Their wives were part of our family, and we were absolutely close. Then all four men and their spouses took two trips together and never asked us. Connie and I were very hurt, and they made some big excuses. Connie told me, "Pradeep, these four with their Indian wives want Indians only." I definitely know that the Indians in my circle always wanted to be Indians in the United States.

I told my friends and relatives bluntly, "You think you are in the United States, but you do not have a single American friend. Regardless of how intelligent or educated you are, you all get together like a big carnival and remain Indians." We decided that it is better for us, because we had different taste and style, and a different approach to being private. Immediately we did a self-evaluation and got the answer that we truly do not want to go with anyone, but just us. Later, many other friends wanted us to go together, but we decided against it. This is a very important point. We truly wanted to be by ourselves, and until Connie's demise, we were together. I did not want or need to see anyone, not even my own members of my family. father's sister's children.

These four Indian men and their wives went to Australia and New Zealand. They never asked Connie and me to go with them. The fact is they called and told me and Connie that we must see the countries someday. I asked them how come they did not ask us, because we would have gone. I will always regret that Connie was not able to go to Australia and New Zealand. There is no way I would ever think of going to these two places now.

Connie's memory, her love, her passion, and our pure love made us inseparable. Connie and Pradeep now is only Pradeep. Connie is gone. This pain is a sharp edge, and there is no treatment, no compensation.

My Present Life—Pain After Connie

It is so painful for me to think of going anywhere without Connie. Sometimes I feel I should try to go to a restaurant and travel by myself, to see how I'd feel. Right away, my brain and heart tell me no. This is due to the fact that during our lives, we always went together, except when we were working. I had to travel quite a lot, and so did Connie. I have not gone anywhere without Connie in the last ten years. The only exception was that I used to go to India every year for two weeks, and that was difficult. Even then, I would have panic attacks at the thought of leaving Connie for two weeks. Connie used to make the decision that I might as well go. I still did not want to go, because leaving her was difficult. I would go to India, but I would miss her. From the moment she dropped me at the airport, it was extremely difficult for me. I debated whether I should forget about going to India and come back home to Connie. Connie was strong, and she used to give me the power to go; otherwise, I would regret leaving her, and after a few days, I would be on the phone booking return flights. The decision to go or to stay was difficult. In the end, I would decide to travel, but my mind was always on Connie. I would call her five or six times a day and have long talks with her. Connie used to tell me, "Either go or don't go. If you go, I can keep busy with cleaning the drawers and organizing my stuff." This statement, and knowing we would be in touch over the phone for hours, made my yearly trip to India possible. It was a struggle then. Now, the same struggle is still there when I leave the house alone. In reality, these are signs of our love.

Once in a while, I think I wouldn't mind going somewhere, but the thought of going or even taking a flight reminds me of Connie. It scares me and makes me upset, and immediately my heart tells me no. Finally,

I don't even think of going. Her unbearable absence stops me from going anywhere. The only place where I can go is to see my elder brother and his family in India. But even that has become upsetting—to leave our home, her chair, her table, her computer, her walker, her oxygen, her study room, and all the rest. Even leaving the car and the garage is hard. How much pain I have to face and will always have to keep facing. Repeating this is not good writing, but it has a soothing yet painful effect on me. I never want to stop saying the same message. For someone in my situation, or perhaps for someone who has not fallen in true love, perhaps this book may give some solace. At that time, you may forgive me that this book was no good, and you might appreciate the depth of our love. Leaving home to go to India is unbearable. My mind tells me I should forget going anywhere. Home becomes my favorite place to stay. I had mentioned this earlier, before I diverted completely into painful memories of our traveling together.

Thoughts of Connie and her memory shake me. My mind is thinking of the most painful episode I went through, and I start wondering if it is true that Connie is gone. Again, I block my mind and want to believe Connie is in her study. I totally forget that events like her cremation, the chapel of peace ceremony, and the interment of her ashes in her plot next to her parents were all performed—by me. I wonder how I could do all of that. Is it true that I was brave enough to do all that? The answer is that my love and God gave me the strength to do it. My shock and pain were due to the deepest love. I had never gone through that painful episode of losing someone, losing my wife and my world. I was upset and in deep pain. However, I could not bear the pain of knowing that Connie's body was in a funeral home. My wife was not a charity case, and I wanted to have her cremation and burial done immediately.

I am again repeating this episode many times; it is due to my constantly thinking about Connie, and due to the deep love that I have lost. Even after nine months of living in pain and suffering, nothing has changed. The saying that time heals pain has no truth; rather, my suffering increases. One common saying is that any incident of some fall, cut, or little burn looks like it is fine, but its effect is worse the next day. I am giving one instance, though I have seen many painful events. One of my uncles died at a very young age. My aunt was grieving very hard. Her mother-in-law's sister said to her, "Right now, you are surrounded by lots of family members and friends. Once they go to their homes, you will have to bear this loss and pain by yourself." Connie's fall, the ambulance taking her for a checkup at the hospital, and staying with the hope of coming back the same day or the next day was painful. The happiness of coming home on February 22, 2015 was tolerable. However, the evening before her cardiac arrest absolutely shook me. Her lying on the hospital bed with tubes in her mouth was unbearable, fighting at the time for her tubes was painful for me, and taking the tubes out shook me each minute. Her demise broke me down completely. I don't know how I could handle all that. Later, her cremation and the interment of her ashes in her plot was another trauma. That trauma still haunts me after nine months. At that time of great shock and pain, I had to ensure the best cremation and select the best of caskets and urns, along with talking to a priest about the services. My mind was occupied, and that pain took a different direction to do many things. After all that, a different kind of pain took over as I began to do the legal work, and so many things occupied my mind and life. This pain definitely came in different waves. I haven't had that experience before. My priorities were to ensure that she had the world's best funeral. I know that was done.

I am writing about Connie's demise and the whole episode again and again. There are two reasons. First, it's my pain. Second, that is how the human brain works, and how many new brain cells that are not used open up. God has given us billions and billions of brain cells, but on the average, we don't use half of them. I would say, at least for me, that new brain cells opened, and some of the cells I was using, I now feel I am no longer using. This is a new segment of my life, and our relationship is making me write all these things. I still have no answer for this, and I doubt if I would ever find the answer.

Today, April 27, 2016, I was coming back on the train at rush hour, when so many people travel to go home from work. I especially wanted to observe the younger generation in their twenties and thirties; some were working, and some were students. It was extremely soothing to see them with their smart phones and earphones. All of them were busy with their phones, which is happening now in many countries, both developed and underdeveloped. I saw the same in Delhi, in the two times I have been back since Connie's death. Honestly, gong to Delhi was nice, but it brings me painful memories of Connie.

From the 1970s to the 1990s, traveling on the train was different. Most of the middle and senior management people were nicely dressed in suits and ties while reading papers; it was a half hour of leisure for them. Offices opened at 8:15 a.m., and after reaching the office, the senior managers would have the same newspapers in the office. It was mandatory to read those papers to find out about business news and to research market shares, the strategic planning of companies, and the ratings of Fortune 500 companies. All of that was like a PhD student's workload, in addition to the fifty to sixty hours per week that they worked. I did very well. It was a very happy life, working and sometimes spending 80 percent of my workday traveling, staying in top hotels and living off of the company expenses. I used to think that I was a king and was happy because Connie was also a professional and had to leave by 7:15 a.m. to be at colleges and schools where she taught Spanish and French. Punctuality was a must for her. For me, with the amount of traveling I did, if I was a few minutes late, that would be mitigated by my work. I used to work sixteen hours a day when I traveled, and many of my juniors would say, "Pradeep, it is 5:00 p.m. You are leaving early? What a good life. You enjoy your easy independence. No one is there to say anything to you. We have to work another hour, but you get to leave early." This was a very sarcastic remark, and it used to make me mad.

I used to tell them, "You sit on your rear ends the whole day, doing nothing, and you take a two-hour lunch. Your productivity is zero, and that is why you have to stay long hours. Why don't you work hard from eight fifteen to five, and cut your personal phone calls and lunches? I wish I could get rid of you, because you are a burden on the payroll and get paid for doing nothing." I hated those sarcastic comments. Later, senior management was informed of this, because they kept track of the efficiency and productivity of their employees Our chairman started firing the unproductive employees. He openly told me he wanted the best employees, and five professional development courses were required to stay there, in the largest worldwide finance company. There was a lot of hard work, but there were many awards and rewards in return. Our motto was, "We are playing to win." That became my theme: I wanted to be a winner at any cost. Connie was a winner, because she was teaching, and at that time there was much less political rivalry and jealousy in education. One of the reasons is that the economy was good; unemployment was very low compared to today's 10 percent unemployment rate. I would say that the rate is worse than that, because many people have stopped working and cannot find jobs, and unemployment benefits beyond forty-eight weeks are not available. As such, those are not part of the census, and therefore the figure is distorted.

I would say that when Connie and I were in senior positions at work, this was the best time of our lives. We had no cell phones and no computers until 1988, although we both became experts at computers and smart phones. "Necessity is the mother of invention." That was the life I had with Connie. Now, I feel I am lost in an unknown world without her. I find her in our sweet home, because she is still with me. All these forgotten things have come to my new eyes and new brain after going through the traumatic period that began in April 2013.

In 1998, she contracted PRP. Her immune system was weak with the stress of PRP. I am distant from my old friends, and I keep myself busy the whole day by writing this book, doing household work, and taking care of some legal things after Connie's death, including the cancelation of many magazines and other things. I have many other errands I have to sort out, and it's an unbelievable busy life in the absence of Connie. I have realized how much work my career-oriented Connie did; she was an excellent wife. She was good at, teaching, household work, shopping, grocery, laundry, ironing, buying clothes, scheduling car service, looking after her parents, doing volunteer work, cooking. She was not my slave; I helped her in many other ways, cooking Indian food, serving her, shopping with her or alone, and picking up her things. We used to go together wherever we went. After I left my senior management consulting, Connie took early retirement to travel the world, including cruises in Norway. Denmark,

Budapest, Amsterdam, France, Germany, the Black Mountains, Spain, Morocco, Alaska, Santa Fe, the French Quarter, Palm Springs, California, Wisconsin, Michigan, and India. We went to Broadway shows, Mozart symphonies, movies, theaters, and fine dining.

Connie Was Efficient in Everything

Connie was so efficient in each and every thing, whether at home, grocery shopping, taking care of the laundry, ironing, or keeping our clothes properly folded. She was also efficient at accounting and keeping inventory of the house, including our clothing, silver, furniture, paintings, crystal, glasses and other kitchen wares, carpets, and more. She was very particular about the cleaning of the house, ensuring that the carpets were regularly cleaned, the table was polished, and the oven and granite counters were cleaned. She kept track of our monthly expenses of food with receipts, house assessment, electric bills, telephone, and Internet. She also compared television and Internet bills for accuracy. By doing this, she saved us lots of money when the company billed us the wrong amount. She used to cut coupons from every Sunday newspaper to save our hard-earned money. I am convinced that due to these habits, she must have saved over thirty thousand dollars in forty years. It was not that she was miserly or cheap. She was conservative, and the money she saved was used for shopping, traveling, dining out, or whatever. This habit of hers also made me save money when I did shopping for her, for the house, and for myself.

Today, I can still do all of these things, but I am heartbroken and don't shop much; neither do I care about money. Her demise has taken away all these qualities. I get lost again and again about these things, and the pain brings back memories of everything. I will keep repeating all of this about Connie and her qualities. I have taken her demise very hard. I don't think I will see a ray of happiness.

Our karma reminds me of Connie's many great deeds, and mine too.

In March 1993, my Uncle Behl told me that I should come back to India to handle his pharmaceutical companies and four charitable hospitals, provided that Connie agreed. It was a great opportunity for me, however I was confused about it. Connie told me that she could try living six months in India and six months in the United States, to look after her mother. Although we both were ready to sacrifice for each other, it was a difficult decision to make. Finally, I went back to the United States and was promoted to a very senior position. I hired many employees, and they had to be trained because they had little experience in my field. It was a great challenge, and there were times I regretted passing on my uncle's opportunity. But later, it worked out well for over five years.

At that time, one employee didn't have the minimum experience of fifteen years, but I trained him well in the most basic work in less than four years. In this way, I was able to help him, his wife, and their children. After almost four years, he decided to apply for the same kind of a position, but earning a few thousand dollars per year more. I advised him not to go and to spend more time to learn from me, but he was sure that he knew everything. I could have given him more money, but I didn't because I had to train him again. He left his position with me for a few thousand dollars, and I told him that he was not trained and a few thousand dollars might not be worth the experience he would lose. Afterward, he was always in touch with me and Connie. Connie always told me, "Pradeep, you are a very kind man and are always willing to help others. That is a good thing. However, I hate to interfere in your feelings, but many people take advantage of your soft heart. You have been hurt so many times, so think before you try to do good. These people are users and call when they need your help." I knew Connie was right, but I was still the same.

Now, after the demise of Connie, I realized all that and am extremely angry that people, friends, and relatives have betrayed me. Connie is not there anymore to see how correct and smart she was, and I didn't take her advice seriously. I must admit now that I am changed, and I will not allow people to take advantage of my soft heart or the fact that I am always ready to please them. I never want to see those ungrateful people and users. Connie's demise has shattered me and changed my happiness, and to some degree I'm an angry man, except toward my brother and his family, and some unknown people. I would always be nice and helpful to outsiders.

I spent Christmas and Thanksgiving alone in 2015 for the first time in the forty-two years I have lived in the United States.

Connie Was My Destiny, Like a True Episode on the TV Program Wanted

In memory of my Connie, there was an excellent weekly TV show twenty years ago, *Wanted*. Connie and I always watched this program. The program requested the audience inform the FBI if anyone had seen or had knowledge of the featured hardcore criminals. The journalist used to ask that if a viewer had a clue about them, to please inform the FBI via the phone number provided. One of the programs was very touching and applies to my life. My entire career and its advancement are due to one person, and that is my beautiful wife and friend of forty-one years, my Connie.

The program was about a successful businessman in his late forties. This man, when he was about eleven years old, lost his way and didn't know what to do or how to survive. The same kid was weeping on the TV and had been looking for the man who'd encouraged this kid to remain in the United States and given him an American gal and one dollar in order to explore America and find his fate in the land of opportunity. The kid, after finding success, was looking for the man to meet him and say thanks, and to serve him as his father and his family for any help. The businessman would do anything for him because the man was the person who'd encouraged him to go to the United States. He was weeping and saying, "Please let me know if you recognized this picture of him." The search was being funded by his own money. The boy wanted to thank this person, who he said was not a man but a god for his support.

Connie was amazing to my start in the United States. She was everything for me and for my success. Connie was my best destiny, and she was instrumental to my success. I want to share many incidences that will add to my faith that Connie was my destiny and my life. That is why I was not interested in marriage in India. I was engaged three times by my parents without my permission and my knowledge—and without meeting the girls. This was the way the marriages were conducted back in India. However, things have changed, and now there are mostly marriages for love. I am sure some arranged marriages do take place, but I do not think that is the right way.

The following section includes e-mail messages I have exchanged with friends, family, and organizations.

From the Carleton Alumni Network, Alumni Farewells:

Constance (Fuller) Berry

* September 4, 2015, 2:12 a.m.

I don't know where to start and where to end. I can write and write, but it is no ending story of true love. Yes, I am Pradeep Berry, husband of over 39 years of my most precious, best friend and darling wife, Mrs. Constance Berry (Connie)—Constance Fuller when she graduated. I had the opportunity to visit with Connie at Carleton, I would say six years ago, during her Alumni. I truly enjoyed and the food, and the lectures were great. My Connie's demised on February 28, 2015, was not expected. I wish, in my opinion, she had listened to me to go for another opinion in another hospital in the USA. However, it was too late. My life has changed since then. I don't know what I am going to do without Connie. She was everything for me. We were two bodies and one soul. I pray to the mighty Lord we'll meet again in our next lives, as the same loving couple. "Connie and Pradeep." This hope is giving me the power to live and fulfill the desires of Connie; though physically she is not with me, in a spiritual way she is with me and watching over me. I am also writing a biography for darling Connie and would do my best to bring many parts of our lives, while giving some great quotes from many world scholars and their quotes. I just feel like talking and talking about Connie, which gives me the most power. I could never have imagined I would go through such pain, as I know very well that we all have to go one day. God exists all the time, but human beings and animals have to go. However, when it comes to me and the loss of some special person, knowledge vanishes. I am only quoting this for myself, as each person handles things in their own way. But I have to bear this no ending pain all the time. I pray Connie to give me the power to bear this loss. I can realize the pain of the king who made the wonder of the world Taj Mahal in memory of his wife, Mumtaz Mahel, as she had asked him to build a special monument in her memory, 'so that the world can remember their love."

Pradeep Berry, Loving Husband

September 29, 2015
Dear Mr. [Name Withheld]

I had been reading your articles. I am writing for my darling wife of forty years, Mrs. Constance Ann Berry, a graduate of Carleton and the University of Michigan, with a master's in Spanish and French. The diamond in my life was born in the USA. She was American, highly intellectual, a great reader, and more. We were two bodies and one soul. I should finish with the book in a couple of months.

Thanks.
Sincerely,
Pradeep Berry

Many Tributes for Connie from Our Neighbors

Dear [Name Withheld]

Thanks for coming to the peace ceremony of my darling wife of over 40 years, Connie. I am absolutely at a great loss without her, and she was most important part of my life and would remain that way. I miss and miss her all the times—day and night. I used to go to India for two weeks every year, but I haven't gone since 2011. I was in a different mood then. Now, I am planning to go to see my brother and his family and other family members this weekend for two months, depending upon how I feel. I have not told any of my relatives in India or in the USA about her demise, as I took her death very hard. The only person I told is my elder brother. I have been busy sorting out many things; how the mighty Lord gave me the strength, I don't know. I have to find a way to cope up this never-ending loss. Connie had always thought very high of you. She went suddenly from my life, leaving me alone. I can't believe or imagine. Thanks for your time and support.

Sincerely,
Pradeep

Dear Pradeep,

Thank you so much for this note. It was an honor to attend the service for Connie; I always had such high esteem for her. From the time I moved into this building, she was a source of good sense, good humor, infinite practicality, and kindness. This building overall would have been a much worse place were it not for her, not only in terms of her leadership for all those years, but also in terms of her radiant goodwill. She was truly what the biblical phrase calls "salt of the earth." We all were lucky to have her, but you most of all, of course. Never having been married, I can only imagine what you're going through in terms of the loss you feel at every moment. But I do know from having watched friends and family members move through grief that you *will* get through it. Things will become easier, and you'll be able to let go of things gradually. But grief has its own schedule with every single person; there's no timetable. I am very glad you're going to India, and for such a long time. It will truly give you time and space apart to breathe, to be, to consider what life might hold for you in its very different form now. And you'll be with your brother, another thing about which I'm glad. If I may presume to say so, a person can't do all of this alone. We're put here to lean on and help each other; let your family do that. You deserve to be supported right now.

Take this time for yourself. You have spent years devoting your time to Connie, which of course was the best and the right thing to do, but now the caregiver needs some care.

Godspeed, Pradeep. I hope that when I see you next, you will be refreshed and will have found a measure of peace.

[Name Withheld]

From [Name Withheld]

I pray that the frustration and anger over the bad memories of Connie's care heal, Pradeep. They will only weigh you down. Connie had such a long, beautiful life, Pradeep. I've forgotten how many cancers she survived and all the suffering she experienced, yet kept pulling herself up.

[Name Withheld]

Thanks for your kind words. Yes, you are right: I didn't want to be social anymore, and I wanted all my time with Connie. I was happy if someone wanted to come see Connie and be there for hospitality. Her one friend used to visit every two weeks. I used to serve her cookies and pastries from the bakery, and I'd make different kinds of milkshakes. All these things gave me happiness. As long as we were together, I was happy. When I went to India in May 2015 for a little change, as an American citizen I was invited to the US embassy to celebrate July 4. The program was extremely wonderful, but I was thinking of Connie. There were over one thousand US citizens and their families. There was an honor guard, a band, food, drinks, singers, dancing, fireworks, rides, and things for the kids. They don't allow anyone but US citizens. I talked to the US staff, and Indians were working there, as well as the food preparation people. They don't allow any food from outside. Everyone has to pay for the entrance and food. The Delhi police and military security were there. Diplomatic people live like lords, and there were US tourists, as well as students on exchange programs.

It was nice, but with Connie's absence, I was very depressed and thinking wish she was with me to have a better time; it would have been gold. I will tell you more about it when I get back on July 23. Thanks for your kind words and phrases. Anything you want me to bring? Don't hesitate.

Pradeep

[Name Withheld]

Trust you and your family are doing well. I have been thinking about you for a while, but just didn't write. It is hot, and I stay mostly in the house in air conditioning. I do go to some places, if my brother and his son are going. They offer me to take anywhere I want to go, but I don't think I have a great desire to do much nor. Neither I want to meet anyone, like I used to when Connie was alive. In fact, regarding some of my other family and friends, I don't want to meet them. I am happy with my brother's family, including his two boys, Mona, and the girls. I am waiting to come back to my home, knowing that Connie is not there, but still her lovely decorative place gives me both happiness and unhappiness. Also, going to her cemetery gives me the same mixed feelings. I have practically lost my charm of doing, going, and meeting friends. I am happy meeting people like you, outsiders, like the funeral home ladies who helped me for the cremation.

Dear Pradeep,

It would be presumptuous to say I know your pain. Only the person who is experiencing it knows its depth. Yes, it will be difficult for you to return because you had been so very busy at the time Connie died (making arrangements, taking care of business). Then, you had her with you. Next, you had Mona and the girls with you. Then you went to India. Constant movement. When you return, everything will stand still for you, and you will have to be strong. You will have to lean more than ever on your God. You already know that. Pray for direction. Pray for the right people to be presented to you in your life. Prepare first to feel the grief here, all alone. But if you ask God for direction, you will be led to the right people, places, and things to help you move forward.

Again, Pradeep, I can only say that we are alone in our grief. We can feel alone in a crowd. You will get through this. You will not "get over" it, but you will be able to live a full life with Connie at your side in a different way. You are not giving her up.

Give my love to Mona. She is such a lovely lady and such a good mother. Please don't worry about bringing anything back for me, Pradeep.

Take care of yourself.
[Name Withheld]

You were and still are such an exceptional husband, Pradeep. Not too many women are given that gift. You, Pradeep, will someday have your own spring, your own eternity. For now, all you can do is remember Connie in your heart … in your dreams. She is with you. Talk to her as if she were standing next to you. Now she is all-wise, all-knowing; she can read your mind and your heart without you ever speaking words. They know us more than they did when they were with us.

Take care, Pradeep.
[Name Withheld]

Thanks for your kind words and phrases. I renewed Connie's account, which perhaps I had canceled as I had no desire to read, watch TV, and look at other magazines, and I was still paying for the TV. They billed me saying they would put a hold, but they charged the whole amount and are doing the same thing. The *Consumer Report* person was very nice, and he renewed Connie and yours, and due to the circumstances, he was touched and was charging me less than the regular prize.

Upon Connie's wishes, he gave a great price for you also, and now I will get it till January, and you too I think, when yours is expired. So you will keep getting it, and I would be happy to read on her behalf. [Name Withheld] would still be in the picture and certificate you will have to take, I can tell you, no matter if you say no.

I might leave on October 20, 2015 and, I was thinking of one month or five weeks, but then I made the reservation for December 24. This is due to the fact that I am using my miles, and they have little inventory, but I will keep checking to see if they come early. Please suggest something to me; I am going for a long time. Two things I feel it is long for you to do the things. Second, I would be thinking of Connie's house: she is gone, and the home is alone. I am missing her chairs, her computer, her room, her pictures, and her cemetery, where I go quite often. In fact, I am writing this from the cemetery. Regarding India attractions, I want to see my brother and his family and Grandnieces. However, I can try to come early if I am missing Connie, her rooms, and our home. How much my life and mind have changed due to Connie. I am writing her biography and want to finish at the earliest. I never thought I would be so much upset and suffer pain for the loss of Connie.

[Name Withheld]

Thanks a lot for your kind words and phrases, and I am extremely great full to you for your kindness. Yes, I am truly going through a series of pain and suffering due to my wife of forty-one years dying, and I will be not happy with any of my friends and relatives. Though it may be a temporary diversion of my mind, after that I would be the same. I don't enjoy anything and stopped eating at the super restaurants and traveling. I just make simple food to survive, and that is all. I have no desire to travel like we were doing it. I was the happiest person who has now become totally different. I don't buy anymore that God had a different purpose, and I ask God what bad I did or she did, except helping others and attending the good and bad events of all. I will be happy when her biography is written, but sadness will still be there However, I truly admire your passion for me, and I will try to follow your suggestion.

Thanks,
Pradeep

From: [Name Withheld]
September 19, 2015
Good Day, Sir Pradeep K. Berry,

I am the guy you spoke with earlier over the phone. I decided to send you a message today because I am so worried about your condition, and I really wanted to show my deepest sympathy for the death of your wife. I hope that you will be okay soon and be strong. Remember that God has a purpose for all the things happening in our lives.

I know for certain that we never lose the people we love, even to death.

They continue to participate in every act, thought and decision we make.

Their love leaves an indelible imprint in our memories.

We find comfort in knowing that our lives have been enriched by having shared their love.

—Leo Buscaglia

Return to Alumni Farewells Comments

September 2015
Mona Berry,

I have no words to describe her personality. As much I knew her, she was a wonderful person, full of life, who wanted to explore the whole world, was a dedicated wife. Her farsightedness, and her way to judge, no one can be like her. We all are missing you, Aunty Connie. We have lost a gem of our family.

Constance (Fuller) Berry,

I have no words to describe her personality. As much I knew her, she was …

Thanks for your kind words and phrases and advice about Connie. You are not to feel guilty for your dedication to Connie's memories, nor to continue grieving, Pradeep. It's such a tribute to Connie that your love continues.

Thanks for your kind words and support. I would say once a week, and if it is not too much for you, you can come over and I can show you. Also, I want you to see the collage pictures and other things, I have put together. I love them and I would like you to see the beginning of our forty-one years of marriage pictures, and some in between. I would like to put more later on. That gives happiness and sadness. I therefore live in two worlds, happy and sad. I can't take Connie out from my mind, and neither do I want to believe she is no longer with me. Please let me know if the plants, etc. are too much due to your health. I want you to be frank because your health is first. My flight so far is on the twentieth. If you want any other magazine, please let me know. I would like you to see those pictures and a very rare thing, *Thanka*, which Connie bought thirty-five years ago from India. That was one of her favorite paintings but she wanted to frame it and find a place to hang. I got the framework done over here and asked someone to hang it, along with other pictures. You could suggest if I should try to hang *Thanka* somewhere else. Connie would not have allowed me to hang in the living room. So whenever you have time, come over. Please take care of your health and fitness.

Regards,
Pradeep

Thank you for all your trouble, Pradeep. It's the small things that make some people happy. Hope your trip arrangements are going smoothly.

[Name Withheld]

Hello Pradeep,

What a lovely idea. I think it will be a wonderful, and therapeutic, thing for you to write about your cherished life with dear Connie. Such a dynamic, well-rounded, thoughtful, and humane person should be memorialized in writing. And you, who knew her best of all, are the perfect person to put her into words. I'm so sorry for your pain. I miss Connie, as I'm sure several of us in the building do. Her intelligent, benevolent presence leaves a great void.

Pradeep, I hope this is of at least a little aid.

Please take care of yourself.
[Name Withheld]

Dear [Name Withheld]

It was in my mind for some time that I talk to you. I am writing a biography about Connie and bringing out our love destiny, true love, and quotes from the world's scholars, going back to 520 BC. I discuss the painful end, my suffering, her education, reading, love for world travel, our house that was her life, the best restaurants and food, our experience of travel, some true episodes, and some of her best things she always remembered. I mention her role as a wife, best friend, sister, and mother, with evidence of this written in India centuries ago. I bring up books with proof, messages from Gandhi, Nelson Mandela, and Martin Luther King Jr. Some of the other experience include the Broadway shows, Las Vegas shows, Mozart and Vienna, her character, her charity, her contributions in exposing me to US culture forty-one years ago, and so many things under different headings.

I was wondering if you know someone who can proofread and edit his, giving a second eye. I have great respect for you, and Connie was happy for your personality as a team player. Hope you are doing well. It is 7:00 a.m. People are going to work, and I am going to sleep. How life has changed for me without Connie, who meant the world to me. I am truly living in the pain and the trauma. I was in the hospital from February 20–28, 2015, and had lived on three to four hours' sleep. I don't know how I was able to do all that. More later.

Thanks,
Pradeep.

[Name Withheld],

Trust you and your family are doing well. I also hope your knee is better and better. I am doing well with my family and family, going to the market just to pass time. I do go to gym for one hour, as there is no indoor swimming pool. I am also getting pain in my legs, which started on May 22, and when I came from India on July 23, I saw a few doctors and went for physical therapy.

How is everything in the building and our apartment? Connie always remains in my heart and soul all the time, and I can't believe that she is not more with me. I would never be able to forget Connie, who was my world and precious diamond. I am writing a biography, but it has been slow. I am going to spend four to five hours daily. I was writing the whole day, sometimes till 6:00 a.m. in the USA. I have to proofread and edit again and again. Please be in touch.

Pradeep

Dear [Name Withheld],

Trust you are doing well. My name is Pradeep Berry, and I am the husband of my darling wife and best friend, Constance Berry (Constance Fuller before marriage), a graduate of Carleton College in Minnesota and the University of Michigan. Constance and I were married for over forty-one years. We were two bodies and one soul. We had been getting messages from the University of Michigan for forty-one years and have taken many trips with the University of Michigan alumni. To name some, Crotona, Tuscany, Ireland, Budapest, and Amsterdam. Later, we cruised with Vantage to Norway and Europe.

It breaks my heart and soul to inform you and the university that Connie, my world, expired unexpectedly. Later, after many painful episodes and a series of traumatic things she and I went through, I think about her every movement of my day. I lost my battle and saw my wife taking her last four breaths, and I could not do anything. I have lost my life and don't think I will do anything, including travel, dining, symphony, Broadway shows, and Oscar-winning movies, to name some.

Finally, I would like to be connected with the University of Michigan. She left money for Carleton and the University of Michigan. I would like to continue sending some small donations. I left a very high-powered senior management position in 2005 for my darling and never looked back. Connie wanted to enjoy life and travel more and more. We truly enjoyed whatever Connie wanted. Having said all that, we had been working and traveling to the United States, India, Europe, Alaska, and the Caribbean. In our forty-one years of marriage, we were both extremely happy. I wrote this long as a part of tribute to Connie.

Thanks,
Pradeep Berry

Thank you, Mr. Berry, for the e-mail and information. I have made progress on reviewing the records and expect to be finished by the end of the week, and I will reach out to you then. Please feel free to provide me any additional information in the interim. Thanks again.

I miss all but would not go and remember that with pain, as Connie is not with me physically. I would put all in her biography, including the following: seven trips to India, our ten-thousand-year civilization, Lord Krishna, Chanakya in 520 BC, Egypt, mummies, many world scholars, Nelson Mandela, Gandhi, Dr. Martin Luther King Jr., her favorite music, our happiness, and being two bodies and one soul. Her clothing, her shoes, her walker, oxygen, her house that I want spotless. I am going to have a cleaning girl here for hours weekly, I want to do things that used to make Connie happy I go to her cemetery every week, or twice a week.

[Name Withheld],

Thanks for your kind words of wisdom and the prompt response. The reason I wrote for the 27th was Krishna's birthday is on the 26th, and she was keen. However, Mona decided that they can have a party on the 10th, and she has no problem if I leave on the 12th. I have confirmed seats on the 12th and can change for the 27th. I am not worried about Christmas, and I would not mind being alone. After all, I have to come either the 12th or 27th. Regardless, I miss Connie's empty room, her cemetery, and our home. I am not doing a whole lot, even if I am busy with kids and in the market. Still, I am not in a mood. I didn't want to go for two days, whether I would have to bear it on the 12th or 27th. Again, I would not feel lonely during holidays. I am lonely to some extent here too. I am writing her biography, and I have to find a proofreader and to do the editing. I would be happy, if you desire to do so. I don't want to hurt you, but I definitely would like to pay for that. I strongly mean that. Please don't get me wrong or feel hurt about that.

Maybe in one or two months. I didn't get a lot of chances to do it here due to the other things, like going out with my brother and talking with my family. After all, they want me to spend time with them. Thanks for your kind words and phrases, and your time.

Regards,
Pradeep

Pradeep,

Your coming home on the 27th doesn't affect me. The weather has turned snowy and very cold these last two days. It's supposed to warm up for Thanksgiving.

Perhaps you should research what the weather will be like in this area for the winter. At the same time, you will be able to get an idea of what the weather would be like when your plane arrives here. It's such a shock to leave warm weather and walk off the plane into drifts of snow!

For no other reason, you can escape bad weather for those two extra weeks. Winter is long and depressing here.

[Name Withheld]

P.S., I just realized, Pradeep, Christmas here will be very lonely for you. Even if you are not in the mood for Christmas, if you are here alone, you will feel all the gaiety and joy around you of other families and on the TV shows blasting Christmas music. I never tell people what to do, Pradeep, so it's surprising I'm going to say this: You should return on the 27th and remain there for the holidays. Oh, I just realized—perhaps a trip will be difficult to plan if people are coming and going on flights for Christmas, and then again for New Year's Day. That's a hectic time for travel. You need to research this too.

[Name Withheld]

It is 6:00 a.m., and I was busy, so I will be brief. If I come on December 27 rather than December 12, would there be any problem? I sometimes don't think I can stay longer than the 12th because I miss Connie, our house, and everything. But still, I thought if you have any questions or suggestions …? In a way, the 27th looks long compared to the 12th, and I may stick to the 12th. However, I hope you are doing well, and good luck with your own home and family, and your health.

Thanks, Pradeep

Enjoy the remainder of your stay, Pradeep. I assume you don't have any holiday in India on our Thanksgiving Day (11/26), which pertains to a part of the history of America. It must be difficult having "a foot in two countries."

Hi XB,

Thanks for your reply and its contents. Regarding Thanksgiving, you are absolutely right. India never celebrates, and most people don't know about it. Thanksgiving was an extremely important part of my forty-one years of marriage with Connie. It was so great. Connie and I always celebrated every year. Practically every year, Connie used to have Thanksgiving and Easter with great style, silver plates, cranberry sauce, mashed potatoes, broccoli, rice, snacks of many kinds, turkey filling on the barbeque, drinks, and three kind of desserts. We had banana cream pie, pumpkin pie, and nutmeg pie (special only on Thanksgiving). Connie used to make everything from the scratch, and it was perfect and absolutely selective. There used to be over twenty family members, and Connie used to cook. We used to go to people's houses, including her parents and her one sibling's family. I would say those were golden days. I used to help Connie with the whole table setup, wine, whiskey, snacks—you name it, I was there.

I know we were happy when we were overjoyed, and Connie did an excellent job in renovating and furniture. Later, we started going out to Prairie Grass in Northbrook, and three to four times we took S. Prairie Grass has an excellent Thanksgiving special, but it's little expensive. In January 2011, we bought the garage We were happy to have a garage, especially for Connie. I had promised Connie I would definitely make sure she had a garage, and we were looking for different houses. But my words came true, and we got the garage. After coming back from Sanibel in 2012 and in August 2012, we bought a new car, and a garage was there for Connie's Toyota Camry. I started parking inside the garage we were renting from P. After buying the car, Connie drove the Lexus for fifteen minutes when we went to Lake Geneva to try a Lexus. I encouraged Connie and said, "I would do anything to make you happy."

After Connie's mother died in August 2006, Connie and I arranged all the last rites, and Connie paid quite a lot for her share for the last rites, along with her one sibling. I gave my tributes to her mother, and Connie was very happy that I gave wonderful tributes to her mother. I bet it was nothing but great, and Connie and I used to work days, nights, and weekends to do a perfect job.

I am missing Connie. For Thanksgiving and now Christmas, regardless of where I am and would live, I'm in pain when I think of these two holidays. I would enjoy it in my house, alone with her pictures and candles, and I'd go to the cemetery. Mona gave that advice to me today. I must say that for Thanksgiving and Christmas, I was always with Connie. Last Thanksgiving, I made a good dinner for her at home. For Christmas, I bought some nice things and cakes. No matter what it was, being with Connie every moment in her room, movie watching, reading, and just being with her, just next to her, next to her in the car, next to sit in the kitchen, taking her to the hospital, carrying her to the wheelchair, taking her wheelchair to bathroom in the hospital, giving a shower to Connie, taking her to her room. Filling her water in the morning and afternoon and night, her green glass on kitchen table; you can see water there and in her room, in the bedroom, which I am still doing and will keep on doing. I'm praying for her three to four times, sleeping with her pictures in my home, in India, in my bedroom. I'm full of her pictures everywhere and go anywhere with her pictures in my pocket. Her ashes are still in our house in urns. (Though according to Hindu religion, ashes have to disbursed, I took a little in the urn from the funeral home, in two beautiful urns.) I used to pray to those in our house because they are sealed and cannot be opened. I pray to them and feel closer, but I still live in pain. I am writing all the family about our episodes: hospitals, our love, our education, her qualities, her love for cooking and traveling, books, magazines, charity, and Sanibel. I have cut down going out, and I'm not traveling or spending on clothes. Anything Connie wanted, I would do that, but I would live very simple. Now Connie is gone, and that is how I am going to go through my life. The most difficult period and painful part of my life.

M,

Thanks for your nice compliments about our marriage and, most important, Connie. I truly can't describe Connie's beauties along with all the great qualities, knowledge, and responsibility in every aspect. I can't find any fault whatsoever. "People who think they knew Connie did not know Connie. People who knew her can't describe Connie." This quote will be in my book. Thanksgiving and Christmas were extremely important in our lives, and so were Easter and many other things. Now, I will not enjoy any of these things. Marriage is never going to happen; no way can I think of that. Connie was Connie.

If God gives me my Connie again, I will be more than a king. It will end all my sorrows. But I can't have that unless God personally makes it happen. I know I am dreaming, but sometimes dreams and God's blessing upon seeing one's devotion can happen. It may be Connie as a wife, sister, mother, or father. I would accept her in any form, as long as it's her face and her voice and the qualities she had.

I think my mind is that I want to be there on Christmas and will put flowers on her cemetery, as I did one day before going to India. It was pitch dark at six thirty, but I managed with my cell phone and a flashlight app you can download free from Google. You would like it; they are great. Later, I brought the car and turned on the lights. Peace of mind and sadness is what I get, but I still like to go for my happiness. Connie's brother and his whole family of sixteen people have never visited Connie's parents' gravesites, which is next to Connie. Pradeep Berry is the only person Connie can expect to visit, and I like to do so with great pleasure and happiness. I become upset if I don't go there once or twice a week.

You do give me great advice about how to get over this most painful thing of my life, but it may not be able to treat the problem soon. I showed your e-mail to [name withheld].

Sincerely,
Pradeep

Very few people have those type of memories. So many couples struggle with their partners and marriages. You were both so blessed, Pradeep. Such a wonderful life.

[Name Withheld]

I envy Connie her skills. I was never a great cook or hostess, although when the kids were being raised and my husband was alive, I did have family over. It was a struggle for me—even to this day. I burn things and am a bundle of nerves. You were blessed to have Connie create such a beautiful ambiance for those times.

Please don't feel badly that you gave me much of the story at length; it is so healthy to vent and let things out, Pradeep. You painted a beautiful picture of all Connie created in your lives. Keep hope within you that when your grief lifts, good things may come to you. Don't say no, because I have seen it in my own family's lives. I will say good night, Pradeep.

[Name Withheld]

Pradeep,

Thanks again for calling last week, and it was great to hear from you. I'm so happy that you and Connie are doing well, and in particular that you're now engaged with teaching and writing. And happy belated seventieth birthday last July 29!

I'll be happy to share with you my thoughts and observations regarding yourself and Connie as you requested; please also let me know more specifically what might be helpful. What I've largely observed is that you've been an exceptionally devoted and close couple. This is all the more remarkable with you being from India and not having your immediate family here, your heavy job-related travel commitments, and Connie's health issues in more recent years. But you've managed to maintain a close and enduring bond through it all for forty years. Altogether, your closeness as a couple is what I aspire to for myself.

I've been most recently busy working as a credit and portfolio manager in commercial lending at a $700 million New York–based thrift headquartered in the Bronx. The bank, historically as a thrift, has been principally engaged in residential and commercial mortgages, but it was recently expanded into commercial lending, including ABL and SBA loans. I've been pleased to continue to work in banking and advance my career here in New York, especially because I turn sixty in January, and it gets harder as one gets older. And as I've said, as much as a I miss seeing people such as you in Chicago, to whom I was close, I've benefited on balance being where I have better opportunities.

The biggest event in my life is meeting and marrying on Saturday, November 26, in Great Neck, New York, a special woman, Karen Ferrare. Karen is an attorney who was born in Brooklyn and grew up in Long Island. Karen is previously married with no children. This will be my third and final wedding in life, and my final shot at complete happiness. We've been together for over a year and have shared an apartment on Manhattan's Upper East Side since early June. You and Connie are cordially invited, and please give me your address for an invitation. Please also feel free to visit us at any time. As you know, there's always so much in do and see in the Big Apple.

I plan on coming back to Chicago next spring but have too much going on till then. In the meantime, let's be sure to continue to stay in touch, and I hope to see you in November for my wedding.

Ed Muller, Senior VP, Banking, New York

Dear Ed,

I am very grateful to you for your sincere compliments, and I know you mean this. I have known you since 1993, and we have been close friends. The time we spent at ABL consulting was one of the better times. Connie is Connie. I truly mean that. I have never seen another person like Connie. I am writing this from the core of the heart. My Connie is absolutely special. You recall going with Connie and me to Monticello, Indiana, for the company in my white Toyota in 1994 or 1995? A small town, and I recall you going to the library there. How much love was developed with Victoria, and how much fun was that? Then there's the time you came to Sanibel, and we took you to Captiva and had grouper, fresh lemon pie. The drive was beautiful, and we had a two-bedroom condominium. We asked you to stay with us, but you had to go to work on Monday. Those memories are good and bad, but the reality is there. People avoid good or bad past, but I think it is nice to remember and share with those people. I am going to thank you again, and Connie is very appreciative of what we are doing. Thanks for the nice letter. Best wishes to you and Karen. I am sure you will find yourself in a world of joy with Karen.

Best wishes,
Pradeep

For Whomsoever This Note Is For:

I have had the great good fortune to have maintained a close and valued friendship with Pradeep for over twenty years. During this time, he has been as loyal and devoted a friend as anyone could wish.

I can honestly and truthfully assert that I have never known as close and devoted a couple as Pradeep and Connie. Their abiding love and complete dedication have been abundantly evident. This is particularly noteworthy given Connie health issues in recent years. If I even come close to attaining this level of dedication in my own impending marriage, I'll be completely happy.

Ed Muller. Vice President, Banking, New York

In Memory of Connie, I Am Writing a Few Things about My Birth and Childhood

Years back, I was listening to a radio program in Delhi that allowed listeners to phone in with their queries about the mysteries and mystique of the historic Mughal city. I found the program inviting because there used to be one expert who would competently provide fascinating details and explanations. I found the half-hour show absorbing because as an old and proud Dilliwalla, I thought I knew almost everything there was to know about the walled city. But here was someone who knew much more and unloaded absolutely delicious nuggets of history week after week. Years later, I was to discover this wonderful repository of historical tidbits.

Delhi is the capital centre of an empire. The very site on the banks of the Yamuna that Emperor Shahjahan chose to locate his capital was, in fact, associated with Hindu myth and tradition. This spot, called Nigambodhak, was deemed to have been blessed by Bhagwan Vishnu. "A knowledge of the Vedas could be gained simply by taking a dip in the waters." "By establishing a capital city here, the Mughals could reinforce their legitimacy to rule in the eyes of the people." Now, this Nigambodhak Ghats, where people were cremated and ashes were collected the next day to disburse in Ganga in Haridwar, about six hours' drive by car.

It was the only place in Delhi where I witnessed many deaths. To start with, there was my second mother, Kanta Mummy, when I was close to five years old. Later came my two uncles in 1964 and 1966, my grandparents in 1969.

Later, I came to the United States and attended five to six cremations in Illinois. The most painful cremation was of my wife, my world, which I would never forget. It was on March 3, 2015, and her ashes were put in her plot in Illinois on March 4. On April 10, I ordered one of the most beautiful granite stones for her plot, where I go at least twice week. Now, I do not want to visit or see any other cremation or funeral. My Connie's cremation, pressing the red button and seeing her body burning in the caskets, was the most terrible thing I saw, and it took away all my happiness and peace of mind. Her stone, where I have put paid for a yearly contract to provide flowers, is soothing, and I will keep doing that till I die.

I had to see my lovely wife in cardiac arrest in the hospital, and later on the artificial ventilator. Her vitals were going down from sixty to ten, and after her last four breaths, she died. I will remember that particular time, at 1:10 a.m. on Saturday morning, February 28, 2015. I had to watch and keep my mind in the situation, knowing that I had to do her cremation and get her ashes to her plot. There were no family members of mine or of hers. I do not care for that, because it was my duty and my destiny that I had to do that. I got two days of video made by a professional, and I have watched it many times. It provides me most difficult pain but also some solace. It is about my love, and I watch it by myself. No one else has seen this video except my brother and his family, and one of my aunties in India. My sister also saw it. Yes, Prina and Sanjay Mehrotra were there, along with my neighbors, at the cremation ground and at the chapel of peace.

Going back to the radio program, it manages to bring out the fundamental principles of statecraft. The king has to work for the welfare of all his subjects. The Mughal rulers "had seen themselves as rulers of all the people of India, irrespective of class and religious beliefs." Not only that, but the Mughal emperors went out of their way to acknowledge Hindu festive occasions. "On Holi and Diwali, the emperor bathes in the water of seven wells," and the "palace was specially lit for Diwali." Special durbars used to be held during the Hindu festivals. This was a glimpse of the composite culture.

Then there is always the need to impress and intimidate the subjects. The basic feature of the city was designed to showcase the imperial majesty. "The broad main streets were designed to enable impressive processions. As the emperor went to pray at the Jama Masjid, or as he left the city to the north or to the south, his magnificent procession of elephants, horses, palanquins and carriages made an impressive spectacle." (Today, we have the special police and officers aimed at intimidating the citizens every time the prime minister steps out.)

The British also took a leaf out of the Mughal book. For example, the durbar of 1877 was organized, in the words of Viceroy Lytton, to "place the Queen's authority upon the ancient throne of the Moguls, with which the imagination and tradition of (our) Indian subjects associate the splendour of supreme power." This suddenly makes us realize that till this day, we continue to replicate the imperial rites of splendor. Our Republic Day parade and the Beating Retreat ceremonies can be traced to the "imperial need" to demonstratively establish hierarchy and authority. The walled city was known for its kahwe khane (coffee shops).

I am surprised that the program did not mention the rich Kahatri families of Katra Neel and Chunamal Haveli during 1893, and going into Katra Neel and Bagh Diwar. From there, one can walk over to Old Delhi Railway Station, one of the largest in Delhi. With the gangsters Katra Neel, R. Guru, and Late B, wealth was flowing in the Katra Neel Kahatri family. I belong to one of those families. My late grandfather, Lala Durga Parshad Berry, and the late Seth M. M., whose son was the late Dr. J. M. S. The doctor was in the United States teaching in the elite universities, and he started an Indian and drug pharmaceutical company in Rishikesh, India. Dr. V. M. S. was a mathematics professor in many universities, and finally he was in the University of W. They both were in the same high school in Bagh Diwar, in L. N. Girdhari Lal Karari Upark School.

Right across the Katra Neel is Ballimaron, a heavily Muslin residential and commercial place. The late Mirza Ghalib's palace is a tourist attraction in Chandni Chowk. Chuna Mal Haveli is too. This hovel was part of my childhood till I came to the United States. Haveli is still there in the Katra

Neel. Connie's loss is more than money. Ghantewwal Halwaie was closed a few years ago and was started in 1839 during Sahajaha. Fathepuri Majdid, Khari Baouli, Katra Ishawr Bhawn, and Lahori Gate, (G. B. Road, a red light area)—all this history would have been discussed on the radio or TV programs. I am extremely proud to say that I am from the rich family of Lala Durga Parshad Berry. I came to the United States from Katra Neel Chandni Chowk.

Worries of My Connie

Connie was right when she told me, "Pradeep, I worry if something happens to me, you will be left alone, and I am very upset over that." She also told me, "I feel angry that you and your brother had a horrible childhood. Now I am sick, and I do not want to you to ever leave the United States. Don't go to India for a few months and spend time with your brother and his family. Do not leave America." Those words are written in my heart and soul, just like the *Ten Commandments* with Charlton Heston, where he draws the Ten Commandments on the wall at the very end of the movie. Yule Brenner played his role so well. This movie is shown every year during Christmas, and it's the most famous movie in the history of Hollywood, along with *The Sound of Music,* which is also played every holiday season. Now, I don't imagine watching those because they bring memories of Connie.

I enjoyed each and every thing, no matter how small or big, as long as Connie was with me. I could not live without her for an hour, and now she has been dead for 14,450 hours, or twenty months. I have not seen her except for pictures and my memories. Our house is my temple, or I go to her grave. Today, October 30, was Diwali, the most famous festival of India. I went to her cemetery in the evening to pray for her and ask her to give me power. I have turned on all the house lights, and that is the way I personally celebrate Diwali. This year I was by myself. Last year, I was in India, and before that I was always with Connie. She used to give me Diwali gifts, take me out for dinner, and buy sweets for me. She'd wish me a happy Diwali with a big kiss and love. It was the same for Christmas, Thanksgiving, Easter, and New Year's. At midnight, we had a big kiss between husband and wife, and it was the greatest thing and a sign of a happy couple.

Now I have a title: widower. I hate that, but do I have any choice? No. How painful this word is. Of course, divorce is bad, but still one can remarry or do whatever he wants. But certainly I will remain a widower all my life. I have no intention of remarrying. That is due to my love toward Connie. Let people and readers form their own opinion, but Connie's husband, Pradeep, will not listen and will remain widowed. For the last twenty months, I have been without Connie. Now I am facing a choice of an isolated life because I am going through the pain of losing Connie. With her watching over me, going to her cemetery regularly gives me a big boost, but also pain. I say at the cemetery, "Connie, please give me the strength so that I can get us justice for the medical negligence you suffered."

My Connie would never have requested a DNR order, and she wanted full code. She told me this by body language after her cardiac arrest. The delay before she got CPR was the worst thing I saw. Later, on the afternoon of February 27, when I made the sin of leaving her room for one hour, the medical staff did what they wanted to save themselves from their negligence. I pray that I get justice, otherwise in the court of the Lord, the supreme power of this world, they will be punished millions of times over until they pay their dues. It will happen. Connie's last wishes, her soul, my destroyed life, and the curses from the core of my heart will never forgive them. That is how we feel. Many people have been very cruel.

There was a story about a writer who wanted respect and recognition of his work but later realized that he was a candle that will have to burn, giving light to others. This writer cum director and producer was Guru Dutt.

I was thinking and moved around. I saw several other gravestones that had the same color and design as other people's families, and they had "beloved son" "beloved wife," and "beloved father."

I have been thinking about Connie and many new and old memories; happiness and pain are combined in my life. I am unable to believe that Connie has died, and I keep looking at the bedside where she fell down on February 20, 2015. That was her last journey from her house, leaving behind her medicine, her glass of water, her sandals, her clock, and her clothes. Now I put pictures in those places and on her pillows. Her water glass is filled up every night. The Clock is working. He bedside is empty, with the sheets clean and her beautiful, expensive pillow covers. Two brand-new pairs are in her drawers for future use. Connie never made it back to home after her fall, and she died on February 28, 2015.

Is that what God wanted to give me in return for my devotion? I must blame someone for sure, and I know that, but I am not disclosing that in this book about Connie. It was never expected that Connie would not come back to have breakfast with me in our house, at our dining table in the kitchen. I would have served her in our regular dining room with excellent decoration, for a celebration. That day did not come. Now the dining table, the placemats, the silver, her glasses, her medicine box, and her pen and pencil are still sitting. Her special sea salt and black pepper are part of the memories haunting me day and night.

Connie was my girl in my life, and she was a lovely and devoted wife. I had everything. We were two bodies and one soul. That is what I call the love of my life. Lust is not love. Love is love without lust. My wife means everything. Man without his wife is nothing. The wife is the engine of the family, and she is the sensible and is the incarnation of silence and sacrifice. She surrenders herself to her husband. Evil and inhuman are those who never treat their wives well. So what am I going through with my Connie, and how do I get my life happy back?

When we met, we looked in each other's eyes and saw the love. Then we held hands, and our tune started. We danced and got married right away, eloping without our families. Some family members were happy, and some were angry. Later, we were the apple of their eyes, and we overtook them with our charm. They praised my wife. She was a beautiful life, and our beautiful love shined day by day. Now, I hold her pictures and sleep in the same bedroom on my side, with lovely pictures of Connie all over.

I was thinking of a song by Cliff Richard, who was born in Lucknow, India. He used to come to India around the time that I had finished high school and was sixteen years old. My brother and our very close friends who liked music used to listen to his concerts, and we saw the hit movies *Bachelor Boy* and *Summer Holiday*. I was a good singer, and so was my brother. I wrote the following lyrics for my Connie, along with the score composition, but I can't attach the music in the book.

When the girl in your heart, when the girl in your soul arm, then you get everything of the world. Ohe-yoy. My Connie, Connie. My and mine, only mine. You are in my dreams; you are with me. I am with you in your heart and soul. Here now, I am bachelor. When I came from India in your life, and you were single, and in one meeting it turns my wife, and we both found our dreams. Our first trip after three years, to India, was the time when we were surrounded by a hundred people at the airport. And later we had trips to Kashmir, Taj, Missouri, Jaipur. I could see Kashmir because of you; otherwise I would have been without seeing that. Again, now I am single, or what. But my mind says I am married, and that's what I say to myself. Oh, my Connie is with me. But I see her in my life. This book is yours. I am yours, and we both are living in two worlds now. And that's what I say to myself. But the reality: I have to write my status on legal forms, the marriage certificate. I still write I am married; in my mind, I am. I got the best in my life, Connie, whom I called my girl. I sang when Connie was in my arms. She is in my mind, and then I get everything. Her hands, her shining face, are more than my happiness. I miss and miss my girl. When she left my hand and left me, to hold to her memories. That's what now I want: to hold you and sing the same. My girl, the great Connie. We are still together in our lives, and others have left. We are as close as ever.

I remembered just in time what my daddy said to me. "Happy to be a bachelor boy until my dying day."

Connie always followed the great message of Gandhi, the father of India. We should be humble and contribute either money or time to teach and give free education to the unprivileged or the weaker sections of the community. Connie always wanted to see the weaker section progress, and she devoted time for teaching and giving her research papers to students all over, so they could read and gain knowledge to advance their careers. Her habit of reading and writing during work and after teaching, and they coming home to be a great housewife, kept her busy most of the time. She was extremely productive every minute of her time for most of our marriage. She loved going out to social events, functions, marriages, birthdays, and dancing, and she was full of joy and fun. We enjoyed a few light drinks. I was a scotch lover, and she joined me to keep me company. I'd have two drinks more or less daily, and when I quit drinking twenty-six years ago, she was happy that we could enjoy our dinner around 6:00 p.m. and have the whole evening to work and study books, journals, and papers, or perhaps watch award-winning films and intellectual shows. She chose the movies we would watch in theaters and on Netflix. I cannot think of that anymore.

All of those shows, whether on Broadway or TV, are in the past for me. I now watch the news and a few programs like *20/20,* or I'll catch Jimmy Fallon or Seth Meyers, but that is simply to occupy my mind. I turn on the TV, but these programs take me back to Connie. I am watching, but in truth I am remembering Connie. Then I doze off in her memories and suddenly realize that I was watching Connie's life with me. It is a daily routine. My mind, no matter what I am doing, is half on my work and half on Connie. Today, June 7, it is 2:15 a.m., and I am writing, but 90 percent of my mind is on Connie. I want to write nonstop for forty-eight hours. However, I think of my sleep and health, and I have to force myself to stop writing. I wish God would give me twenty-eight hours to a day.

In memory of Connie, I want to share a true episode that happened over 5,500 years ago in India, during the time of Lord Rama, who was an incarnation of Lord Vishnu. Rama; his wife, Sita; and his younger brother, Laxman, were exiled to the jungles for fourteen years on the order of their stepmother, who wanted her own son to take the throne. However, after their exile, her son Bharat also went into exile with Rama. His younger brother Shatrugan-ji handled the kingdom without sitting on Rama's throne or wearing his crown for fourteen years, until Rama returned. This is celebrated in the greatest festival of Diwali, Deppawali, in memory of the return of Lord Rama. During that time, Lord Rama had to fight with one of the greatest scholars in Indian history, King Ravana, who had devoted his life to praying to Lord Shiva and was extremely powerful and wise, with the intelligence of ten human beings. King Ravana was destroyed and was told that he can only be killed by an arrow in his stomach. His wife had made him drink amrit (an antidote) in his sleep, so he did not know if he could ever be killed by anyone. Ravana's wife was scared that if Ravana found out he had amrit in his stomach, he would destroy the world. Only his wife and one of his brothers, Vibushan, knew this. His family begged Ravana not to fight with Lord Rama, and not to abduct Sita. He abducted Sita to see the true power of Rama.

When Ravana disregarded their pleas, his brother Vibushan, a secret follower of Rama, told Rama how Ravana could be killed. During the battle between Lord Rama and Ravana, Lord Rama shot an arrow into Ravana's stomach, to bleed the amrit out of his body, and he died. Lord Rama asked his brother Laxman to go to the dying Ravana and request that he share his knowledge before dying. Laxman-ji went to Ravana and asked him to share his knowledge, but Ravana refused because Laxman had approached his head rather than his feet. Finally, Lord Rama went to Ravana's feet and asked, "Oh, King Ravana, please do not take all of your knowledge away. Please share some knowledge before you die. You were my enemy before, but now I have killed you, you are not my enemy. Please consider me your disciple and share your knowledge."

Ravana said, "I wish I was your teacher and had not kidnapped your wife. I wish instead I would have acted as your teacher." He further narrated that humans have a tendency to do bad things first and good things later. Please do not postpone good things; they postpone bad things. We should withhold our ego and act to help humanity. Immediately after that, King Ravana died. Even to this day, many people in India worship King Ravana or Shanni Maharajah on each Saturday, and people put coins and other things to the devotees. Some beggars come with mustard oil in a big pot and ask people to see their shadows.

This is very important in my life, and especially when Connie was sick and was a victim of the conspiracy by her doctors. I prayed to both Rama and King Ravana to save Connie from her cardiac arrest. I hope that someone should appear in the form of Lord Rama or King Ravana to save my

Connie, and I was sure the same episode of amrit, in the form of oxygen or anything, would save Connie. But the conspiracy of the doctors was so strong that my prayers and amrit became dangerous, and Connie was gone. I was praying to both the lords all the prayers of our ancestors. I prayed with our friend's wife, and nothing happened.

Connie took her last breath while I was touching her hands and feet; she died in my presence. I have a video, and during her cremation, I can be seen touching her feet and asking for forgiveness and kissing her forehead while she was dying—feet and head, feet and head. But I lost my battle like Ravana, because the conspiracy was much stronger, with three doctors and their staff. I wish I had not gone that sixty minutes and only had to face one doctor, rather than the ten medical staff I faced. No one can win ten against one. That is what I saw and faced. I wish I had called many of my friends to be with me, but I was totally absorbed, and my mind was blocked. My innocent bad karmas were stronger than my good karmas. One dirty fish spoils the whole pool. I am paying for that as long as I am alive. Connie has gone, and I cannot ask anyone to bring her back. There must have been some lack of devotion some years ago. That sixty minutes was my biggest mistake, and it caused the biggest loss of my life. It will haunt me every second of my life.

People tell me that I should concentrate on the good times of our forty years of marriage and love, but I cannot accept that. I will continue thinking as long as I live, "Why did I leave her with good faith on the assurance of the hospital staff that I could be gone for an hour?" That absence of sixty minutes will never go away.

Her death took away all the knowledge. I am hoping that my Connie will be with me in our next lives. That hope will continue to keep me positive and will keep me doing humanitarian deeds. Thanks, Connie, for all you did for me. I have no words to thank you. You are the one. You made my career and my success in the United States. I pray that your soul rests in peace.

Your loving, lonely husband,
Pradeep Berry

A Few More Great Messages
in Memory of My Connie

These messages are from *Chankya Neeti* (*Chankya's Philosophy*).

1. "A wise person will come to grief if he does the unwise acts of giving advice to a foolish pupil, looking after woman of loose character and keeping company of a sad one who has lost his fortune." —quote 4, page 8
2. "It is living death to stay in a house where there is an evil natured, badmouthing woman of low morals. Or a cunning and deceitful friend, or an impolite talkative servant, or possibility of the presence of a snake." —quote 5, page 9
3. "If you were to choose between evil person and a snake to keep company with, opt for the snake. Because a snake will bite only in self-defense, but an evil person can put a bite for any reason and any time or always." —page 31
4. "Skill is man's friend in a foreign land. A good natured wife is the man's friend. Medicine is a sick man's friend, and charitable deeds are one's only friend after death." —quote 15, page 63

Connie uttered her last words: "Pradeep, my own siblings cannot even call me on Valentine's Day and on my birthday." Also, I must mention that at her cremation on Tuesday, March 3, I had a few friends and neighbors with priest service. The next day, her ashes were at the peace of chapel, with a priest service. When the ashes were to be disbursed in her plot with a priest service, a few of my friends were there. Connie and I had no family there. I did not inform any of my cousins at all. Connie's siblings knew, and I told them after Connie's death. It was their choice not to come till today, October 31, 2016. I can assert that I do not want to keep in contact with them. For Thanksgiving 2015, they wanted me to come to their home, but I said no. Connie always loved her brother and his four children and seven grandchildren. I can honestly assert that Connie was the best aunt I have seen to her family. They appreciated her.

Now, I am at a new junction of my life, and later I'll forgot all that. I have now forgotten that chapter and moved forward to my next chapter. I believe what goes around, comes around. I never wanted this to come true, but now I do agree with this message, and I have accepted that message. It is in my heart and in my soul, with full pain and anger when I think of all that. I try to calm down. God's stick is very silent, and when it gets hurt, it acts like a fire. I might write another book, and I would like to mention many things that happened between 2013 and February 28, 2015, and even the next year. Currently, I have relations with Connie's siblings, but I do not want to go alone because it's a three-hour drive. I do not like to drive long distances without Connie.

I got lots of sympathy cards from Connie's friends, who were known to me for years. Later, as people found out, I started getting phone calls and visits of condolences from some of those friends. I must mention that many of my own close working friends—twenty of them, who were very close to me and Connie, including their kids—have not been in touch since 2013. I have not disclosed to them Connie's demise. I know this is my anger and unhappiness. I want to be left alone rather than tell everyone the whole episode. Many of my outside friends, whom I met at the health club, are always nice to me and respect me. I have also written to the Universities of Michigan and Carlton, as well as her common friends, and they showed sympathy to me.

The important thing is if Connie's friends find out, they will be sorry for me and upset about Connie. However, at the end of the day, I have to count on myself because all of them have their own lives and own problems. I therefore have accepted that no one can heal my wounds and my sorrows. I will have to bear the loss of Connie myself. I have to find a way to cope and live. I am still figuring it out how I can be slightly distanced for few hours or half a day, for peace of mind, but it is a long process. My happiness is our home with her pictures all over. I am living in her temple. At the end of the day, I am all by myself. People will show sympathy at one time, but later everyone is busy. I do not blame them because they may have had many problems or deaths in their own families. No one can escape from hard times as long as this planet is in place.

Buddha's message is a revision that has been mentioned before. Also, Connie and I have few regrets. One is that we took the second opinion of her sickness from another top US hospital, and their doctors were right, but it was too late. In my own opinion, had we gone there before, I am sure Connie would still be with me. I will also regret forever that on February 27, 2015, I went out to discuss a very important thing with someone for sixty minutes, while Connie was in the hospital under the care of the nurses. Something happened in that sixty minutes, which I have decided not to reveal in this book. In my opinion, that was not the right thing. I have to regret that sixty minutes all my life. Why did I left Connie for sixty minutes? Those sixty minutes cost me pain. I have one satisfaction: after that, I was with Connie every minute, holding her hands and exchanging words till her death. The most important thing was I was there when she took her last breaths, and I stayed with her body till it was taken to the funeral home.

The next morning, I made all the arrangements for her cremation, the peace ceremony, the lunch for friends who attended, all more. I feel that was the best thing for her noble soul that I could do. Thank God that I was alive to do all that for her. This was the best thing I could do for my darling wife. Otherwise, who would have done that? That thought, when it comes in my mind, is like death and breaks my heart. It gives me happiness that God kept me alive to do the best for her. There was no question of compromising quality for her cremation, ashes, and peace of chapel. I told the funeral people that I would go for the very best. This thing is giving me a power and life so that I could do all that. Going forward, I have not compromised. I did not compromise on her stone, decoration, grave, flowers, cleaning the place, or flowers. I make my regular visits three to four times a week, standing for a few hours and sitting; it gives me happiness for my pain. Truly, I am the only person who has gone there, except for Mona, my grandnieces, and a few friends the day the stone was put out, April 10, 2015. Mona and my grandnieces went again in May 2016. There is no one else who has come, and I don't want anyone to come. I am happy.

Her death was the end of our forty-two years as a best couple. With her death, our relationship is formed into spiritual love. This is true, because her pictures from all those years are with me, decorating the house. It's a temple or holy place for me, and I do not have to go to any religious place. Her house is a religious place. Wherever, I go in my house, I see one thing: Connie. That is my faith, that is my worship, that is my devotion, that is my love, and that is my life. A drowning person needs one hand to be pulled out from the water, or sometimes a stick or rope. In the same way, I have found a way to pull out from the deep water of sorrow and pain, and that is being in our home and her temple.

We need hope to survive. My hope and my prayers are in my house, in my heart, with her pictures and the places where she used to sit. I sit there now to feel that I am sitting with Connie. Everybody finds a way to survive after a deep loss. I have found 1 percent to satisfy myself, but I'm still 99 percent in pain. How could I possibly forget my Connie after forty-two years? The best things is that I have her memories in my heart and body.

My biological brother and his family live in India. I talk to them quite often. After forty-two years of our marriage, on behalf of my wife, Connie, I say, "Connie, if God heard your pain, he would give you justice and reward for your noble cause, for your loyalty, for your one sibling and extended family. Connie, you were special, and I will not find that rare gem again. I hope I can ask God for your justice and what you did for your family and for your loving husband."

Quote 4 is 100 percent true for Connie. She lived honestly, did good deeds, was self-made, and was the best wife. Her deeds, even after death, are helping many charities, students, cancer patients, and blind schools.

However, Connie's loss has made me very bitter. I had forgotten until now that I am happy to not ask for my inheritance from my family. Once again, the moment Connie and Pradeep met, my childhood tragedies vanished. The worst and the most devastating thing was Connie's sickness and death. That smashed me to no end, and I lost all my happiness forever until the day my book is published. However, that does not mean that my happiness is back. It a is a fraction of relief for my love, and I will have to find a way to write more books, as well as find a way to survive without Connie.

There are many variables I went through when I landed in the United States over forty years ago. At that time, I had some hope that my variables and unknown future could be good, or else I could back to India. That dilemma suddenly changed into the best destiny when I met Constance A. Fuller. Soon she was my precious wife, and she immediately opted to change her name to Mrs. Constance A. Berry. I called her Connie. We never thought that marriage was a gamble, knowing that the sixty minutes of our first meeting were enough to judge and decide that this commitment was our future. We were the happiest couple and were two parts of one soul.

Now, with her demise, a new chapter has opened with a blank page. What will go in it is Connie's memories, along with my heart and soul. Our families and friends are not part of my life, and again I am brand-new in the United States. I now live in our love house, and I fill paper with Connie. I go back and forth to India to see my brother and his family. The economy changes, and nature changes; morning comes, and then evening comes. There are dark clouds and rain, then a shining day. Nature plays by its own rules. Now I would have to include Connie in that great part of my life. It is the beginning of a new life. I get maximum happiness when I stay in our home, which is Nirvana. Her gravesite gives peace of mind, but there's pain in every part of my body, today and forever.

> Everything on earth lives
> according to the law of nature,
> and from that law emerges the
> glory and joy of liberty; but man
> is denied this fortune, because

he set for the God-given soul a
limited and earthly law of his own.
Man built a narrow and painful
prison in which he secluded
his affections and desires.
—Khalil Gibran

**Surely, none can ever remain inactive even for a moment;
for, everyone is helplessly driven to action by nature-born
qualities. He whose mind is deluded by egoism, thinks: "I
am the doer," whereas all actions are being performed by
the modes of nature. —Gita**

Sickness, accidents, and death. All over the world, they have been happening, and they will keep happening, especially death. Birth is also part of God, and to some degree, humans have more control over the birth. One can decide to remain a bachelor, or even marry but decide that he does not want to have children. I have seen people want to adopt rather than have their own kids, to help the children in poor countries. Many examples are there. I simply want to show how man has some control over birth.

He also has control over death, to some degree. He can avoid car accidents, drunk driving, drugs, shootings, and fighting over small things. A sickness that was uncalled for has taken my Connie from me. There is a very important saying: "Different people, different mouths." Every individual will say what he thinks is best. Connie was an expert to use her own mind and brain while taking advice from different people. If something was convincing, she would take the advice seriously. However, she did not always listen to people and take their opinions.

You are the one who has to make a decision. Connie used to respect and listen to everyone, and if someone said something nice and she agreed, she followed. She was very humble and private, and she would not cry or weep to talk about herself. She would accept the consequences. She did not ask people to decide things for her. Some people have a wavering mind and ask the same question to different people, but in the end they do what makes them happy.

Many cultures have their own faiths and beliefs. I am fully aware that it is not always God who takes away human beings. Many times, someone dies from a sudden gunshot, car accident, or medical negligence. Someone may commit suicide. Do we truly want to believe that it was God's decision? Does God want his creatures shot dead, or killed in a car because there were slippery roads? There were mistakes and errors by the doctors, and the doctor is playing a second god to save his patients, unless he does not care and is used to seeing death. He becomes a hard soul and doesn't care after seeing so many deaths in the hospitals; he becomes emotionless. That is perhaps one of the great contributing factors I have heard from many families and friends. They openly tell me, "Pradeep, that doctor did spoil the case by giving the wrong medicine." He could not find out what it was, what kind of a sickness. The doctor thought it was a heart attack, but it was not. He treated it and did surgery, but he found out it was her lungs. There was water in her lings but no sign of cardiac attack.

Who is at fault? God? Really? No. It is not God. God would never do that to his own people. These human beings become doctors after education in the medical school for seven years. Does it mean that because they have the title, they are always right? No. They are still human beings.

Connie spent eight years before graduation, taught in high school, and worked very long hours grading papers and preparing exams. I spent nine years after high school for undergraduate, chartered accountant classes, and two MBAs. Why do we give so much value to the doctors when they do medical negligence? The law protects them, and attorneys protect them. They protect each other because no doctor would write, "Breach of trust in medical care." Get me that from a doctor. I bet no doctor would go against another. That is why we give up all that medical negligence, and the law protects them by giving only two years to sue otherwise; after that, the law bans the victim's family from suing. This debate over two years is not even clear to many attorneys. The police or the FBI cannot take action against medical negligence. They say it is a civil case, and it has to be handled by the attorney, who in return takes the case only if he or the firm can make millions.

I am writing the medical system in the United States to raise awareness in memory of my Connie. In other countries, it may be happening too. In my opinion, it happens across the world. My grandniece was to have a treatment when she was six months old in 2006. A renowned doctor outside the United States in a developing country did the wrong surgery. She was to have a child cardiologist, but apparently the adult cardiologist was sure he would a better job because he was renowned Cardiologist, But that cardiologist did the wrong surgery and treatment. It is a miracle that my grandniece got timely help from the child cardiologist, and the surgery was performed in an emergency; she was saved from the clutches of death. That was a miracle, and now she is doing great. That incident was alarming. Doctors are not God. People may say anything, but I do believe that there are many medical negligence cases I have seen in my life, especially in poor countries. Developed and rich countries are no exception, and it happens there too. I have seen it myself. But people can afford the time or money to be the winner.

In my opinion, Connie and I had thought many times to go for a second opinion, but when her doctor did not suggest that Connie get another opinion, it was a error. We should have gone, but Connie trusted her doctor. Later we both wanted a second opinion, and finally we went to see another top US doctor. However, by ten it was not great news.

God has taken my Connie, and only God can give her back to me, in this life or in the next life. Only God can return my Connie to me. Also, many times family members do not care about their own flesh and blood. They can be one's worst enemy. It's a big shame to humanity and is a bad lesson for society. However, now I will try to forget and forgive all. Connie has gone, and it's not worth it. We will meet again, and I will never a be able to get her out of my mind. I miss her each second of my life. I know Connie and I are still very attached to each other, and I do not have time to think anything other than her. I would rather think of doing charitable, humanity care and following the path of Connie.

I was angry when I started writing the book, and now it's close to two years since Connie died. Let God take care of the bad deeds of others. I must concentrate on the on my life and the miracles that happen every day. We will meet again for sure, in this life or in the next life. My great faith and confidence, as well as my pain, my suffering, and my anger, is evidence of our love. Love needs sacrifice like plants need water. Love is immortal and is forever, All the anger and inheritance lost in my life is meaningless. What gives me happiness is to think of Connie and follow her path of being noble. I think of her education, reading, writing, housework, smile, knowledge, charm, and most important her true love for me. This love will shine, and regardless of anything, it is not going to diminish; rather it will keep increasing every day. All these things are enough in my mind, in my thoughts, throughout the day. I see gravesite, and all the memorable things of fine dining, world traveling, and more in our house. Her life was my life. Her time was my time. Her happiness was my happiness. Her unhappiness, especially when she was not well, was hurtful to me.

Our forty-two years together was a gift from God and was worth much more than any wealth in the world. All these thoughts carry forward in my life, showing a new path. Whatever circumstances I have to live, I will do so in the hope we are going to meet again. Connie knows how much love we had, and we will remain together as long as this world is here. Our love will stand on top.

Thank you, Connie, for all the best things you gave me. I will try to repay it by doing anything for you. I will live for you with this hope that we are going to meet again and restart our marriage and evergreen love. All this and my daily prayers to you are my true companion, and I hope it gives me the strength to overcome my crushed life. Thanks my Connie for everything, and I keep concentrating on those two words: my Connie.

This is my sincere, loving, and heartfelt tribute to my wife. My Connie, my wife, my life, my world.

I'm always your loving husband, and our true love will last forever. I'll love my Connie forever, till the next life.

PRADEEP KUMAR BERRY
February 16, 2017

I do not express any anger or any bad feelings to any of our family, friends, and other people involved. This book is my life with Connie. It's not a book where I have to mention the bad examples, because I have no power to change the behaviors of others. People do what they know, or what they think they know. They may realize they were wrong. I want to concentrate on my second book for Connie, focusing on our academic career, education, humanity, and legacy for the coming generation.

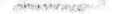

TO MY WONDERFUL HUSBAND
I LOVE YOU

THE ALUMNI ASSOCIATION OF THE UNIVERSITY OF MICHIGAN

takes great honor in awarding this Certificate of Achievement to

Constance A. Berry

having successfully completed Italian, Etruscan, and Renaissance Studies
at the Alumni College in Tuscany amid the grandeur of the region's rolling hills,
magnificent vineyards, and olive groves.
Presented in this month of April nineteen hundred and ninety-nine.

Nadine Hogan
Alumni Association Representatives

Phil & Judy Meyers
Alumni Campus Abroad Representatives

Printed in the United States
By Bookmasters